DATE DUE

GAYLORD			PRINTED IN U..S.A.

READING IN YOUR SCHOOL

Reading in Your School

J. ROY NEWTON

Professor of Education
State University of New York
College of Education at Albany

McGRAW-HILL BOOK COMPANY, INC.

NEW YORK   TORONTO   LONDON

1960

READING IN YOUR SCHOOL

PREFACE

This book seeks to increase understanding in a much misunderstood field so that the reading process in schools may go forward smoothly, intelligently, and purposefully. It indicates solutions to reading problems from an orientational, cooperative, and administrative point of view. Wherever possible, alternative measures are considered in order that a school may evaluate several approaches before determining what is best for its particular requirements.

The educational self-examination that America is going through implies an awareness of the need for increased emphasis on the realization of potential ability. At the precise time when our schools are being confronted with an ever-increasing wave of learners, we are becoming conscious that individual excellence cannot be mass-produced. If the individual learner is to achieve—or even approach —his potential, he must be able to use his reading and study skills effectively.

This book is based on the conviction that continuing growth of a boy or girl is dependent upon a harmonious and exacting program designed to encourage the greatest possible development of the individual. Areas in which reexamination, rethinking, and reorganization may be necessary are suggested and discussed.

No one person or single group of people can be held responsible for developing individual excellence. Besides the student who is involved, we have the school, the community, and the home all contributing. Consequently the ideas suggested here stress the interdependence of teachers in training, beginning and experienced teachers, administrators, specialists, the PTA, parents, and special services.

In reading, as in other branches of learning, our schools should react positively to criticism. They must recognize that there is much that may justly be questioned and that coordinated effort is needed in order to maintain public confidence in public education.

Appendix A suggests some twenty books and several magazines which might form the nucleus for a professional library on reading. Appendix B presents a check list for determining the reading climate of a school. Appendix C shows a sample check list which the school may adapt, as required, for use as an addition to the cumulative folder; and Appendix D shows sample reading control report forms for use within the school itself and in reporting to parents.

The author is indebted to those teachers in his classes who have often spoken of the problems they face in their schools in the establishment and improvement of reading programs. Acknowledgment should also be made to the author's wife for the help he has received from her and to publishers who have granted permission to quote from their publications. To all these the author expresses his sincere gratitude.

J. Roy Newton

CONTENTS

ILLUSTRATIONS

Chapter 1

WHY READING IS EVERYBODY'S BUSINESS

Since reading is basic to learning and learning is basic to survival, we all have a stake in the reading program of our school. Teachers, whatever the grade or the subject they teach, are involved in the improvement of reading. Elementary, secondary, and postsecondary teachers can develop reading skills in various subject-matter areas to the end that each individual may become a proficient reader. Members of a community have a right to know how well their schools are achieving this goal.

Most children of average intelligence, or above, can master the mechanics of reading by the end of the primary grades. Reading, however, does not end there, since further refinement becomes necessary as the demands upon reading increase.

While certain individuals may never learn to read and a larger number may never develop the skills necessary to read with adequate understanding, there is another fact of even greater importance. Many who have the ability to become proficient readers never attain that proficiency. Naturally, inadequacies in reading have invited condemnation.

REVIEW OF CRITICISM OF READING INSTRUCTION

Seldom has public denunciation of our schools been as wholesale as it has been on the subject of reading instruction. Some critics claim that modern methods promote guessing, and propose to solve the problem by returning to the alphabet approach to reading. Others intimate that the number of poor readers is on the increase and suspect that European countries do not suffer from a similar problem. Reading readiness, some say, is an educational hoax perpetrated for the express purpose of delaying reading, with the result

1

that American students are at least a year behind those of other countries. Basal readers, others say, with their controlled vocabulary, odious repetition, and insipid illustrations, make a travesty out of the reading process. Having looked at the present and found it wanting, many of those who are critical advocate a return to the good old days and the way they themselves were taught to read.

Parents. One of the groups most outspoken in their disapproval of our schools has been the parents. Naturally enough it is those whose children are not doing well in school who tend to be the most critical. Parents can understand, although they are loath to admit it, when a child of limited intelligence has difficulty learning to read. What they have trouble comprehending is the reason why a child of apparently average or above-average mental ability fails to achieve.

With newer methods of teaching reading, parents simply do not understand what our schools are doing. As teachers have moved away from an alphabet-spelling approach to reading, mothers and fathers are left more and more in the dark concerning reading instruction. Parents who are left in ignorance regarding methods and purposes of reading instruction, or who become frustrated in their attempts to help their own children, quickly become critical. They see in a return to simple and apparently logical procedures an easy answer to a perplexing problem. Pressnall [19], in a recent survey of parental opinion, found that while 60 per cent thought former methods were as good as, or better than, present-day fourth- and fifth-grade reading instruction, only 16 per cent felt modern methods to be superior. Thus a large segment of the population, who should be friendly to our schools, are frankly critical. Or perhaps it would be more accurate to say that a vocal minority tends to speak for this large segment.

General Public. In the past, schools have been judged by their graduates' academic success in college. While this continues to be true, it is equally true that secondary schools are now being judged more and more by the business and industrial records of the students they graduate. By graduating students, the schools place the stamp of approval upon them in effect. While many of them are a credit to their schools, unfortunately, some present an erroneous impression of what the schools are doing. The general public—not always as well informed as it should be regarding the meaning of universal education—is prone to blame the classroom. A local businessman who has hired one of the less gifted high school graduates to work in his office can very easily check on spelling errors, and, as a businessman, he has ample opportunity for publicizing the failings of modern education.

Self-styled Experts. In addition to parents and local business executives, another group which is critical of our schools consists of self-styled experts. Many of the articles that have appeared in popular magazines and books are the result of biased or unrealistic thinking and do little constructive good. The suggestions they give are often panaceas which, if followed, would only cause still greater confusion.

ANSWERS TO CRITICISM

A major part of the information refuting the charges made against current procedures in reading instruction is to be found in professional magazines. Gray and Iverson's "What Should Be the Profession's Attitude toward Lay Criticism of the Schools? With Special Reference to Reading" is particularly appropriate [9]. General articles defending the schools have been written by Russell [22] and Witty [31]. The NEA [18] has assembled a portfolio of the answers to the recent book by Flesch [8]. A useful summary of evidence is to be found in the booklet *Are We Teaching Reading?* by Spache [26].

In the popular press, Dunbar [5], Hersey [11], Larrick [14], and Wilson [30] have articles appearing in such widely different media as the *Chicago Sun-Times, Life, The Saturday Review,* and *Harper's Magazine.* While at times questioning some aspects of reading instruction, they seek to interpret what our schools are doing.

Past vs. Present. The claim for the superiority of older forms of reading instruction is not borne out by research. Spache [26] lists twelve experiments in which tests used up to one hundred years ago have been readministered to contemporary classes. In an overwhelming majority of the cases, present-day readers proved superior. Oral reading, which is the type of reading by which parents are most likely to judge their children, was the area where the older methods showed to some advantage—probably because of our current shift in emphasis from oral to silent reading. The superiority of the past is shown to be largely a nostalgic figment of the imagination.

Superiority of Foreign Countries. A second criticism which is commonly heard is that boys and girls read better in other countries. One author [8] has gone so far as to imply that reading problems exist in no other country except the United States. Karlson's article [13] "We Have Remedial Reading in Europe Too" refutes this. The claim that European children are at least a year ahead, educationally speaking, is actually based on several differences in their schooling—greater employment of male teachers in the lower grades, the introduction of many subjects at an earlier age, a longer school day, and a longer school year. In England and most of Europe, a very different philosophy of education prevails.

Guessing in Current Methods. Yet another criticism of reading instruction is that modern methods foster guessing and that a return to a phonetic approach is indicated. The spelling of English words, unlike words in many other languages, is highly irregular. For this reason, teachers regularly introduce phonics in conjunction with the acquisition of a basic sight vocabulary, rather than employing an abstract phonetic prereading technique. McDowell [16] tested the relative merits of the two approaches and found that the evidence favored the combined approach. Phonic analysis should be regularly taught as one means of word attack [10]. Because a somewhat more mature mentality is required, a large part of phonics instruction occurs in second and third grades [23]. Thus a child in first or second grade, encountering words not in his basic reading vocabulary, tends to guess, since his methods of phonic attack are limited. As more phonic work is introduced and mastered, the tendency to guess lessens. By fourth grade, a child making normal progress should be able to sound out unfamiliar words. A delay in beginning reading instruction until a child has reached a mental age of six years avoids many of the pitfalls that might otherwise be encountered (see Chapter 4). Schonell [24], one of the leading English reading specialists, agrees that a mental age of six years or more is desirable. While it is possible to teach children who are mentally younger, little is to be gained.

Basal Readers. Three criticisms of graded basal readers have been directed against repetition, controlled vocabulary, and the insipid character of the illustrations. A certain amount of repetition is necessary for learning, and in the early stages of reading instruction the frequency factor plays an important part. The result is reading material which from the adult point of view appears deadly, but which from the child's viewpoint gives a sense of familiarity and security. That repetition, as such, does not bother children is amply proved by nursery rhymes and the rereading of stories already familiar. The dislike of repetition may be largely an expression of an adult feeling.

However, the repetition of words does sometimes result in rather too small a vocabulary being introduced in some basal readers as Hersey [11] notes. While vocabulary control is necessary [12], every effort is made to encourage children to read widely in supplementary materials from first grade onward. This supplies additional practice in recognizing words introduced in basal readers as they appear in a different context. Supplementary readers also can be read silently so that another important reading skill is being emphasized.

The third criticism, that concerning the illustrations, is in part true. Publishers have tried children's own drawings and stick figures in addition to the more conventional pictures. Photographs and marginal drawings have not been widely used but are of potential worth in illustrating some stories.

Increasing Number of Poor Readers. Some critics contend that poor readers are more numerous today than ever before. This is probably true. Chronological promotion and advances in the school-leaving age tend to keep poor readers in school longer. The rapid increase in school population has further augmented this number. However, it should be remembered that the number of good readers has risen also, and this fact is of even greater significance.

WHY READING REMAINS AN ISSUE

The refutation of much of the above criticism of current reading instruction should cause us no complacency. Many of today's improved teaching methods are a direct consequence of such criticism.

These methods—the result of teachers, children, reading specialists, and publishers working together—represent the best thinking, the best materials, and the best procedures that self-appraisal, experiment, and cooperative effort have so far produced.

Yet there is much that is wrong with reading instruction and much that may be done to better it. Reading instruction will remain an issue for several fundamental reasons. Stressing reading at the beginning level and neglecting its development at the upper levels is an ineffectual procedure, since reading is inextricably involved in the instructional pattern of the school. Learning can take place by other means, but reading remains the most efficient way of gaining knowledge and is available at all times and in all places.

Many of the criticisms of secondary education may be traced to the neglect of instruction in reading. To neglect, ignore, or separate from instruction so important a thought-gaining process as reading compounds difficulties in areas of curriculum, mental health, and public relations. The contention offered here is that, within the present framework, there is ample room for improvement in reading. Two groups in our schools should be able to throw some light on the shortcomings of reading instruction. These two groups are the teachers and the students themselves.

Teachers. Even before the recent furore, many teachers realized that not all boys and girls worked up to their capacity. Of course, there are many reasons for this failure to achieve. In some, it is laziness; in others, lack of interest. Poor teaching is to blame for much poor learning; poor attitudes, both in school and in the home, negate good teaching.

At least some teachers have come to realize that lack of sufficient mastery of the reading skills necessary for the work of the grade or subject is yet another reason for underachievement. In the elementary grades the teacher usually follows a basal series for reading instruction. She may or may not have various sections of children grouped according to reading ability. Almost inevitably the teacher who recognizes different levels of ability in the narrative type of reading encountered in the basal series will violate this principle when using science, social studies, and health materials.

The teacher of secondary school boys and girls usually knows very little about reading as it has been taught. Indeed, he may be ignorant of the reading skills necessary to the successful reading of his subject. Again, he may understand both what has gone before and the skills required but still feel that it is not his job to teach boys and girls how to read his subject. He has to use the materials supplied him, so it is easier to keep everyone together in the same book. Besides, he has only so much time and the demands of examinations have to be met. Thus, he reasons, reading instruction is not for him.

But is he right?

High School Students. The following are a few of the answers a sophomore girl gave on an open-ended questionnaire about her reasons for dropping out of school:

> *The subject giving me the most trouble*—"anything with reading in it."
> *School is*—"pretty good until it comes to reading."
> *Teachers could have helped me by*—"showing me how to read my assignments."
> *If I were a "big wheel," I'd see to it that*—"my teachers knew how to teach reading."

Leaving school before graduation is an apparently easy solution to a complex problem; complex problems usually call for multiple solutions. It is indeed naïve to suggest that continued instruction in reading will solve the dropout problem, but such instruction is one of the possible solutions.

High school students, at least the conscientious ones, realize if and when their reading skills are weak. Very frequently they may not be able to tell what specific skills they need to improve; more than likely they will say, "I read too slowly. I need to speed up my reading." While this is often true, there are usually things wrong with their reading other than lack of speed. They may spend hours reading an assignment that the teacher intended them to complete in thirty or forty minutes, but the poorer students are apt to close their books when the time they have allotted to preparation is up, regardless of their comprehension of the material. Both the conscientious and the less eager students need help.

Often the better-than-average students are the most retarded from a reading point of view. An example may clear up this apparently contradictory statement. Charles, in the eighth grade, has a mental-

grade age of eighth grade and three months (8.3).[1] He is about
average mentally. His reading, as determined by standardized reading tests, is about 8.2. Therefore, his reading is about commensurate
with his ability. George, also in the eighth grade, is reading at about
the same level as Charles, but his intelligence is in the neighborhood
of 10.2. He is not reading up to his mental ability. He is what
reading specialists would term a *reading-disability case*. Many of
our more intelligent, so-called "academic" students are sadly retarded in reading. This is an appalling educational waste that the
critics of reading instruction pass over unnoticed.

The Dropout. Many school systems are plagued by their loss of
students at the legal school-leaving age. This lack of holding power
results in what are popularly called dropouts. In larger schools,
organized in homogeneous classes, many drop out because the simple materials employed in the slower sections fail to hold their interest. Far too often the above-average students are to be found
dropping out of smaller schools because a single-track instructional
program fails to challenge them.

Together with those who are not challenged by the school's offering, many students are dropouts or potential dropouts because they
are unable to do the work of the grade or subject [20]. By and large
their interests are the same as those of their more endowed classmates, but they are limited by a restricted reading ability which is
sometimes the result of low mental ability. They have been passed
on from grade to grade, never being quite able to do the work.
Frustrated as they undoubtedly are by being given books that they
cannot read with adequate comprehension, they seek the easy way
out by leaving school at the earliest possible time.

Terminal Students. Yet another group presents a reading problem. This group consists of boys and girls for whom high school is
terminal. Because of lack of ambition, ability, or financial resources,
they will complete their formal education with high school. There
is much controversy regarding the type of education they should
receive. On the one hand, there are educators who argue that they

---

[1] Both chronological age and mental age are stated in terms of years and
months, but mental-grade age and reading-grade age are stated in decimals
because the school year is regarded as being ten months long.

should be exposed to the same instruction and content as those who are preparing for college [2]. On the other hand, there are those who feel that everything should be made practical. Undoubtedly reading ability is one of the factors governing the development of suitable curricula for these terminal students. For those of lower ability, a serious and sustained effort must be made to improve reading ability. Instruction should, in all probability, be centered about the skills and concepts necessary to enable them to earn a living. For the others of average ability or above, who lack the ambition or financial means to further their education, the problem is more complex.

We have all read a good deal about life adjustment education. Educators are prone to talk in glowing terms, but they sometimes forget that boys and girls are more interested in the present than in preparing for some future millennium when they will be working a thirty-hour week.

Many teachers continue to teach necessary concepts from outmoded textbooks and literary masterpieces because they are familiar with these materials or, as they say, "I love to teach _____." These teachers sometimes forget that the young people attending our schools today are different from those of past generations in some respects, and are likely to ask, "Why do we have to do this?" Such teachers should realize that they are suspiciously close to being in a rut from an effective teaching point of view. The worthwhile concepts, the concepts upon which society depends, can often be taught more effectively from current sources. The overthrow of everything just because it is old is not advocated. However, teachers would do well to examine newer materials while reevaluating the appropriateness of older writing.

Poor readers need, above all else, books, magazines, and articles of interest within their somewhat limited reading abilities. The effect of selecting more modern writing is to reduce the reading difficulty and provide selections which are more likely to be of inherent interest.

College Students. Turning to the college student, we find that a parallel difficulty in reading exists. Colleges have gone on record as expecting secondary schools to teach their students to think, to write, to listen, and to read. This is precisely what the language arts program of the elementary school seeks to do. Somewhere along the line we are failing.

Many college students are not reading up to their capacities. They are young men and women of better-than-average intelligence whose reading is frequently far below their mental abilities. Once more they complain of being slow readers. And once more this is not the main fault with their reading. They have not learned how to adjust their reading speed to the type of material encountered and therefore tend to plod through everything at the same relatively slow speed. Their comprehension is frequently faulty, while their vocabularies are woefully limited. Some are tempted to ascribe these deficiencies of college students to the fact that they have not done enough reading. This is doubtless partly true, but the more important contributing cause is that they have not had sufficient instruction in the refinement of the basic reading skills. In short, they have not had continuous and continuing reading instruction.

The College Dropout. The dropout in some coeducational colleges has reached as high as 50 per cent. Financial troubles, a desire to start earning a living, and, of course, matrimony are but some of the causes for leaving college. In a large number of cases the underlying reason is a fundamental inability to cope with the required reading. In an effort to combat the dropout, colleges are showing a comparatively recent trend toward the establishment of personal reading courses for their students [1].

Criticism of Secondary Schools. The secondary schools are beginning to feel the pressure, situated as they are between the elementary schools on the one hand and liberal arts, technical, and professional colleges and technological institutes and junior colleges on the other. To put it more bluntly, they are being criticized by both elementary schools and postsecondary institutions. The elementary schools wonder why reading instruction—call it study habits, if you will—cannot be continued. The colleges for their part wonder why it is that young people who are intelligent enough to pass entrance examinations are unable to stay in college and do college work. Obviously, lack of reading ability is only part of the answer. Listening, writing, and thinking are equally important.

Indeed, all four of the language arts components are closely related [17]. If reading is thinking the author's thoughts with him, then so is listening, except the ear is substituted for the eye. Similarly, speaking and writing are ways of expressing one's own thoughts. In order to speak and write convincingly, one must have something about which to speak and write. Both direct and vicarious experiences—gained through reading and in other ways— furnish the ideas, while writing and listening improve organization.

Contributions of Reading. Teachers of the upper elementary grades and junior high school are realizing today more than ever before that they have a particular and unique contribution to make to the thinking process of boys and girls by the upward extension of reading instruction. Much of our information of the past and present, even though ably assisted by moving pictures, slides, filmstrips, and television, must still be derived from the printed page.

A grave danger appears to be that teachers tend to substitute factual knowledge for the ability to organize one's thoughts and the thoughts of others [20]. Possibly undue reliance on objective examinations with their tendency to check only factual information is partly to blame. Yet there would appear to be a deeper reason and a far more serious danger. Americans have long been accused of being a people who, instead of engaging in athletics for their own sake, are more interested in spectator sports. Can it be that this phenomenon of the sporting world is being carried over into our classrooms? Are we creating a generation of students who expect to learn by passive watching and listening, who prefer predigested information, selected and analyzed for them, rather than students who are willing to exert mental effort? We do not improve reading by avoiding it.

Audio-visual aids have much to contribute to the reading program. Depth, color, and tone are added to reading by judicious employment of recordings, movies, graphs, models, and illustrations. They add much as interest arousers, convey specific details clearly, and summarize succinctly. But to short-circuit the reading process in an effort to make learning as painless as possible is, to say the least, a misuse of a valuable teaching aid.

Conclusions. What is the evidence against the schools? First, in high school we have students with above-average ability getting by with, for them, inferior reading. Second, we have an alarming dropout both in high school and college, with the result that both secondary and postsecondary institutions are becoming alarmed at the situation.

The simple expedient is to blame methods of teaching reading presently used in the primary grades. This is the course that most of the public criticism of reading instruction has taken. Is the problem so simple? Reading readiness and primary grade reading instruction are based on the theory that reading is developmental; that is to say, individuals are ready to read at different chronological ages and progress at varying rates. To start with such a theory should imply that it is understood and accepted throughout the school system. To employ it in one grade and ignore it at another defeats the effectiveness of such a program.

Therefore, a principal cause of the reading problem really lies in the school's failure to recognize the reading level of the student. Such failure may occur at any grade in the system. With materials suited to his age and interest, and at the rate best suited to him, the school can help each individual to develop his reading skills so that he is able, in all normal situations, to function on his own as an independent reader. In such a school, reading instruction is based on a continuous-process theory embodying the idea that a student starts from where he is, not from where he should be.

READING IMPROVEMENT COMMITTEE

Obviously such continuing instruction is no one-man job, since reading permeates all subjects and all areas of the curriculum. One of the first steps in organizing a whole-school approach to reading may well be the setting up of a committee to consider such questions as (1) who should teach reading? (2) what students are involved? and (3) how should the program fit into the academic pattern of the school? [25]

At this point a decision may have to be made as to whether such a committee is to operate independently as a Reading Improvement Committee or whether it is to be made part of a larger curriculum-evaluation study. Once a school is alerted to the reading needs of the various groups of students that it serves, readjustments of curriculum content and materials are inevitable. In the interest of simplicity, the independent Reading Improvement Committee will be considered.

Evaluation of Present Practices. At the beginning such a committee will concern itself with evaluating present practices in order to discover (1) general principles of child growth that apply to reading instruction, (2) practices which are acceptable in their present form, (3) changes which will lead to improved practices, and (4) practices which are out of harmony [29]. Appendix B provides a check list which should help the committee in its preliminary work. In such evaluation, members of the committee will find that Durrell's listing [7] of weaknesses common to elementary reading programs a useful guide.

Committee Organization. Simpson [25] indicates an organizational form for a high school reading committee which includes representatives of instructional departments, reading-related services, students, and parents. Such a committee should be expanded to include both elementary and junior high members. Adequate representation is essential both because many good ideas will otherwise be lost [4] and because proposed changes are likely to involve, directly or indirectly, all departments of the school. Furthermore, in order to support a program, the community must be informed.

Undoubtedly such a group will be too unwieldy for working sessions in all but the smaller school systems. Durrell [6] says little is to be gained from a first-to-twelfth-grade approach when it comes to discussing specific reading practices. The over-all committee will want to subdivide, sometimes meeting by grades in the elementary school or by subject-matter departments in secondary school. At other times the nature of the problems under discussion will dictate a primary, intermediate, junior high, or senior high approach. To provide the necessary continuity of instruction all levels of the school should be involved, but provision must also be made for smaller groups to work on problems of immediate concern.

Figure 1 indicates one of the possible ways of organizing the Reading Improvement Committee. Membership of the committee includes representatives from both the school and community. An advisory council, which may itself act as a planning board, is composed of chairmen of the special interest groups plus members of the

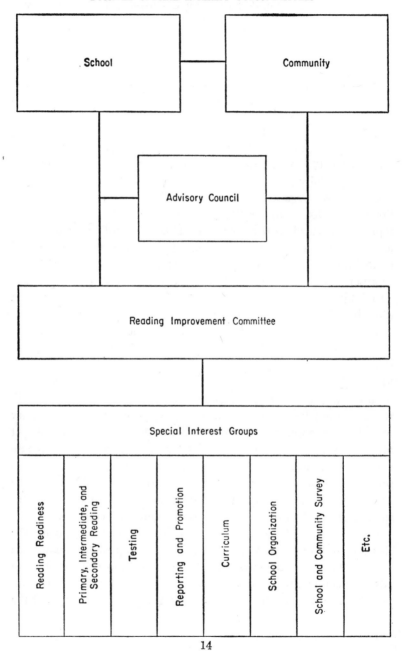

administrative staff. Thus each special interest group is free to conduct its own working sessions but has direct communication with the advisory council.

The advisory council may be composed of some or all of the following:

    A. Administration
        1. Principals
        2. Assistant principals
        3. Supervisors
    B. Community
        1. Board of Education representative
        2. Social agencies representatives
        3. Community leaders
        4. PTA representatives
    C. Special (reading-related) services
        1. Curriculum coordinator
        2. Guidance director
        3. Librarian
        4. Psychologist
        5. Reading specialist
        6. School doctor
        7. School nurse
        8. Speech therapist
        9. Visual-aids director
    D. Teaching staff
        1. Grade-teacher representatives
        2. Subject department chairmen

Both the size of the school and the degree of involvement or interest of individuals will be deciding factors in the selection of the advisory council.

Available Resources. Individual staff members may feel that the formation of such a Reading Improvement Committee is too complicated for the resources of the school. However, in a cooperative undertaking such as this, much assistance will usually be forthcoming. Given a chance to contribute, an elementary supervisor, a department head in the secondary school, or a classroom teacher will prove invaluable. A reading teacher assigned to the intermediate department or a secondary school counterpart, if there is one, can work with smaller groups. Finally, neighboring colleges can frequently provide consultant help [27].

Another resource available to the Reading Improvement Committee is visitation. While this practice is commonly provided for in elementary schools, it is not always efficiently organized. The elementary supervisor or principal should know what neighboring schools possess good reading programs on paper and which are actually putting such plans into action. Visitation should be extended to secondary schools, and department heads should compare notes at professional meetings so that their teachers may learn about various methods of reading instruction which are in actual classroom use. This necessitates providing funds for travel and hiring the required substitutes.

Frequently, a previsitation trip by a supervisor, reading specialist, or department head will ensure a more profitable experience for classroom teachers. Details of schedule, materials to aid in the observation, and an opportunity for an unhurried postobservation conference should be arranged. An unplanned visitation frequently results in mutual embarrassment and a feeling of lack of accomplishment.

Widening Interests. What starts out as a desire to improve reading instruction in a school frequently brings concomitant rewards. Teachers share enthusiasms and—what is equally significant—they learn from each other. Despite all our efforts, this aspect of learning from the experience of others is too often neglected. Woodring [32] recognizes its efficacy in training young teachers. Information concerning better-than-average reading programs, obtained through professional reading and by visitation, is translated into a dynamic program which can be shared with others in turn.

The further in-service training possibilities inherent in the reading-committee approach to the problem of reading are apparent. Such training possibilities become increasingly important as schools face the prospect of a continued shortage of adequately trained and experienced teachers. The nucleus of some twenty books suggested in Appendix A will serve as a guide to the setting up of a professional library in the area of reading instruction.

Of almost equal significance is the fact that what started out as a concern for reading will inevitably lead to changes in the testing program; in instruction for the slow and the able learner, with resultant strengthening of the curriculum; in the promotion, marking, and diploma policies of the school; and in an improved professional attitude toward the task of the teacher in schools providing universal education.

Bestor [2], Conant [3], Flesch [8], Lynd [15], Rickover [20], Townsend [28], Woodring [32] and other recent writers have been critical of our present-day schools and much of their criticism has had some basis in fact. The methods some of these critics have advocated to correct shortcomings have not always been sane, unbiased, or realistic. Individual school systems have it within their power to correct obvious failings, improve the school's total educational offering, and, above all else, provide instruction that will help each student achieve to his maximum capacity [21].

SUMMARY

Parents, the general public, and certain self-styled experts are critical of contemporary reading methods. The evidence indicates that today's boys and girls read better than did their mothers and fathers. Yet the teachers of high school and college students know that there is much room for improvement in the reading of young people. The alarming dropout and the provision for personal reading that colleges have found necessary are two indications of this.

Secondary schools are being criticized by both elementary teachers and college professors for not continuing instruction in the language arts, particularly in reading. Reliance upon purely factual knowledge and the substitution of passive for active learning are partly to blame, but the real cause is the failure of some teachers in the upper elementary and secondary schools to realize that reading is, and should be, a continuous and continuing process which must be incorporated in subject-matter teaching.

The formation of a Reading Improvement Committee will aid such teachers while focusing the attention of all departments upon the basic problems of reading instruction.

18

REFERENCES

1. Barbe, Walter B.: "Reading-improvement Service in Colleges and Universities," *School and Society*, vol. 74, pp. 6–7, July 7, 1951.

2. Bestor, Arthur D.: *Educational Wastelands*, University of Illinois Press, Urbana, Ill., 1953.

3. Conant, James Bryant: *The American High School Today*, McGraw-Hill Book Company, Inc., New York, 1959.

4. Covert, Marshall: "Enlisting Faculty-wide Cooperation for Improvement of Reading Skills in Senior High School," in Nancy Larrick (ed.), *Reading in Action*, International Reading Association Conference Proceedings, vol. 2, Scholastic Magazines, New York, 1957, pp. 100–102.

5. Dunbar, Ruth: "Can Johnny Read?" *Chicago Sun-Times*, May 29–June 7, 1955.

6. Durrell, Donald D.: "How Can We Maintain Continuity in the Teaching of Reading Skills?" in Nancy Larrick (ed.), *Reading in Action*, International Reading Association Conference Proceedings, vol. 2, Scholastic Magazines, New York, 1957, pp. 102–105.

° 7. Durrell, Donald D.: *Improving Reading Instruction*, World Book Company, Yonkers, N.Y., 1956.

8. Flesch, Rudolf: *Why Johnny Can't Read and What You Can Do about It*, Harper & Brothers, New York, 1955.

9. Gray, William S., and William S. Iverson: "What Should Be the Profession's Attitude toward Lay Criticism of the Schools? With Special Reference to Reading," *Elementary School Journal*, vol. 53, p. 24, September, 1952.

° 10. Harris, Albert J.: *How to Increase Reading Ability*, 3d ed., Longmans, Green & Co., Inc., New York, 1956.

11. Hersey, John: "Why Do Students Bog Down on First R?" *Life*, vol. 36, pp. 136–140, May 24, 1954.

12. Hester, Kathleen B.: "The Nature and Scope of Reading Programs Adapted to Today's Needs," in William S. Gray and Nancy Larrick (eds.), *Better Readers for Our Times*, International Reading Association Conference Proceedings, vol. 1, Scholastic Magazines, New York, 1956, p. 23.

13. Karlson, Bjorn: "We Have Remedial Reading in Europe Too," *CTA Journal*, vol. 51, May, 1955.

14. Larrick, Nancy: "But Children Do Read Nowadays," *The Saturday Review*, vol. 37, pp. 65–66, Nov. 13, 1954.

15. Lynd, Albert: *Quackery in the Public Schools,* Little Brown & Company, Boston, 1950.

16. McDowell, John B.: "A Report on the Phonetic Method of Teaching Children to Read," *Catholic Educational Review,* vol. 53, pp. 505–519, October, 1953.

* 17. McKee, Paul: *The Teaching of Reading in the Elementary School,* Houghton Mifflin Company, Boston, 1948.

18. National School Public Relations Association: *This Business about Johnny and His Reading: A Portfolio,* National Education Association, Washington, 1956.

19. Pressnall, Hugo: "Parents' Opinions of Reading Instruction," *Elementary English,* vol. 33, pp. 29–33, January, 1956.

20. Rickover, Hyman G.: *Education and Freedom,* E. P. Dutton & Co., Inc., New York, 1959.

21. Robinson, H. A., and R. M. Udall: "All School Reading Program," *High School Journal,* vol. 39, pp. 91–96, November, 1955.

22. Russell, David H.: "What Is Right with Our Public Schools," *NEA Journal,* vol. 39, pp. 366–367, May, 1950.

23. Russell, David H.: "Teachers' Views on Phonics," *Elementary English,* vol. 32, pp. 371–375, October, 1955.

24. Schonell, Fred J.: *Backwardness in the Basic School Subjects,* 4th ed., Oliver & Boyd, Ltd., Edinburgh and London, 1948.

25. Simpson, Elizabeth A.: *Helping High-school Students Read Better,* Science Research Associates, Inc., Chicago, 1954.

* 26. Spache, George D.: *Are We Teaching Reading?* University of Florida, Gainesville, Fla., 1956.

* 27. Strang, Ruth, and Dorothy Kendall Bracken: *Making Better Readers,* D. C. Heath and Company, Boston, 1957.

* 28. Townsend, Agatha (ed.): *College Freshmen Speak Out,* Committee on School and College Relations of the Educational Records Bureau, Harper & Brothers, New York, 1956.

* 29. Traenkenschuh, Amelia, and Earl H. Hanson: "Superintendent, Supervisor and Principal as Resource Persons," in *Guidance in the Curriculum,* 1955 Yearbook of the Association for Supervision and Curriculum Development, National Education Association, Washington, 1955, pp. 127–146.

30. Wilson, Sloan: "Public Schools Are Better Than You Think," *Harper's Magazine,* vol. 215, pp. 29–33, September, 1955.

31. Witty, Paul A.: "Are Children Learning to Read?" *School and Society,* vol. 75, pp. 289–294, May 10, 1952.

32. Woodring, Paul: *A Fourth of a Nation,* McGraw-Hill Book Company, Inc., New York, 1957.

* See Appendix A for annotated list of books for the professional library in schools.

Chapter 2

CAUSES OF POOR READING

School personnel seeking to determine the causes of poor reading are not likely to find a ready answer. McKillop [8] has pointed out that a number of factors often operate together to inhibit reading. These factors vary from student to student and sometimes even within the individual. Poor reading may be due to physical, mental, or emotional causes, or any combination of them. Emotional factors may be intensified by social conditions prevailing in the home or in the school. Before steps may be taken toward the elimination of these causes, they must be recognized and fully understood. Bond and Tinker [3] summarize the implications of recent studies.

PHYSICAL FACTORS AFFECTING READING

The relative importance of seemingly slight physical handicaps is often misunderstood. A number of mental and emotional factors may each be contributing to a child's poor reading. This child may well find that the addition of a physical limitation, in itself not serious, raises the sum total of his disabilities to the point where he seeks to withdraw from the activity.

Visual Defects. Robinson [9] has shown that the incidence of physical defects of vision in good and poor readers is about equal. On the basis of her sampling, this establishes the fact that both good and poor readers have vision difficulties. The good readers were good in spite of handicaps. The poor readers, beset by additional problems, such as lack of success and emotional instability, often unconsciously used the physical limitation as an excuse for not reading.

The manner in which the two eyes work together in reading is as important as the acuity of each eye working individually. Studies have shown that fusion and acuity at reading distance and depth perception are of particular importance [9]. *Fusion* is the ability of the two eyes to merge the picture seen by each eye into one single and distinct image. *Acuity* at reading distance is the clarity of vision when the viewed object is held some 14 inches from the eyes. *Depth perception* is the ability of the two eyes working together to give the feeling of a third dimension.

Auditory Defects. At first the connection between hearing and reading is not readily obvious. A child with a limited impairment, however, may have trouble hearing the endings of words and, in some cases, certain letter combinations. We are not interested here in the ability to distinguish the particular sounds of letters so much as in the acuteness of the hearing function. Poor auditory acuity tends to limit the listening vocabulary which in turn limits the speaking vocabulary. Since a majority of the words included in the reading vocabularies of the early grades are words which are, or should be, familiar to the child in the home, at play, or in school, a hearing loss may affect listening and speaking vocabularies adversely and, through them, the child's reading vocabulary.

A child may have acceptable auditory acuity and yet have trouble hearing the beginnings, middles, or endings of words. He may also have difficulty distinguishing between certain letter combinations. A child so handicapped is lacking in auditory perception skills and is likely to profit little from phonic instruction until discrimination between the sounds of letters has been taught [5].

Speech Defects. Similarly, anything hindering normal participation in speech activities affects future reading adversely. Undue prolongation of baby talk, while often a source of entertainment to doting parents, may prove a serious hindrance, once reading is started. Such baby talk is likely to affect the auditory discrimination necessary for successful phonic instruction, in addition to making the subject appear ridiculous.

Specialists should be called in where malformation of the mouth and teeth exists. Normally, operations for cleft palate are completed well before schooling starts so that a child so afflicted may have a number of years of normal, or near normal, speech development before reading is started.

Parents who follow the proverb "Children should be seen and not heard" tend to limit the speaking vocabulary of their children. A more recent phenomenon leading to a similar limitation is the neglect brought about by the situation existing when both parents work. Much the same result occurs if the parents place social commitments before those of raising their children. Sharing prereading experiences, having something to say and having someone to say it to—both of these play an important part in getting ready for school. Later on, anything which makes an individual's speech different from that of his contemporaries will tend to prove a limitation in oral reading and a deterrent to group participation. If a person so affected is forced to take part against his will, detrimental emotional situations often occur [2].

General Health. The school values the general health of all boys and girls and takes necessary steps to safeguard their well-being. Of particular importance from a reading point of view are glandular disturbances involving the endocrine glands. General listlessness, lack of coordination, and a tendency toward being overweight are some of the symptoms.

Children who are having trouble adjusting to the instructional program of the school need to have sufficient rest. The school must depend upon the parents to see that a child is free from fatigue. Many parents, cognizant of social values, plan a heavy extracurricular program for their children. Dancing class, boy and girl scouts, religious instruction, elocution lessons, and horseback riding —all worthwhile in and of themselves—often make excessive inroads into a child's program. The school is able to regulate the activities engaged in by limiting the number of clubs at the junior high level, but it is less effective in limiting the out-of-school activities. Boys and girls need time for themselves, for unscheduled fun and recreation. One of the suggestions often made to parents by reading specialists is that the child should not seek to participate in everything that is going on. After a frank discussion, the truth frequently emerges that the child does not want to do all these things; but that the parents insist either because it is "good," i.e., socially acceptable, for their child or because they feel that they missed certain activities when they were growing up. A feeling of accomplishment in a restricted number of activities is often more beneficial to a child than the possible feeling of frustration which may be caused by forced participation in too many organizations.

Vitamin deficiency is not an illness that would be expected in the United States. With both parents working, however, many children who get enough to eat fail to get a properly balanced diet. Busy parents take the easy way out in meal preparation with the result that both general vitality and eyesight sometimes suffer.

Another general health consideration is that of excessive absence from school. Since reading is a progressive subject, work lost through absence should be made up. The teacher could usually find time to give the necessary individual instruction when classes were smaller. Today, with larger classes, this is rarely the case. The poor reader who falls behind has little to look forward to except missing the work completely, or, in elementary school, dropping back to a slower reading group. When a child is not doing well, he seeks to avoid school at every chance. Gullible parents, abetting such absences, quickly set up a vicious circle.

EMOTIONAL FACTORS AFFECTING READING

Most parents and school authorities are quick to recognize physical factors affecting reading—hearing, vision, speech, and general health. In a majority of cases, they are also quick to take the necessary steps to correct them. Most schools have access to funds furnished by civic-minded groups in the community to supply glasses, hearing aids, or medical treatment to children whose parents cannot, or will not, afford them. A similar situation does not exist when factors affecting reading are emotional. These tend to be both more difficult to discover; more difficult to comprehend when discovered; and more time consuming, hence more expensive, to remedy than physical handicaps.

Emotional Stability. Emotional stability is one of the prime requirements for successful reading. A child should be as free as possible from emotional stress as reading instruction is begun and continued. Both parents and teachers frequently fail to recognize this need—probably because they are too closely involved to be able to maintain a clear perspective. For example, the teacher who loses her temper and shouts, or the teacher who is extremely strict one day and very lenient the next, is likely to intensify the emotional problems of boys and girls at exactly the time when children need some adult on whom they can depend. Parents also need to set an example of stability. One of the principal causes for worry on the part of a child is the parents' habit of talking about his lack of success in reading or other school activities in his presence. The child soon realizes that the parents are worried and may react in any one of several ways—usually with unfortunate results.

Psychological Ways of Revealing Emotional Instability. Any person who has worked with boys and girls should be able to recognize the ways in which they reveal insecurity [6]. We should be aware of their methods of covering up emotional instability. There are four well-known ways in which an individual seeks to compensate for his environment by personality adjustments.

1. *Withdrawing.* The subject turns into himself. We often hear teachers say, "George is a good boy. He doesn't cause any trouble but just sits in the back of the room." In an educational sense he is lost to the teacher. If he were reacting to his environment by causing trouble, he might be better off. As it is, he has sunk for the third time and has withdrawn into himself.

2. *Escape.* Probably all individuals indulge in this form of adjustment to some extent. It is only when such behavior becomes excessive that it is to be regarded as a danger signal. The individual seeks to escape from unpleasant tasks at which he is unsuccessful by attending moving pictures, watching television, reading comics, or daydreaming.

3. *Substitution.* This is a method of adjustment whereby the individual substitutes something he likes to do, and can succeed in, for an activity which he dislikes, usually because he lacks success in it. Very often participation in athletics is a form of substitution which enables boys to continue school.

4. *Boasting and belittling.* Scoffing at an activity is another way of covering up insecurity. "Reading is sissy stuff" frequently denotes emotional instability brought about by failure to do well in reading.

Causes of Emotional Instability in the Home. Of the many ways in which the home environment may adversely affect the emotional life of the child, three appear to be most important: sibling rivalry, unequal parental discipline, and broken homes. To these, various parental attitudes may be added.

1. *Sibling rivalry.* Several different kinds of brotherly and sisterly competition come under the heading of sibling rivalry. In all cases the problem child feels inferior. In some instances the child in question is older. He may regret the transfer of affection, real or fancied, to a younger brother or sister. If he is slow to learn to read and does not do too well in school, if the younger child learns to read quickly and, as sometimes happens, overtakes him in school, we have all the ingredients for trouble. On the other hand, a brighter elder sibling may be held up as an example with equally distressing results. Both parents and teachers are tempted to say, "If you're like your brother, you'll do well in school." The younger child knows he isn't like his elder sibling although he is continually being forced to compete with him. The competition is equally keen and even more direct in the case of twins, one of whom may not be as gifted as the other.

2. *Unequal discipline.* The second major cause of emotional instability found in the home is unequal parental discipline. This may appear to be a somewhat trivial thing, but to the mind of a child who needs a continuing sense of security it often looms large. Frequently, the father is out of the home working, so the mother disciplines the children. During the comparatively short periods the father is with his children he may be indulgent or he may be overstrict. Whichever extreme he takes often leads to family disharmony, and the child senses the lack of parental accord.

3. *Broken homes.* An even greater cause of emotional insecurity results from divorce or separation. There are many more problem reading cases among children who come from broken homes than among those from homes where both parents share the task of raising the children. There is no need here to go into the effect on susceptible children of the incidents leading to the breakdown of family life.

4. *Parental anxiety.* When the child comes from a home where the family is a tightly knit unit, there is the danger that parents will be overanxious regarding the child's success in reading. Often, despite the efforts of the school to prepare parents for the delay in

beginning reading brought about by the reading readiness program, they feel that there is something wrong with their child if he doesn't learn to read the first day of school. If at such a time overeager or apprehensive parents unwittingly express their feelings, the child will often sense and reflect this anxiety.

5. *Parental indifference.* Almost equally injurious to the child's emotional stability is the indifference of parents to the child's initial successes in school. This may range from neglect caused by over-emphasis on social activities, through preoccupation with economic affairs in homes where both parents work, to studied indifference resulting from a well-meaning but ill-judged attempt not to appear overanxious. It is not easy to steer between anxiety and indifference.

6. *Sex pressures.* Another factor which merits consideration is the difference in what is expected of boys and girls. Girls do not have to meet the same pressures as do boys. For example, a girl is not held to the same standards of behavior. She may cry without being exhorted to be a little man. Furthermore, families are prone to expect their sons to attend college, preferably the father's college if he went to one, so that success in beginning reading tends to become more important for boys than for girls.

7. *Growing up.* Boys and girls look upon reading as an adult accomplishment, so that learning to read becomes a very real meas-ure of growing up. The immature child may tend to resist this activ-ity, which apparently leads to independence. This resistance is in-tensified in a home where the child sees, feels, or senses that the adults involved are not in harmony. If being an adult is not a pleasurable state, the child may well avoid what, for him, is one of the first measures he encounters of growing up.

School Causes of Emotional Instability. Emotional troubles may cause lack of success in reading, or the failure in reading may give rise to emotional problems [10]. Thus a well-adjusted child com-ing from a good home environment may become emotionally upset by certain school practices. A child who enters in an unsettled condition has trouble adjusting to school.

The school may be a party to emotional instability, assisting the child's defeat in initial reading experiences [1] by introducing reading before he is ready or through a well-meaning overemphasis upon reading. A feeling of tenseness and unsureness develops when he becomes aware that the pace is too fast. Confusion sets in when too many new words are introduced before he has had a chance to assimilate what has already been taught. There is also a danger that the school day may be too reading centered. In such a case, a child already bewildered in reading finds that other activities which should be pleasurable are clouded by the feeling of frustration he develops in reading class. Long reading periods, beyond the child's power of concentration, may also contribute toward the difficulty. Another trouble spot is the setting up of goals so early in the year that slower children find they cannot accomplish what is expected of them. Many reading problems are directly attributable to lack of initial success in reading.

Not all the school-induced causes of emotional insecurity are to be found in the first grade. At any level above this grade a child's emotional troubles may be increased by undue forcing. This is particularly true if the school ignores the principles necessary to developmental learning. Thus, a child who is not making average progress in narrative-type materials is likely to have difficulty when he encounters study-type reading in upper grades. Poor study habits frequently result from overlong assignments, while the pressure of too many extracurricular activities also creates a feeling of frustration.

MENTAL FACTORS AFFECTING READING

For a good reader, reading is an apparently simple, yet effective, process. Not until the reading breaks down do we realize just how complicated it is. In this respect reading may be compared to an automobile engine. When every part is functioning, one only has to get behind the wheel and drive. Yet let one seemingly minor part fail to perform correctly and the whole mechanism fails to respond. Reading, creative reading in which the reader both thinks and reacts to the author's thoughts, is without doubt the most complicated of our mental processes.

Restricted Mental Ability. It is not surprising to find that limited mental ability is one of the prime causes of poor reading. Provided the psychometric tests give a true picture of the individual's ability or lack of it, there is very little that can be done to improve reading above the limit set by intelligence. True, carefully planned reading instruction sometimes results in some raising of intelligence scores, especially those dealing with vocabulary and other verbal items [7]. Also, in rather infrequent cases, a substantial amelioration of home environment promotes better emotional adjustment, with a resultant improvement of mental ability as measured by subsequent tests. Yet these two statements do not belie the fact that a low mental ability is a basic reason for poor reading. Unfortunately, the reverse is not equally true, for a high mental ability does not result, per se, in good reading. It should be remembered that progress is definitely restricted by low mental ability, provided the estimate is correct. Reading instruction will be a slow and tedious process, demanding constant repetition in meaningful and interesting situations.

Limits of Progress. A child having an IQ of 80, as determined by group and individual intelligence tests, should be able to read at fourth-grade level by the time he reaches the chronological age of twelve. By the time he is fifteen years old he may read sixth-grade materials, provided he has received proper instruction. Beginning reading would necessarily have been delayed two or more years, and the amount of progress per school year would be less than normal. Presumably he would be promoted each year. Each teacher would build, making allowances for considerable forgetting, on what had been accomplished the previous year. But the important thing is that he would be working up to his capacity. Harris [7] compares the limitations of mental ability with regard to possible reading achievement.

Brain Injury. Another curb on reading is that of brain injury. Such injury is sometimes the result of an instrument delivery or a fall sustained before the hardening of the bones of the skull. Certain childhood diseases which are characterized by sustained periods of high fever may also result in injury to the brain. In all cases of suspected injury, parents should be encouraged to consult a specialist. Certain clinics and learning-disability centers are now doing remarkable work with this type of case.

Lateral Dominance. In seeking causes of poor reading, we should also consider lateral dominance. Usually a child is right-handed and right-eyed, or alternatively left-handed and left-eyed. These present no reading problems as such, but occasionally a child may be right-handed and left-eyed or vice versa. Sometimes, also, dominance is not established. Both these possibilities are termed *mixed dominance.*

Some specialists feel that mixed dominance causes confusion in left-to-right eye movements in reading, which may lead to possible reversals. Robinson [9], writing in 1946, said, "It appears that dominance should not be entirely neglected as a cause for reading failure until further research has been done." Today, the evidence is still inconclusive.

Tests of lateral dominance [7] should be administered when causes of poor reading are being investigated. The danger is that a diagnosis of mixed dominance may be taken as the cause of difficulty and that other contributing factors may be ignored. A child may make reversals because he has not mastered left-to-right eye movements, or because common reversals such as the reading of "was" for "saw" have not been corrected. The fact that he is also mixed dominant may be coincidental.

Directional Confusion. Another complication affecting the normal movement of the eyes is to be found in the study of certain languages that are read from right to left. For a good reader who has mastered the left-to-right eye movements necessary for reading English, the study of a language which employs the reverse eye movements creates little directional difficulty. However, for a poor reader, who is likely to have some directional trouble in English even as high as the third grade, the introduction of a language such as Hebrew may cause unnecessary confusion. The postponement of the second language until reading in English is progressing satisfactorily would seem to be a sensible solution to the problem where directional confusion does exist.

SOCIAL CAUSES OF POOR READING

The School

The general public is prone to blame the classroom teacher for many educational shortcomings, including lack of success in reading. It is just as easy for teachers to blame parents. Both are probably right, since reading difficulties usually result from a combination of causes, as we have seen. However, it should not be a question of who is to blame, for if we understand *why* reading problems exist, we shall be in a better position to move toward the elimination of many of the causes of poor reading.

Crowded Classrooms. The increasing number of boys and girls attending our schools today has brought about two factors which tend to limit reading achievement. They are (1) crowded classrooms in the primary grades and (2) the lack of school buildings, which forces some school systems to adopt a split-session school day. Especially in the primary grades, the size of classes needs to be carefully regulated. With three to five reading groups in the average primary grade classroom, the teacher has trouble getting around to everyone when the number of children exceeds twenty-five. Already some schools are faced with the necessity of forming classes twice this size. As a consequence of these overcrowded conditions, much of the careless reading encountered in the middle and upper grades is actually "taught" in the first three grades.

Teacher Shortage. Another condition existing in our schools which tends to reduce the quality of reading instruction is the lack of experienced teachers. Unfortunately, when a teacher resigns, it is not at all unusual for a class to have a succession of at least two or three substitutes before a permanent appointment is made.

The employment of an untrained, or partially trained, lay person in the capacity of "baby sitter," so that the teacher may spread herself even more thinly by devoting all of her time to instruction should not be condoned by teachers' organizations. Seat work and much group work other than reading should be regarded as an integral part of primary instruction.

Ineffective Teaching. Finally, one of the causes of poor reading achievement is ineffective teaching. There are a number of reasons for this. (1) The teacher may be a subject-matter-at-all-costs specialist who ignores the fact that his charges have varying abilities. He may feel that he has a certain amount of ground to cover. The result is often what Durrell calls "solo-flight" teaching. The teacher takes off at the beginning of the school year, knows where he is going, and lands safely in June—only to find that the members of the class who took off with him in September have dropped out one by one, mentally if not physically. (2) Teachers vary a great deal in their relative effectiveness with different groups of boys and girls. Increased class size has rendered this situation more acute. Some are temperamentally suited to working with slower children, while others are more effective when teaching able learners. Another consideration is the age of the groups to which they are assigned. (3) Some teachers, otherwise well-prepared, are ineffective in that they either do not comprehend what must be done before a class is ready to read, or they do not select appropriate topics for study. This latter situation is frequently brought about by lack of suitable materials. (4) Much ineffectual teaching is the result of poor classroom organization. No matter how carefully the administration may have planned classes, provided adequate materials, and helped teachers evolve a suitable curriculum, in the last analysis, the individual teacher tends to sink or swim depending upon his success in organizing materials, methods, and techniques within the four walls of his own classroom.

The Home

The home must assume responsibility for a number of factors tending to limit reading achievement. Of course, in a very real sense, the fact that our schools are presently short of both school buildings and teachers may be attributed to the home, since parents are taxpayers. Certain other aspects of the problem seem more likely to originate in the home itself.

Poor Start in Reading. The home, as well as the school, sometimes contributes toward getting children off to a poor start in reading. Families are on the move today more than at any other time in the history of our country. During the period following World War II, we were getting in our secondary schools boys and girls who attended primary grades during the war years. During those grades—the most important ones from a reading point of view—families frequently followed the father from army camp to army camp. The adjustment period following a global war, complicated by overseas peacetime service and foreign marriages, is likely to be long and far-reaching in its consequences. One of the results has been that, instead of getting a good start in reading, many children attended two or more schools during these formative years.

Another group also is in constant motion. These are the children

of migrant farm workers. Moving with their parents from South to
North as crops are harvested, these boys and girls also attend many
schools. Their case is often complicated by a foreign-language
barrier. So acute has the problem become in many states that the
Federal government has had to step in to ensure a continuing educational program. While these two groups may not be typical of
the nation as a whole, it is true that there is much less tendency
for families to remain stationary than was formerly the case.

Changing Moral Values. A more subtle factor which tends to
inhibit full reading achievement is a changing sense of moral values
brought about by unsettled world conditions. Children tend to
absorb the attitudes expressed or implied in the home. Many
homes today mirror the chaos of nations. A feeling that the world
and school owe them a living is, unfortunately, relatively prevalent.
Children often do not have daily chores to do. Hard work is not
the way to success in business; application to studies is not the
way to recognition in school life. Social successes, meeting the
right people, joining the right sororities and fraternities—all these
tend to replace a sound schooling as a preparation for living.

Parental Discipline. Home life in yet another area is working at
cross purposes to school and reading instruction. Many parents
seemingly lack an understanding of sensible parental discipline. A
child who is allowed to do pretty much as he pleases in the early
formative years is faced with a serious adjustment problem when
he enters school. Studies show that children attending good nursery
schools and kindergartens make the adjustment to school much
more easily than do those whose first contact with school is delayed
until the first grade. Indeed, this beginning often enables boys and
girls to make such a start in reading during the first grade that they
are seldom outdistanced. A firm, but not harsh, parental discipline
effectively bridges the gap between home and school by condition-
ing boys and girls to the orderly behavior necessary to public
school learning.

Reading Atmosphere. Another environmental factor is the amount
of reading done by the parents, father as well as mother, at times
when children can observe them as they derive satisfaction from
reading. The number of books and magazines available in the
home directly affects a child's interest in reading. Books are ac-

cepted by children who want to enjoy them as their parents do. The example is before them all the time so that, in a very real sense, parents are responsible if their children do not learn to love books and reading.

Head of the Household. To some, the following suggested cause of poor reading may seem very far-fetched. However, if they will think of families they know, in their own and other socioeconomic groups, they may make some rather startling discoveries.

Boys naturally look to their father as the epitome of manliness. Yet in many families the mother is better educated, better dressed, handles the family income, makes the majority of the social decisions, and, in short, gives at least the outward indication of being the head of the household. In such a situation a boy is scarcely motivated to emulate his father's academic or intellectual accomplishments.

Conclusion. Apparently, in the complex of factors affecting success in reading, there are more operating against boys being successful than against girls. In comparison to the number of girls, the number of boys experiencing difficulty in reading is increasing from the 3 to 1 ratio formerly recognized.

CHANGED SCHOOL POPULATION

At a time when schools are least well-prepared to meet the challenge in terms of physical plant and suitable teachers, they are admitting boys and girls who, often through no fault of their own, are poorly equipped to undertake the task of learning to read. Going even deeper than this is the lack of home training which would, in part, enable them to become successful readers. Our schools are more and more being called upon to take over duties and responsibilities that formerly were the province of the home.

Quality of Students. Not only are our schools crowded and our home life disrupted, but there are also changes affecting the quality as well as the quantity of our school population. As is often true in social change, there are many contributing causes [2]. One of these is that there are relatively few jobs for teen-agers. More and more employers are demanding a high school education as a prerequisite for a position. As automation increases, with the resultant decrease in demand for manual labor, the premium placed on education increases. There are also indications that young people themselves do not desire to work in positions demanding physical effort alone. This would suggest that the youth of our country is fairly unanimous in regarding a high school education as socially acceptable. From the parents' point of view also, economic conditions now make it financially possible to keep boys and girls in school at least through the completion of high school. Then, too, many parents who did not receive such an education now desire it for their children. This desire for a secondary education, laudable as it is in theory, means that secondary schools are now opening their doors to students who, in the past, would not have considered pursuing their education at this level.

Chronological or Social Promotion. Another factor to be considered is chronological or social promotion. The theory advocates yearly promotion of children with relatively few exceptions. The exceptions are usually based on individual considerations, such as absence during prolonged illness, extreme retardation, and in some very few cases at the request of the parent. Social promotion is predicated on the belief that a child tends to adjust better with his own age mates, since he has interests in common with that age group. It further predicates that rates of learning are not uniform, and that it is better educational procedure to permit a child to get what he can from the instructional programs in several grades than to have him repeat the same grade and substantially the same program for an equal number of years. The alternative to social promotion is a return to grade standards, a concept under which children must complete the work of the grade before being promoted. This worked fairly well when a relatively small percentage of those entering first grade sought to enter junior high school. Now, with practically all the children who enter first grade entering junior high school, adherence to such a policy becomes physically impossible. Over the years our educational philosophy has shifted from a policy of the education of the fittest to a policy of educating practically all the children of all the people.

Psychologically, social or chronological promotion is sound. It must be pointed out, however, that such promotion complicates the task of the teacher, places the school in a position of being misunderstood, and graduates a body of students differing widely in capabilities.

Compulsory Attendance. Finally, the age at which boys and girls are legally permitted to leave the secondary school is increasing. From age twelve, the figure has been advanced to age sixteen. Some states, not having already done this, are contemplating the change in the very near future.

Factors Making for Change. The combination of scarcity of jobs for young people, a desire on the part of boys and girls and their parents for a high school education which is now financially possible, the adoption of chronological promotion, and the increase in the school-leaving age—all these factors make a changing school population a reality.

Factors to Continue. There is every indication that the combination of factors making for a changed and changing school population will be present in the future. In fact, many of these conditions will be intensified. A secondary education is likely to be increasingly demanded by industry. Whether the school-leaving age is advanced still further may be subject to question. In a very real sense, however, it is already eighteen to twenty for many of our students. The increased enrollments in technical institutes and junior college have, in a certain sense, effectively postponed the school-leaving age.

Colleges, at least some of them, are forced into a position similar to that currently faced by the secondary school. The pressure is on them to accept larger and larger numbers of secondary school graduates differing widely in ability. How will these colleges, long critical of public education, resolve the problem?

THE TEACHERS' DILEMMA

The sum total of these factors is to admit to the lower grades of the secondary school boys and girls who formerly never were promoted from the elementary school. Many of these are above average in ability. Some, of course, are merely waiting until they are old enough to leave school. Faced with this dilemma, teachers have three alternatives: (1) to condemn present methods of reading instruction, (2) to advocate the return to grade standards, and (3) to give a developmental reading program a chance to prove its effectiveness.

Criticism of Present Methods. Under the grade-standard concept of promotion, the slow learners usually did not enter junior high school. Thus the existence of such a group of students did not materially affect the secondary school teacher. Now he is aware of them and, in some cases, he is both puzzled and perturbed by them. A first reaction, and a very unfortunate one, is to criticize the reading methods employed in the elementary school. The bulk of the criticism has been made by persons who are ignorant of the practices and purposes of current reading instruction. No one claims that present methods result in the ultimately desirable program, but they are the best obtainable to date. By and large, the elementary school is doing an excellent job in the face of the many limitations which now exist, as we have seen.

Return to Grade Standards. A second reaction of the secondary school teacher, also unfortunate and unfair to the boys and girls involved, is to seek to impose grade standards beginning at the seventh- or eighth-grade level. In some areas, state examinations are used as an excuse for this practice. In fairness to the state departments of education concerned, it should be said that this is not the intent of the examination. To promote boys and girls under a chronological or social promotion scheme in grades 1 to 6 and then to impose grade standards at the junior high level is coming perilously close to changing the rules in the middle of the game. The result of imposing grade standards halfway through the educational program rather than adopting a continuous policy of reading instruction is to force many slow learners and some very able students to leave school. The persons dropping out of school stand little chance of securing suitable employment, become prime recruits for teen-age gangs, and form a potential source of juvenile delinquency.

Developmental Reading Program. One of the causes of poor reading is that the schools have not—at every grade and in every subject—accepted the fact that widely differing levels of ability are present. Under a developmental reading program it is impossible to impose grade standards. If we are going to educate all the children of all the people, schools are forced to adopt a realistic attitude.

The third alternative open to teachers and administrators who are seeking to learn the causes of poor reading is to accept the implications inherent in a developmental reading philosophy. When we adopt a reading readiness program in kindergarten and first grade and when we actually make provision for individual differences in learning ability, we are recognizing the fact that all children do not progress at the same rate. So instead of everyone being capable of doing the work of the seventh grade, we find in the seventh grade of the present and future a wide spread of reading abilities. Reading specialists expect to find a spread of ability of plus or minus five grades. In the average heterogeneous seventh grade, this would mean a range of reading abilities extending from second to twelfth grade. A realistic attitude would include accepting the fact that this wide diversity of reading levels will be found in all grades—the upper grades of elementary school as well as in the secondary school. This spread of abilities is not caused by poor instruction but by the fact that reading is a developmental subject.

SUMMARY

Causes of poor reading are frequently many. Among the physical causes are poor vision, hearing, speech, and general health. Emotional handicaps are usually more difficult to discover and remedy than are physical ones. Low mental ability and brain injury tend to limit reading achievement.

Among the causes of poor reading which may be attributed to the school are crowded classrooms, a shortage of experienced teachers, and ineffectual teaching. By inculcating an adverse set of moral values, by failing to maintain sensible discipline, and by setting a poor example, the home often fosters poor reading.

Chronological promotion, compulsory attendance, and the social necessity of obtaining an education have contributed to the establishment of a changed school population which is characterized by wide differences in reading ability.

The dilemma of the secondary school teacher and administrator is whether to go along with the critics and condemn present methods of reading instruction, to seek to return to grade standards, or to accept the implications of developmental reading.

REFERENCES

* 1. Blair, Glenn Myers: *Diagnostic and Remedial Teaching,* rev. ed., The Macmillan Company, New York, 1956.

* 2. Bond, Guy L., and Eva Bond: *Developmental Reading in High School,* The Macmillan Company, New York, 1941.

* 3. Bond, Guy L., and Miles A. Tinker: *Reading Difficulties, Their Diagnosis and Correction,* Appleton-Century-Crofts, Inc., New York, 1957.

4. Dolch, Edward William: *A Manual for Remedial Reading,* 2d ed., Garrard Press, Champaign, Ill., 1945.

5. Durrell, Donald D., and Helen Murphy: "The Auditory Discrimination Factor in Reading Readiness and Reading Disability," *Education,* vol. 73, pp. 556–560, 1953.

6. Gates, Arthur I.: "The Role of Personality Maladjustment in Reading Disability," *Journal of Genetic Psychology,* vol. 59, pp. 77–83, September, 1941.

* 7. Harris, Albert J.: *How to Increase Reading Ability,* 3d ed., Longmans, Green & Co., Inc., New York, 1956.

8. McKillop, Anne: "Why Many Children and Youth Are Retarded in Reading," in William S. Gray and Nancy Larrick (eds.), *Better Readers for Our Times,* International Reading Association Conference Proceedings, vol. 1, Scholastic Magazines, New York, 1956, pp. 120–124.

* 9. Robinson, Helen M.: *Why Pupils Fail in Reading,* University of Chicago Press, Chicago, 1946.

* 10. Strang, Ruth, Constance M. McCullough, and Arthur E. Traxler: *Problems in the Improvement of Reading,* 2d ed., McGraw-Hill Book Company, Inc., New York, 1955.

* See Appendix A for annotated list of books for the professional library in schools.

Chapter 3

ELIMINATION OF THE CAUSES
OF POOR READING

A school staff, aware that there is some justification for the current criticism of reading instruction and knowing some of the more common causes of poor reading, will first seek to eliminate as many of these causes as possible. This and succeeding chapters indicate what steps may profitably be taken.

In most schools it is not a question of starting at the beginning, since usually some parts of the reading program are functioning more or less effectively. Reading readiness and primary grade instruction may be satisfactory, but instruction may break down in the intermediate grades. Or the reading program of the elementary schools may be progressing well, while the early years of the secondary school may demand attention. Again, the contributions of individual teachers may be excellent, yet their work may lack coordination. Often the screening program for the early detection of physical handicaps to learning may be archaic.

A survey form or check list, Appendix B, will facilitate evaluation of the total reading program of the school. The Reading Improvement Committee should realize that there is much more to this survey than the administration of reading and intelligence tests.

SCREENING FOR PHYSICAL HANDICAPS

Screening for vision and hearing deficiencies is quite regularly regarded as one of the logical first steps toward the elimination of these causes of poor reading. Physical handicaps, as we have seen, are to some extent more easily determined and corrected than emotional ones. The purpose of such screening is to discover and refer for possible correction certain physical limitations, *not always serious in and of themselves,* which may contribute to reading deficiencies [6].

Vision Screening. Most parents recognize the wisdom of taking children to the dentist twice a year, although a routine dental examination is still a part of the school physical examination. Unfortunately, parents do not yet recognize the importance of periodic visual examinations. School authorities will welcome the time when parents place eye health in a category similar to that occupied by dental health. Until such a time does come, however, the school must fulfill its obligation by providing the most effective vision-screening program at its command.

Unfortunately, there is some misunderstanding on the part of two professional groups, the ophthalmologists and the optometrists, regarding the school's concern in vision screening. The sole purpose is, and should be, to screen for abnormalities, calling the parents' attention to such cases so that referral to the proper medical authority may be made. It is not the intent of the school to trespass upon the domain of the eye specialist.

A major reason for the occasional antipathy of eye specialists toward school vision-screening programs is often attributable to lack of communication. The purpose of the school's interest in visual problems is not understood. For this reason, someone in the school system—very often the administrator—should inform the local specialists of the exact purpose of the program *before* the school embarks on it. How this may be done depends largely on the size of the community and the number of specialists in the area. Individual conferences become impossible where large numbers of ophthalmologists and optometrists are concerned. However, local and county meetings present opportunities for the administrator to meet those engaged in the treatment and correction of vision problems and afford him a chance to explain the true purpose of the school's screening program.

In deference to the eye specialists, they sometimes do have cause for complaint since the better vision tests do permit the examiner to diagnose the correctional effects of refraction. When such equipment is being used, the examiner should be careful to remember that the school is not concerned with diagnosis but with referral to the proper medical authority.

A clear understanding needs to be had of the fact that eye specialists are not reading experts; neither are reading specialists qualified vision experts. Diseases and malfunctionings of the eyes call for professional care by ophthalmologists and optometrists. Meanwhile existing personnel, the school physician and the school nurse, should perform regular screening examinations and work closely with the guidance department and the reading specialist. Lack of understanding of the school's purpose may tempt optometrists in some communities to want to enter schools in order to do the screening themselves; and lack of an adequate reading program or poor communication may, in effect, force optometrists to embark on the teaching of reading. Both situations should be avoided. By improving screening and reading programs and by keeping channels of communication open, the school can most effectively fulfill its role—to the end that vision abnormalities may be detected so that these handicaps are not added to other possible causes of reading failure.

In communities where a professional rivalry exists between ophthalmologists and optometrists, the Reading Improvement Committee and the chief school administrator would do well to approach the matter of vision screening cautiously. Apparently, the facts they should consider are these. The school nurse, acting with and for the school doctor, tends to use tests such as the Snellen Chart and the Massachusetts Vision Test. Neither of these even begins to do an adequate job where the working together of the two eyes is concerned. Yet this binocular use of the eyes is of extreme importance in reading. Naturally the sight of each eye separately is equally important. So in some situations, the school nurse uses equipment which only screens for about half of the problem. Indeed, these two screening tests are the only ones recognized for school use in some states. The result is that boys and girls who have binocular-vision problems which *may contribute* to reading difficulties escape detection.

The situation is further complicated by the fact that some vision tests, shortened for school use, tend to omit tests of binocular vision.

Whether this is an attempt to make them acceptable for school purposes or whether the shortening is a legitimate attempt to save time in the screening process is difficult to say. This "simplification" has resulted in making the selection of effective equipment more complicated.

The controversy regarding vision screening is difficult to condone, since the welfare of boys and girls transcends, or should transcend, all other considerations. However, competent ophthalmologists recognize that binocular vision as well as the health of each individual eye must be considered in connection with reading. On the other hand, competent optometrists refer cases that properly lie outside their competency to the proper medical authority. If the Reading Improvement Committee, local educational board, and the administration can secure any one of the more adequate pieces of equipment and see that it is properly used, parents' attention can be drawn to a child's specific need for referral. But parents still need general education concerning the importance of eye health and binocular vision.

Classroom Identification of Possible Vision Problems. Handicaps to vision may be revealed through a child's behavior in the classroom. He may avoid close work or become tense while doing it. The child may rub his eyes, frown, blink, or scowl excessively, hold reading materials very close to his eyes or at a peculiar angle. He may move his head excessively while reading or he may lose his place frequently. Bond and Tinker [2] suggest that a combination of observation and screening leads to more accurate referral.

Equipment for Vision Screening. Much progress has been made in the design and development of equipment for vision screening. In an area of such vital importance to reading as eyesight, there is little excuse for employing anything but the best equipment. By grouping schools, a single piece of screening equipment may be kept in full use.

One of the oldest and most commonly used screening devices is the Snellen Chart. This test, administered at 20 feet, is quite regularly found in the office of the school nurse. Because it is easily memorized and because it does not check vision at reading distance or measure the way in which the two eyes work together and because it is often administered either under poor light or at the incorrect distance, it has little to recommend it for reading purposes [4]. Parts of the Snellen Chart are used by other tests.

The Eames Eye Test, Revised Edition, is a relatively inexpensive screening test. Approximately ten minutes is required for each examination.

The Massachusetts Vision Test has the advantage of being very rapid; as soon as a child fails a test the examination is finished. Glasses of different types are used in testing. Because of this, children who wear glasses normally, when tested without them, are usually found to need glasses. This presents one advantage of the Massachusetts Vision Test; the person doing the screening is not able to pass judgment on the refraction afforded by the subject's glasses. The test could be improved for reading purposes by the inclusion of tests of both eyes working together, especially at reading distance. A revised version of the Massachusetts Vision Test, known as the A O School Vision Screening Test, is now available. The individual tests are much the same as those included in the parent test.

Another piece of vision-screening equipment is known as the Keystone Visual-survey Service for Schools. A long and a short form of the test are obtainable. The instrument, which is called a telebinocular, checks both distance and near vision; several tests of both eyes working together are included. The subject may be tested both with and without glasses.

The Ortho-rater is available both in an industrial model and in a modified model for school use known as the School Vision Test. The longer form is to be preferred.

The cost involved in the purchase of vision-screening equipment warrants careful investigation of the comparative merits of various devices currently obtainable. State boards of health and education might well follow the lead given by California in publishing a booklet on vision screening [3]. To be of greatest use, such a bulletin should be revised periodically to keep up with manufacturing changes and improvements.

Robinson and Huelsman [7], reporting on the relationship between vision and reading-test results with groups of children at first-, fourth-, and seventh-grade levels, found measures of depth perception and near acuity most significant. Not one of the vision-

screening tests used by them was deemed entirely satisfactory. The
same reference [7] outlines in chart form the various eye tests incorporated in each vision-screening device. Several changes have
been made since 1953.

Harris [4] reports that the Ortho-rater and the Massachusetts
Vision Test agreed most nearly with subsequent optometric tests.
The Keystone Visual-survey Service tended to overrefer, although
this defect has subsequently been partially corrected by increasing
the tolerances for several of the tests. The Eames Eye Test agreed
least with optometric findings. The Ortho-rater and the Keystone
Telebinocular have the advantage of testing both eyes working
together at both far point and near point. Harris [4] offers some
very practical and relatively inexpensive suggestions for those
schools not wishing to purchase any of the above equipment.

Screening for Hearing Loss. Because of the connection between
hearing and reading via auditory discrimination, vocabulary, and
phonics, children should be screened for possible hearing loss [2].
The preliminary testing should be completed, if possible, before
entrance into the first grade.

Both the watch-tick test and the whisper test have been largely
replaced by more effective measuring devices. The watch-tick test
is administered in a quiet room by holding a watch possessing a
relatively loud tick to each ear of the subject. A child of normal
hearing should be able to hear the tick at a distance of approximately 4 feet. The whisper test is given in a similar manner at from
5 to 20 feet. A certain amount of experimentation is necessary to
determine distances.

The watch-tick test and the whisper test are old-fashioned and
are relatively poor substitutes for more scientific tests. Both tend
to test hearing at a single frequency and may fail to identify a
person having a substantial hearing loss at a higher frequency,
which might effectively prevent his hearing the endings or, in some
cases, the beginnings of words.

The modern equipment most frequently used to screen for possible hearing loss is called the audiometer. Several companies manu-
facture this device. Two distinct types of audiometer are generally
available. The first is a machine with multiple earphones, and it is
capable of screening an entire class at one time, provided the chil-

dren can all write. The other type of audiometer is a more precise individual testing device not dependent upon writing and therefore usable in the early primary grades. If a school cannot afford both, the individual machine is probably superior, although more staff time must necessarily be devoted to the administration of individual tests. Where both are used, the individual testing equipment should be employed as a further check on atypical cases detected by the group-testing machine. Alternatively, the watch-tick test or the whisper test could be used for preliminary screening and the individual audiometer could be employed for follow-up work. Special attention should be given to boys and girls who have difficulty in hearing or pronouncing the endings of words.

Screening for hearing loss is provided by law in many states and is usually checked at the time of the physical examination. Provision should be made for referral at any time during the school year when lowered acuity is suspected. Accidents, aftereffects of certain illnesses, and the transfer into a school system of new students make this practice desirable.

Screening for Speech Faults. Unlike tests for hearing and vision, screening for speech difficulties requires no special equipment, although the audiometer is regularly used to locate possible hearing loss. Speech testing, somewhat informal in that it does not depend on mechanical measurement, necessitates a fully qualified speech teacher. Correction of baby talk and lisping should start as early as possible. Learning correct placement of the tongue and lips, with a proper amount of drill, is often enough to overcome slight speech defects.

Parents should consult an orthodontist for corrective work on teeth. The prolonged presence of first or baby teeth or the existence of too many permanent teeth for the size of the jaw—either of these conditions is likely to promote speech difficulties in the upper grades of elementary school and junior high school.

Stuttering and complex speech problems which may occur in some spastic cases require the services of a speech clinic or speech therapist. Minor speech difficulties—regional mispronunciations and the improper pronunciation of consonants, vowels, and combinations of letters—can usually be handled by the classroom teacher in conjunction with work in phonics. The specialist may be helpful in diagnosing and planning corrective drill in special cases.

General Health. The routine health examination, whether performed by school doctor or by family physician, is largely preventive medical work as required by law. Such examination serves much the same purpose as do the screening tests in hearing, vision, and speech; it provides a record of childhood diseases which is important in forming a profile of the child's physical health. In cases of suspected learning disability, whether discovered at the time of the physical examination or reported through observation by a member of the school staff, the parent should be informed. Referral to the proper medical practitioner or clinic can usually be best effected through the family physician. A school large enough to offer special services or near an existing clinic has a distinct advantage. Unfortunately there are likely to be some families in every community who resent the school's interference in what they consider private matters.

CONSIDERATION OF MENTAL CAUSES OF POOR READING

In considering the relationship of mental ability to reading, it is not a case of eliminating causes but of recognizing limitations. The most important prerequisite is the setting up of a satisfactory testing program, including group and individual tests of both intelligence and reading. The results of these and other tests will form, in part, the basis for such grouping as may be decided upon.

Mental Limitations. The commonly accepted statement that a mental age of six to six and a half years is necessary for beginning reading needs to be examined. Harris [4] summarizes the evidence and points out that the statement originated from a Morphett-Washburne study. The report showed that with the reading materials then employed, children having a mental age of from 6 to 6.5 years were most successful. While children having a mental age lower than this can be taught to read, especially since the trend has been toward the simplification of initial reading materials or preprimers, little is actually to be gained. On the other hand, much harm may be done by forcing the mentally immature into reading. Perhaps the controversy may best be resolved by saying that such a mental age is desirable.

If the school-entering age tends to center around 5 years and 9 months, not all first-grade children are ready to read at the beginning of the year. A well-conceived and well-administered reading readiness program is a necessary adjustment of reading instruction to mental limitations. The absence of such a program, or the rushing of children into reading before they are physically and mentally ready, accounts for a large percentage of the reading failures that are discovered later in school.

As long as chronological age is the factor determining school entrance, teachers and administrators will be faced with the necessity of providing for differences in mental development. The reading readiness program is the most common provision, but some schools are experimenting with the ungraded primary. However, there remains another alternative which deserves consideration. This is abolishing the age criterion for school entrance. Some children could profit from delaying the beginning of school by a year or more; others are ready earlier. Of course, the majority would start as they now do in the first grade at a mental age of approximately six years.

The abolishment of chronological age as a basis for school entrance might subject the school to all sorts of external pressures, with the result that a new series of administrative problems would develop. However, the substitution of mental for chronological age needs to be advanced as a possible alternative to the present system.

Correlation between Reading and Intelligence. Many teachers are puzzled by what appears to be a relatively low correlation between reading and intelligence. Strang, McCullough, and Traxler [8] report three studies which indicate that the relationship of reading and intelligence is between .5 and .8 when reading comprehension is correlated with verbal factors of intelligence. Since reading is admittedly one of the most complicated of mental tasks, one might expect a higher correlation. Yet when the problem is examined closely, this correlation will be found to be relatively high.

Considerations which merit attention are these: (1) Reading tests and intelligence tests do not measure the same areas. Or, to state the matter another way, reading is a functional application of some of the factors which are thought to make up intelligence. (2) In the case of reading tests there is less agreement as to what constitutes a good one. As a result, tests vary a great deal and measures of validity are difficult to obtain. (3) Reading and intelligence tests vary greatly in their emphasis upon rate. Both types of test are usually timed, so we would expect to find that both tend to penalize the deliberate worker. However, this is not precisely true, and many intelligence tests have rather generous time allotments. The types of item found in the two tests vary considerably also. Intelligence-test items, in general, are relatively short; but comprehension items of reading tests frequently necessitate the reading and rereading of more than one paragraph. Thus a child who has not learned to adapt his reading rate to the type of material is usually penalized. (4) Many boys and girls of superior and average intelligence read far below their capacity in both speed and comprehension.

Grouping in Accordance with Intelligence and Reading. Quite frequently the guidance department, anxious to help boys and girls realize their individual potential, may wish to section at least partially in accordance with reading ability. For example, the guidance department may wish to organize some form of homogeneous grouping. Such grouping usually improves instruction for reading-disability cases and slow learners. The former would profit from individual or small-group instruction by the reading teacher, while the latter should be given instruction in reading in the regular reading groups in elementary school. In junior and senior high school the reading-disability cases should be handled once more on an individual or small-group basis. The slow learners will need adjusted work in heterogeneous classes, or they might form the nucleus of slower sections in a homogeneously grouped system. The slower groups should be kept small in number, since individuals in these groups need more teaching time and frequently are potential behavior problems. Groupings should be flexible to permit changes for those who may have been incorrectly assigned, since errors of this sort are bound to occur. A more important reason for flexibility is to provide incentive and to permit the reassignment of boys and girls to the most appropriate group. The following groupings are general categories rather than precise and well-defined entities. In other words, they are points on a continuum rather than discrete groupings.

1. *High mental ability and high reading ability.* This group is generally made up of the academically minded students. In the reading readiness program these boys and girls were usually the first to begin reading instruction, and they tend to form the top reading groups throughout elementary school. In junior and senior high school they form the upper sections in homogeneous groups. They need the stimulation of work that challenges them if they are to escape intellectual laziness. While they are not reading problems in the usual sense, they can frequently profit from instruction in specific reading skills such as outlining or developing speed in comprehension. Occasionally some individuals may need a refresher course in senior high school or college.

2. *High mental ability and low reading ability.* This category includes the reading-disability cases who frequently make large gains in reading once the causes of their poor achievement are diagnosed and remediation is instituted. Since they possess relatively high mental ability, they become an asset to the school once their reading improves. In the primary grades these children are often a cause of anxiety to teachers and parents. They form the middle groups in reading and are usually promoted. Very frequently the members of this group are relatively immature or have physical or emotional problems that may contribute to their poor success in reading. Undue absence and changing schools during the primary years or later are also factors. These children should receive special attention from teachers in the primary grades, and they profit from specialized instruction by the reading teacher from the fourth grade through senior high school.

3. *Average mental ability and low reading ability.* This group resembles the previous one in many respects. Indeed, some schools combine the two groups to all intents and purposes. However, because of their somewhat lower intelligence, these students usually are not able to make as much progress as members of the former group. With special instruction they can become good average students. The only valid reason for including them with the previous group is the lack of reading staff to handle them separately. In this case, they make some gains from class instruction in reading, although not as much as they would if they were taken in smaller groups.

4. *Low mental ability and high reading ability.* These boys and

50

girls form a comparatively small number in any school system. They are achieving above and beyond their apparent capacity, and they are not reading problems as such. The guidance department may well be critical of either the psychometric or the reading-test score. Further tests should be given. If these subsequent test results confirm the previous findings, it is probable that they are conscientious plodders, frequently girls, who may be putting an undue amount of time on their studies.

5. *Low mental ability and low reading ability.* These slow learners form another group with whom the reading specialist will work because low reading performance will frequently hold down the intelligence score. This is particularly true where a single-purpose intelligence test such as the Otis is employed. Sometimes the members of this group tend to be neglected in the upper grades. Some of them will do much better on the nonverbal subtests of intelligence than on verbal subtests. While the description is now frowned upon by psychologists, they are the students said to have good native intelligence. Work in reading, from materials that are sufficiently simple and short, often brings desirable results.

Former warnings concerning groupings need to be repeated. It is necessary to keep them flexible and it is unlikely that they can be clearly defined or distinct. While the following situation applies to music, the parallel is obvious. In City X children's voices are tested in the first grade. The good singers are assigned to Choir 1 and sing at special performances. Choir 2 is comprised of the average singers and is used for mass effects and local functions. Choir 3 is composed of those who cannot carry a tune and is never called upon. These choirs continue with no changes through junior high school. A child should not feel that he is assigned to a particular group for the remainder of his school life.

ELIMINATION OF SOCIAL CAUSES OF POOR READING

Unfortunate social conditions, whether of the home or school, frequently lead to emotional problems which in turn may have a deleterious effect upon reading achievement.

Social Causes—the Home. Among the social causes of poor reading attributable to the home are changing moral values, laissez-faire discipline, and the absence of a good reading example or atmosphere. Obviously there can be no easy way to eliminate these environmental factors and they have accomplished their effect by the time a child starts school. Parentcraft apparently has to be taught each new generation of parents. This should not keep us from trying to eliminate these social causes of poor reading. However, the time lag involved in parent education demands that the school accept conditions as they are and at the same time carry on the public relations program which will alleviate these conditions.

Social Causes—the School. The social causes of poor reading mentioned in the previous chapter were crowded classrooms, a shortage of experienced teachers, and ineffective teaching.

Crowded classrooms are the result of building and teacher shortages combined. No easy solution to either of these problems appears possible. It is disturbing, however, to note the trend of school architects toward larger and still larger classrooms. Space is essential for the various learning activities called for by modern methods of instruction. Much more freedom than was thought desirable under older and more traditional teaching methods is now required. The objection comes when architects start speaking of the optimum-sized classroom as seating fifty children. That number may be the most economical from a structural point of view but it is certainly not desirable from an educational standpoint.

One of the causes of poor reading will be eliminated when no single class in the primary grades exceeds twenty-five children and no class in the secondary school has more than thirty students. This may be wishful thinking and it may be both physically and financially improbable. As a goal, however, it is educationally respectable. Even where television is employed for a large group, smaller sections are required for discussion, writing, and reading purposes.

The suggestion has been made that more desirable candidates will be attracted to the teaching profession by better social facilities and living conditions, especially in the smaller towns; improved salaries and working conditions; and a good secondary school recruitment program, consisting of actual apprenticeship in the early elementary school under adequate supervision. Making teaching attractive is the task of everyone in the community who is interested in the welfare of children.

School systems that can afford to do so are making use of a
building-assistants program. More first-year teachers than are
needed are hired to fill vacancies and those for whom there is no
classroom assignment receive in-service training along with other
first-year teachers under the direction of the supervisor. They assist
experienced teachers with small groups, relieve teachers of some
clerical duties, and substitute for short periods of time. While this
plan does not help the teacher shortage in general, it does ensure a
school of adequate replacements and is infinitely more desirable
than employing untrained lay people to assist teachers.

Many classroom teachers, guidance personnel, and administrators
understand that their increased knowledge about reading is an
effective way of helping boys and girls to become better readers.
Most frequently information is requested concerning methods of
determining oral-reading levels and helping poor readers in the
classroom, testing and the uses to be made of test results, and ways
of teaching reading skills necessary to the comprehension of content subjects. Elementary teachers ask about readiness, the place
of phonics, and special-purpose materials for the very severely retarded reader. Secondary teachers desire information on such subjects as grouping for different purposes within the classroom, unit
teaching, methods of teaching vocabulary, and the organization of
special classes in reading. In-service training, covering these and
other topics, goes a long way toward making teaching more effective.

ELIMINATION OF EMOTIONAL CAUSES OF POOR READING

Many of the emotional causes of poor reading are attributable to
the stresses and strains of family life. Parents may be too protective
or too uninterested, expecting too much or too little of their children.

Emotional Causes—the Home. Attempts to solve emotional problems stemming from the home usually meet with great obstacles. In
the first place, it is often difficult to locate the cause of the trouble;
and, even when the cause has been located, parents sometimes feel
that it is not the school's business. Second, parents who wish to
cooperate, realizing the reasons for conflict, often find themselves

so emotionally involved that efforts are soon abandoned. Better results are usually obtained if both home and school attack the problem simultaneously. School systems having resources such as social workers and professional services boards are better able to undertake the improvement of home relationships than are many small schools. Even here the solution of the difficulty is complex and time-consuming. This does not mean that such therapy should not be attempted where possible, but the school frequently cannot afford to wait until home conditions are bettered before doing what it can to improve the situation.

Emotional Causes—the School. The school solution to the poor reader's emotional problem is not easy. However, even more difficulties are encountered when an attempt is made to change home attitudes. Two alternative courses present themselves. First, provide psychiatric help for those having reading difficulty stemming from emotional causes. Second, attack the reading problem directly with the hope that success in reading will enable a student to become better adjusted.

The first alternative would appear to be the better procedure. However, by no means all children reading below their grade level are in need of psychiatric help. Some of them have not received suitable instruction, and some are reading poorly because of low mental ability. Also, the unavailability of psychiatrists—school or general—precludes this course in all but the most favored communities. For these and other reasons, the public school must take the direct approach to the reading problem. Such a course is estimated to be possible in slightly more than 95 per cent of the cases involved [5].

However there are objections to such a program [1]. If a child is seriously upset emotionally, attacking the reading disability before taking care of the emotional condition tends to gloss over the disturbance—should the instruction prove successful. If it is unsuccessful, the child realizes that another attempt to improve his reading has failed, and subsequent attempts at instruction are rendered even more difficult. It is first necessary to separate the reading-disability pupils from those with low mental ability who are achieving as well as can be expected. It is then possible, by reviewing case histories and consulting teachers, to select those for whom a direct attack on reading is indicated. There will remain a few who are so upset emotionally that little can be done until such time as the home and the school seek a combined approach.

The school is interested in the preventive side of the problem at the same time. Often the combination of a qualified adult, taking time to interest himself in the child, plus suitable reading materials (usually not basal readers), will bring favorable results. Creating and keeping a happy, relaxed, tension-free classroom goes a long way toward overcoming anxiety. Personal recognition given when a small success occurs is one of the ways by which all teachers in a school can counter existing emotional conflict.

SUMMARY

A school system interested in setting up a reading program, or in improving an existing program, frequently starts by eliminating as many of the causes of poor reading as possible. A good starting point is the correction of physical handicaps to learning. Equipment is available for screening boys and girls for possible vision and hearing loss. Speech and general health are also important.

Low mental ability is a cause of poor reading which, while it cannot be eliminated, needs to be understood. That reading tests do not correlate any higher than they do with intelligence tests is due to several factors, one of the most significant being the number of students who are not reading up to their capacity. A testing program permits the grouping of students into five groups: (1) high mental ability and high reading ability, (2) high mental ability and low reading ability, (3) average mental ability and low reading ability, (4) low mental ability and high reading ability, (5) low mental ability and low reading ability. Grouping should be both flexible and tentative.

Social conditions in the home and in the school are difficult to change. A better public relations program will help teach parent-craft and arouse the general public to the necessity of alleviating certain school conditions which are conducive to poor learning.

Ideally, home-caused emotional difficulty should be treated before reading instruction or remediation is attempted. This is frequently impossible. Therefore the school starts by eliminating as many as possible of the school causes contributing to emotional upset and proceeds directly with reading instruction—except in the relatively few cases where psychiatric help is obviously needed.

REFERENCES

* 1. Blair, Glenn Myers: *Diagnostic and Remedial Teaching,* rev. ed., The Macmillan Company, New York, 1956.

* 2. Bond, Guy L., and Miles A. Tinker: *Reading Difficulties, Their Diagnosis and Correction,* Appleton-Century-Crofts, Inc., New York, 1957.

3. California State Board of Health: *A Guide to Vision Screening of School Children in the Public Schools of California,* Recommendations of the California State Board of Health and the California State Board of Education, Sacramento, Calif., 1953.

* 4. Harris, Albert J.: *How to Increase Reading Ability,* 3d ed., Longmans, Green & Co., Inc., New York, 1956.

5. Holmes, Jack A.: "Emotional Factors and Reading Disabilities," *The Reading Teacher,* vol. 9, pp. 11–17, October, 1955.

* 6. Robinson, Helen M.: *Why Pupils Fail in Reading,* University of Chicago Press, Chicago, 1946.

7. Robinson, Helen M., and C. B. Huelsman, Jr.: "Visual Efficiency and Progress in Learning to Read," *Clinical Studies in Reading II,* Supplementary Educational Monographs, no. 77, University of Chicago Press, Chicago, January, 1953.

* 8. Strang, Ruth, Constance M. McCullough, and Arthur E. Traxler: *Problems in the Improvement of Reading,* 2d ed., McGraw-Hill Book Company, Inc., New York, 1955.

* See Appendix A for annotated list of books for the professional library in schools.

Chapter 4

PRIMARY READING

Much attention is given to all phases of beginning reading. Children approach school with the idea that school and reading are synonymous. Parents are most actively interested in the first years of schooling; teachers and administrators alike are anxious that children get off to a good start.

Reading readiness, the various methods of teaching reading, and the place of phonic instruction in a modern reading program are some of the focal points in primary reading instruction which are basic to the establishment of a sound reading philosophy.

READING READINESS

The nature and scope of the prereading program in kindergarten and the primary grades form one of the bases for understanding the developmental nature of subsequent work in reading. A good working definition of reading readiness calls it "a state of general maturity which, when reached, allows a child to read without excess difficulty" [4]. Far from being a do-nothing, wait-and-see-while-we-play-games prelude to reading instruction, the readiness program is a dynamic, constructive force enabling each child to adjust, to build up a background of common experiences and language on which he will draw in the reading situations to follow [6].

New Concept of Reading Readiness. Many teachers who spend a few days or weeks using workbooks and then administer a readiness test to their entire group think they are employing a reading readiness program [11]. Actually such procedures are but a small, though nonetheless essential, part of prereading instruction. They represent a phase in the development of a newer concept of reading

56

readiness which now far transcends the limited workbook-test approach. This newer concept includes the activities of the whole school day, so that a teacher seeking to explain the readiness program finds herself including games, excursions, storytelling, and other daily happenings [5].

Functions of Reading Readiness. This enlarged concept of readiness seeks to include activities which are conducive to the social, emotional, physical, psychological, and language growth of the individual child [9]. Kindergarten and first-grade children, coming as they do from varied backgrounds, are to be found in widely differing stages of development. This is further intensified by the fact that, with the chronological minimum age for school entrance being five years nine months many children will be several months older than others. The rate of growth per month is greater at this age than at any other period during the school life of the child. Furthermore, sex differences are such that girls, maturing earlier and talking earlier than boys, tend to have larger vocabularies. A readiness program thus fulfills two important functions. It permits those of suitable maturity to start reading instruction and fosters the development of those who, through differences of environment, age, or sex, are still immature.

The games they play enable the only child, the child of older parents, or the child with few playmates to learn how to get along with his contemporaries. At the same time he is developing socially, the child is also growing emotionally. He learns, for example, that he cannot have his own way all the time and that disappointments have to be overcome. He is building up a sense of security both in his relationships with his age mates and with his teacher. This sense of security stands him in good stead when he faces distressing situations outside the classroom, possibly even in his own home. The activities of the whole school day help him to develop physically, so that he controls the larger muscles of his body. This, of course, is preparatory to the more delicate control of the smaller muscles of eye and hand which he will need to coordinate in reading and writing. In retelling the events of the playground and other happenings, he is developing his command of language. He is developing naturally and talking about things he is interested in, things that he has seen and done. All the while he is also developing mentally, and his periods of concentration are gradually lengthening.

There is, to be sure, a certain amount of workbook instruction. He becomes familiar with the left-to-right eye movements so necessary in reading. He learns to differentiate, to note likenesses and differences, to look for details, and to arrange pictures in sequence. Pictures also tell him a story, and stories now have a definite sequential order.

Assembling Data. During this whole reading readiness program the teacher has been noting individual characteristics of both behavior and learning which will be recorded in the child's cumulative folder. From contacts with parents, aided by the school nurse and the social service worker, the teacher will be gradually building up a picture which will aid her in understanding the child and in determining his readiness for reading. Vision- and hearing-screening tests have been given and speech habits noted. Physical malformations of the mouth and teeth will be reported to parents as will referrals suggested by results of the screening tests. Certain speech abnormalities will be worked on before reading starts; some will be left for the speech specialist; others will be corrected after formal reading has begun.

Purpose of Testing. The school philosophy of testing will indicate what standardized tests are to be given. Some schools will give an intelligence test toward the end of the kindergarten year, others will delay this test until a few weeks after the beginning of first grade. After the reading readiness program has been going on for some time, the teacher will probably want to verify her own judgment by administering a reading readiness test, although some schools depend entirely upon the test of mental development. Whichever procedure is followed, the information derived from the tests will be considered in the light of knowledge of the child's background and demonstrated development in the classroom [1]. Her judgment will be aided by the information she has collected in the child's folder. She will find that she has four groups in her class: (1) those who are ready to read, (2) those who are probably ready to read, (3) those who are probably not ready to read, and (4) those who give every indication of not being ready to read.

The ready-to-read group will start work in reading while at the same time continuing many activities with the three other groups. Sometime later the second and third groups may be given another readiness test, either a different form of the test already administered or a test from a separate battery. On the basis of this information, again supplemented by the teacher's own judgment, a second reading group will be formed. This process is repeated still later in the school year, but the teacher will not be surprised if she finds that there are some individuals who are not ready to read by the end of the first grade.

The above procedure is the one most commonly followed, but alternative measures should be considered. Some school systems provide a preprimary year between kindergarten and first grade. Children who are shown to be immature by both teacher judgment and the testing program take an extra year before starting first grade. Other systems provide for those who are slow to mature by expanding the primary department to a possible four years without the usual grade designations. Some children complete the primary program in the customary three years or less, while those who are slower take the additional year. Another procedure is to retain the immature boy or girl for a second year in the first grade. This is somewhat less desirable in that the child experiences failure. All three procedures are based on much the same philosophy. The policy of delaying initial reading instruction until teacher judgment and test results indicate suitable maturity is better than the policy of forcing an immature child into what is, for him, a meaningless activity which may cause frustration and emotional upset. A child so forced is frequently held back at an upper-grade level, causing additional emotional turmoil and putting him in an almost impossible state of mind for effective remediation. The secondary school is thus concerned with, and involved in, the reading and promotion philosophy of the primary grades. By keeping the time limits for the prereading period flexible, the program may be fitted to the child, not the child to the program.

Even these plans do not completely take care of the situation for there remains the case of the child who is very severely retarded mentally. Thus a child with an IQ between 70 and 79 will be ready to read somewhere between the ages of 7½ or 8½ years [4]. The number of these children is relatively small, possibly a reading group in a medium-sized school, or a class group in a larger system. Under a yearly promotion plan they might be entering the third grade, but under the alternative procedures described in the previous paragraph they would be starting the equivalent of the second grade and would presumably start beginning reading instruction that year.

Parental Information. Early in the year, the teacher will have called parents in for individual or small group conferences which will explain what is being done in the reading work when it begins. The mothers of the not-ready-to-read group are called in so that they may be aware of the situation and learn what they can do to help. As soon as it becomes obvious that the teacher's supposition is correct, the parents of the probably-not-ready-to-read group also have similar conferences. While individual and small group interviews are superior, much information can be disseminated to grade mothers through bulletins and letters. The former should always be employed where there is anything of a highly personal nature to be discussed. Many first-grade teachers feel that the first contact the new parent has should be a group conference. A parent's first contact with the school should definitely not take place because his or her child is not doing well.

The foundations of a good public relations program are established in kindergarten and first grade. Conferences between parents and teachers are of sufficient importance to be dignified by business-like methods. These should include the scheduling of appointments in advance through the school office so that the teacher may plan her time and assemble necessary information for the meeting. Three methods of organization are possible: (1) after school on certain designated afternoons, (2) on released time from school with a suitable meeting place arranged, and (3) one evening per week, the same for all teachers, designated as conference night. The latter method, while not at first popular with teachers, does enable working mothers and fathers to discuss their problems. Four conferences, each about a half-hour long, are about all that should be scheduled for any one evening.

Intelligence Tests. The following is a list of some of the most widely used group intelligence tests for primary and preprimary children:

California Test of Mental Maturity, Preprimary Battery
(long or short form)
Detroit Beginning First Grade Intelligence Test
Kuhlman-Anderson Intelligence Test, Grade 1A
Pintner-Cunningham Primary Test

Those children who are obviously ill-adjusted to group testing situations, or who do very poorly in one or more subtests, should be given individual intelligence tests by the school psychologist. The test most frequently used for this purpose is the Revised Stanford-Binet Intelligence Scale for Children. Approximately one half-hour is required for this individual test for children six years of age.

One particular provision should be made in intelligence and reading readiness testing with this age group. The tests should not be administered to the whole grade but rather to groups of from eight to ten children at a time. This will necessitate making arrangements for children who are not being tested.

Reading Readiness Tests. Among the large number of reading readiness tests available is the Lee-Clark which takes from twenty to thirty minutes. It is a group test and works well when used in conjunction with a group intelligence test. A somewhat longer test (about one hour, to be given in two or three sessions) is the Metropolitan Readiness Tests. Some tests, while mainly administered to small groups, have one or more parts which must be given individually. In this group are the Gates Reading Readiness Tests and the Monroe Reading Aptitude Tests. The Van Wagenan Reading Readiness Test is for individual use and should probably be reserved for special cases. A handy reference list of reading readiness and other standardized reading tests is to be found in Harris, Appendix A [4].

Parental Anxiety. To mothers and fathers who are aware of the importance of learning to read, the readiness period is trying and somewhat frustrating. Parents want to help; yet, with the newer teaching methods of beginning reading, there appears little that they can do in preparation. Actually their contribution far exceeds that of parents of earlier generations who felt satisfied when their children knew the alphabet. Theirs is the job of providing experiences, answering questions, developing language, and contributing to the social, emotional, and physical welfare of the child [11]. The modern school is missing an opportunity to be constructively helpful and neglecting its obligations when it permits this period to pass without enrolling the cooperation of each child's parents.

Looking Ahead. Just as children do not all walk or talk at the same age, so also they do not all learn to read at the same age. Children in the ready-to-read group of first grade are the future junior and senior high students who will, under a developmental reading program, be reading far ahead of their grade placement. Some of the not-ready-to-read group will not start reading until the second grade. Many of these, with remediable handicaps, will eventually make good average progress. Others, of more limited intelligence, will form the slower groups in later years. Thus the origins of the wide differences in levels of reading ability which are encountered in junior and senior high schools are to be found in the reading readiness program.

TEACHING PRIMARY READING

Part of the refutation of the present criticism of reading instruction is to be found in an understanding of the ways in which reading is taught. Elementary teachers and principals should be aware of the different methods and what each seeks to accomplish. For the secondary school teacher and administrator a consideration of method serves yet another purpose, that of supplying a foundation upon which to build a philosophy of developmental reading. A knowledge of primary reading instruction will also promote a better understanding of many of the reading problems encountered in the secondary school.

Summarization of Method. Methods of teaching reading have evolved from teaching parts of the word or individual letters to teaching the whole word, then to teaching the phrase, and finally to teaching the sentence. Historically, the *alphabet method* of teaching reading came first. This method is based on the idea that if a child can spell the individual letters of the word he can read the word. This is the method that many critics of reading advocate. Next came the whole-word approach. Usually a picture of a

familiar object with the word printed below it is shown. This practice has led to the term, frequently used in describing this way of
teaching reading, *look-and-say* method. However, the words that
tend to cause the most trouble to a beginning reader are not the
names of objects but the connecting words, the articles and prepositions. Partly for this reason and partly because the tendency in
learning is toward wholes, the next method was *phrase reading*.
This method gives practice with articles and prepositions in context while lending itself to the learn-by-doing school in such phrases
as "to the door," "in the basket," and "out of the window." From
phrase reading to *sentence reading* was the next step in the evolution of reading methods. Adjuncts to these methods are numerous.
Many teachers employ a story approach by using experience charts.
Such charts or "stories" contain the ideas of several children about
a common experience, such as a visit to a nearby dairy. This approach can be used to supplement basal reading instruction.

One other way of teaching reading must be mentioned. Properly
speaking, it is not a method in itself but rather a useful and important adjunct to all methods. This is *phonics*. *Phonetics* is the term
applied to the study of speech sounds, while phonics is that part
of phonetics which is used in reading and spelling [10]. It is true
that there are a few phonetic approaches to the teaching of reading
which stress sound rather than sense by having boys and girls repeat nonsense syllables for months before actual reading com-
mences. This practice is contrary to the laws of learning since the
"reading" of nonsense syllables cannot be meaningful.

Selection of Method. The above paragraphs suggest a rather
orderly evolution of reading instruction methods. This is far from
the case. The inquiring teacher is likely to find parts of all methods
being used in his own elementary school. There are several reasons
for this. The method employed is determined partly by the philosophy of the reading curriculum of the primary grades and partly by
the philosophy of the elementary supervisor. The method is also
determined by the basal readers selected. The teacher's manual
which accompanies all basal readers offers very complete suggestions
for teaching and reflects the philosophy of the reading specialist
who wrote the series. Finally, the training and experience of the

teacher are influential in determining the method or methods to be employed. Selection is likely to be eclectic, the teacher employing parts of different familiar methods which she has found successful in similar cases. This is as it should be, provided the teacher of reading is willing and eager to test new ideas.

A uniform approach to reading is not always possible or desirable. A teacher may be getting excellent results with an admittedly old-fashioned method. To force her to change and so obtain inferior results for the sake of uniformity is ridiculous. It is possible—even desirable—to have unity in the over-all program without uniformity in teaching approach.

Comparison of Method. Since teachers and administrators are going to find several teaching methods in use, they should know some of the strengths and weaknesses of each, as suggested in Figure 2. Observation will reveal additional advantages and disadvantages.

FIGURE 2. COMPARISON OF READING METHODS

Method	Advantages	Disadvantages
Alphabet	Relatively simple. Possibly aids in spelling. Parents can help. Can be used with kinesthetic approach.	Slowest method of attacking new words. Spelling does not always give key to pronunciation.
Whole Word, Phrase, and Sentence	Stresses comprehension of words in context. More rapid way of teaching reading. Appeals to average and brighter children because it is meaningful. Taught in conjunction with phonics.	Admittedly a harder method for slow learners. May lead to guessing in early stages until phonics is introduced.
Phonetics	Enables child to become self-sufficient in sounding out new words.	May promote oral reading without comprehension (i.e., verbalizing). Often frustrating if introduced too early.

Combination of Method. From the above comparison of methods, the reader will see why a combination of approaches to reading instruction is frankly desirable. This becomes even more obvious when we remember that all individuals do not learn in the same way. This can be illustrated by an adult's approach to the spelling of a difficult word. Some adults say the word over to themselves before they attempt to write it; others write the word on a piece of scrap paper to see if it looks right. This does not mean necessarily that each cannot gain additional insight by developing the other's learning method; but children, like adults, tend to favor one technique over the other.

Whatever way of teaching reading is employed, it should stress (1) the aural approach—hearing the words; (2) the visual approach—seeing the words; (3) the phonic approach—sounding out the words; and (4) the mental approach—knowing the meaning of the words. A fifth possibility, the kinesthetic approach—writing or tracing—is usually reserved for special remedial instruction [2], although it may be used occasionally for individual words causing reading difficulty and later on may be used in teaching spelling. While all this may appear to be like tarring everyone with the same brush, it nevertheless ensures that each child has an opportunity to learn to read by the approach which is appropriate for him. In actual practice, the multiple approach is less complicated than the written explanation indicates.

So far, reading specialists have concentrated mainly on basal reading systems which embody this omnibus approach to learning to read. To this the teacher frequently adds a special form of the whole-story method in which experience charts are developed from the class experiences.

Learning-disability clinics should be able to throw more light on how certain types of atypical children learn to read. In turn, this should lead to refinements in the teaching of beginning reading. For example, psychologists tell us that the phrase, sentence, and story approaches are difficult for children of low mental ability. Research may reveal that a modification of the alphabet method is superior for these children. Research may also indicate that certain mental types learn better by separate and discrete methods. If this is the case, reading readiness and primary grade intelligence tests will be devised to show us which groups should be taught by methods other than those presently used.

PHONICS

No discussion of reading method, however brief, would be complete without the mention of phonics. Some reading methods are frequently referred to as phonic methods of reading. This implies that other methods are nonphonic, which is usually untrue.

Phonics is included in all generally accepted methods of teaching reading. It is a useful adjunct to instruction in two essential parts of the program. The first is a prereading phase which consists mainly of ear training. Auditory training involves listening to correct pronunciation of consonants and blends and learning good enunciation through games, nursery rhymes, and songs. In addition, children learn to relate the sight and sound of words. Labeling objects, using pictorial charts, and selecting words starting with the same letter—all of these stress the connection between eye and ear.

The second phase of phonics deals with the structural analysis of words and is introduced after a small sight vocabulary has been developed. For normal children, this is usually during the second half of the first grade but is delayed until second grade or later for those who are slower to mature.

Phonics is only one of several methods of word analysis. Very frequently it is one of the last methods to be employed when the reader experiences difficulty in recognizing a word. Generally speaking, the methods of word attack are as follows: (1) configuration—the length and shape of the word; (2) contextual clues—the word must be this one because it makes sense; (3) initial and final consonants—a form of phonics often used in conjunction with contextual clues; (4) structural analysis—this includes small words within large words, root or base words with prefixes and suffixes, and syllabication; and (5) phonics—pronounceable combinations of letters.

Methods of word attack have a dual purpose in a reading program: first, to develop as many word-recognition techniques as are necessary to make a fluent and independent reader; and second, to eliminate guessing and confusion through analysis of a part or parts of a word.

The point stressed by all reading methods worthy of the name is that word recognition is the connecting of the symbol (in this case, the letters of the word) with the object (the meaning) represented by the symbol. On the other hand, some phonetic methods —as contrasted with phonic methods—are concerned with making a fluent oral reader with little or no consideration of his understanding of the meaning behind what is being read. The term *verbalizer* is often applied to such oral perfection without comprehension. This, of course, raises the question of what is meant by reading.

Undue emphasis on phonics, the sounding out of combinations of letters, results in a slow, painful form of oral reading for the child so trained. Indeed, undue emphasis on any of the word-analysis techniques tends to do this, for the child applies these techniques to words which should be in his ready-recognition vocabulary. All methods of word attack are crutches, to be used when needed—but they should be used only when needed.

Some children need more phonic instruction than others, just as they may need more time spent on other methods of word analysis. Able learners can almost invariably employ phonics when necessary. Others may benefit greatly from systematic phonics instruction, including aural discrimination. They may need supplementary drills above and beyond the work suggested in teacher's manuals and workbooks. Primary grade teachers should recognize the desirability of introducing as many methods of word attack as is feasible; and teachers of the middle elementary grades should recognize the necessity of continuing such instruction and providing additional emphasis.

Part of the hue and cry over phonics has a very ludicrous history. In the late thirties, because of studies whose implications were partially misunderstood [4], the teaching of phonics became unfashionable. At that time, phonetic instruction frequently consisted of endless and meaningless drill on word families which was engaged in separately—quite apart from work in reading. While this type of instruction was in disrepute, many efficient and discriminating teachers continued to teach phonics in a functional and systematic way as a part of structural analysis. Gray [3] presents the case for the proper place of phonics instruction in modern reading.

This shift of emphasis—from prereading phonetics, through a period during which no phonetics was taught, to the present emphasis on a combined basic sight vocabulary and phonics approach —has resulted in considerable confusion. Thus it is possible to find schools and individual teachers holding various and sometimes contradictory attitudes toward phonic instruction.

At times, progress has been hard to discern as instruction has veered from one extreme to the other. Our experience with the vicissitudes of phonics instruction indicates that although our schools should be alert to new teaching ideas, new practices should be tried experimentally before they are permanently adopted. In this way extremes in reading instruction, which are often the bases for criticism, may be avoided.

The main purpose of reading is finding meaning, so a balance must be kept between reading skills and understanding. Word meaning, comprehension, fluency in reading, interest, and enjoyment should all be combined to help reach the ultimate goal of reading instruction—a thoughtful reader.

Additional information on the language arts approach to primary reading is given by McKee [7]. Yoakam [12] presents a well-balanced explanation of the goals of basal reading instruction.

CLASSROOM INSTRUCTIONAL ORGANIZATION

The teacher, faced with the task of teaching her young charges how to read, has three possible types of classroom organization from which to choose.

She may elect to teach the whole group as though they had similar interests, abilities, and needs. This procedure is the older way of teaching reading; it may still be found in some intermediate classes of teachers who believe that every child in the class should be doing the work of that grade. In attempting to maintain a single standard for the entire class, the teacher generally employs a single-text approach.

The second method of instructional organization calls for the formation of reading groups as a logical continuation of the reading readiness program. This is probably the most common form of organization in the primary grades. Three to five groups are often found. However, the teacher may work with the entire class as she develops auditory discrimination, some forms of phonic work, and other methods of word attack. At other times, the teacher may work individually with the exceptional child, the slow learner, the child who has been absent, and the child who needs extra drill.

The third form of organization for classroom instruction is known as individualized reading. The teacher works with each child as often as she can. Proponents of individualized reading do not advocate this approach to the exclusion of others. This point should be carefully noted. Miel [8] presents many suggestions for developing this plan. While the practice is by no means original, since teachers have been using it in a modified way, the idea of using it as a form of instructional organization for an entire class is relatively new. The procedure may present problems for the inexperienced teacher. A school probably should not require all teachers to use this type of instruction, but should permit some experienced staff members to try the technique and evaluate it. In this way, with the formation of experimental and control groups, the merits of each plan may be ascertained.

SUMMARY

Reading readiness promotes growth in social, emotional, physical, psychological, and language areas. The purpose of such a program is to permit each and every child to begin reading without excess difficulty. Through tests and observation, the teacher forms groups on the basis of the children's readiness. Parents are informed of their child's place in such grouping and are helped to understand what they may do to help. Every attempt is made to fit the school's program to the child.

Methods of teaching reading have evolved from the part to the whole. Each method presents advantages and disadvantages. Teachers and administrators should expect to find a certain amount of individuality in reading instruction within their own systems. By following good basal reading series and the accompanying manuals, the teacher is assured of a combination of techniques, and children learn by hearing, seeing, and saying.

Phonics is an adjunct to all methods of teaching reading rather than a method in itself. It is useful as one of several word-analysis techniques; but, if overemphasized, it can result in poor oral reading. Some children need more phonic instruction than others, but a balance must be kept to ensure thoughtful readers.

The teacher has three types of classroom instructional organization from which to choose. She may treat the entire class as a single group, employ from three to five reading groups, or practice individualized reading. Schools should set up controlled experiments before adopting any one type of organization.

REFERENCES

1. Angus, Marjorie: "Some Essential Reading Readiness Activities," in *Reading for Today's Children*, The National Elementary Principal, vol. 35, no. 1, September, 1955, pp. 29–33.

2. Fernald, Grace: *Remedial Techniques in Basic School Subjects*, McGraw-Hill Book Company, Inc., New York, 1943.

* 3. Gray, William S.: *On Their Own in Reading*, Scott, Foresman and Company, Chicago, 1948.

* 4. Harris, Albert J.: *How to Increase Reading Ability*, 3d ed., Longmans, Green & Co., Inc., New York, 1956.

5. Hildreth, Gertrude: "The Nature and Scope of Reading Programs Adapted to Today's Needs," in William S. Gray and Nancy Larrick (eds.), *Better Readers for Our Times*, International Reading Association Conference Proceedings, vol. 1, Scholastic Magazines, New York, 1956, pp. 18–22.

* 6. Hildreth, Gertrude: *Readiness for School Beginners*, World Book Company, Yonkers, N.Y., 1950.

* 7. McKee, Paul: *The Teaching of Reading in the Elementary School*, Houghton Mifflin Company, Boston, 1948.

8. Miel, Alice (ed.): *Individualizing Reading Practices*, Bureau of Publications, Teachers College, Columbia University, New York, 1958.

9. Russell, David H.: *Children Learn to Read*, Ginn & Company, Boston, 1949.

* 10. Strang, Ruth, and Dorothy Kendall Bracken: *Making Better Readers,* D. C. Heath and Company, Boston, 1957.

* 11. Strang, Ruth, Constance M. McCullough, and Arthur E. Traxler: *Problems in the Improvement of Reading,* 2d ed., McGraw-Hill Book Company, Inc., New York, 1955.

* 12. Yoakam, Gerald A.: *Basal Reading Instruction,* McGraw-Hill Book Company, Inc., New York, 1955.

* See Appendix A for annotated list of books for the professional library in schools.

Chapter 5

DEVELOPMENTAL READING

The first of the three R's, reading instruction, has long been recognized as one of the fundamental purposes of schooling. At first, reading was considered the special province of the primary grades. Thus, in three years, teachers were expected to complete the process and outfit boys and girls with the skills and techniques required for all the reading they were to do for the remainder of their lives. Later, reading instruction was extended through the upper years of elementary school. Admittedly, this was an improvement, but one might as well expect a baseball player to learn all he needs to know for playing in the World Series from the instruction he received in the Little League. Finally, both secondary schools and colleges are tacitly recognizing that continued work in reading should be offered. This expansion of the time devoted to reading is a tardy, but nevertheless realistic, admission that reading is developmental in nature.

THE DEVELOPMENTAL ASPECTS OF READING

As we have already seen, not all boys and girls are ready for the same instruction at the same time, nor do all children progress at the same rate. One of the criticisms of our basal readers is that they are constructed on the erroneous supposition that all children accomplish one year's reading achievement in one academic year. Yet one concept of intelligence suggests that whereas an individual of normal or average intelligence makes a year's progress in a school year, a child whose IQ is 75 can actually make up to 0.75 of a normal child's progress. In other words, he falls behind at the rate of one-fourth of a year each year. By the time he has reached the chronological age of twelve he has the mental ability of a nine-year-old. Yet he has, with relatively few exceptions, the interests of his own age group.

Basis of Developmental Reading. The basic provision of developmental reading is that each child should be taken where he is in reading, that learning takes place at the child's operational level regardless of the grade in which he may be [1]. Theoretically, in a class of twenty-five youngsters, each child might be reading at a different level. This theory is accepted at face value by teachers who practice individual reading instruction [9]. It is much more common, however, for a teacher in the elementary grades to have from three to five reading groups. This takes care of all except the extremely atypical cases. What happens to children from the three, four, or five reading groups when they go to junior high school? If they are fortunate, they may be grouped homogeneously by reading ability and school achievement, but usually there is little provision for the continuation of reading instruction. Yet those from the slowest group may be reading at the third- or fourth-grade level and may have the capacity to improve considerably.

Reading Tests. Obviously, if we are going to take a child where he is in reading, we must first determine at what levels he is actually functioning. This must be done both in oral and silent reading. In the latter years of elementary school and after, where a major portion of the reading encountered is silent, measures of silent-reading ability are most significant. In the primary grades, and where remediation is to be effected, oral reading is more important. Oral-reading tests are naturally time-consuming, since they must be individually administered.

Intelligence Tests. In addition to determining the oral- and silent-reading levels, a very thorough knowledge of mental ability is essential. The reason for this emphasis on intelligence is twofold. First, the classroom teacher will want to discover those who are handicapped by more or less limited mental ability. They are often referred to as slow learners and are usually provided for in the regular classroom, although in larger school systems that allow for homogeneous grouping they are placed in separate sections. Second, a comparison of reading-achievement and intelligence scores will reveal a number of boys and girls who are not reading up to their capacity. They will be helped most by a developmental reading program. When they are so severely retarded as to be reading-disability cases, they will benefit from remedial instruction.

Refinement of Skills. The emphasis in the primary grades is on learning to read, although as soon as possible a sense of purpose in reading is established [13]. Usually by the second or third grade, emphasis is on reading to learn. Yet reading skills already introduced need to be developed and refined. Among these skills are comprehension in silent reading, fluency in oral reading, enlargement of word meanings, development of reading interests, acquisition of a differentiated attack, and the attainment of independence in reading [2].

Oral Reading. In setting up a developmental reading program, one of the debatable topics is how much practice in oral reading should be provided and what form it should take [13]. Since silent reading is used more in subsequent schooling and in adult life, there is a tendency to neglect oral for silent reading. This is unfortunate, since oral reading is usually required in an audience situation. To force a child to read when he is unprepared and likely to do poorly often brings unfortunate results [2]. This is particularly true when boys and girls are called on in turn to read paragraphs from a common textbook. In addition to being a waste of class time, good students tend to be bored and the poor students are embarrassed and frustrated. Purposeful audience reading of plays, reports, stories, and summaries—all of which may be prepared—is superior.

Both Betts [1] and Yoakam [24] suggest other phases of oral-reading instruction. Despite the difficulty of fitting everything into a crowded program, opportunities for oral reading definitely should be provided in all subjects, at least informally, at the secondary school level.

Silent Reading. Silent reading is another complicated combination of skills which needs continued refinement in intermediate and upper grades. Silent reading is, at first, quiet oral reading. As the young reader eliminates his voice and as his word-recognition skills develop so that his ready-recognition vocabulary contains more and more words, silent reading improves.

All the silent-reading skills are taught initially in the primary grades, but there is a great difference between their use in first grade and their use in twelfth grade. For example, the first grader may be asked to tell how he thinks a story will end, while the high school senior may be asked to point out the probable effects of certain proposed legislation. Both are predicting outcomes, but at vastly different levels. During the intervening period, development should not be left to chance. Comparable growth is achieved in other silent-reading skills such as understanding the general significance, reading for details, organizing, summarizing, following directions, forming sensory impressions, and doing critical reading [2].

Comprehension of the material read is fundamental to success in silent reading. In turn, this comprehension depends on the reader's knowledge of the meaning of individual words, phrases, and sentences. Progress is made in much the same manner as a high jumper tops the bar at increasing heights. The reader makes substantially better progress if he is given material of regulated and slightly increasing difficulty. The emphasis is on understanding rather than speed, so that the term *speed of reading* is being replaced by the more meaningful *speed of comprehension* [23]. Durrell [6] charts the increase of speed in both oral and silent reading. Usually speed is one of the last skills stressed, and then only when the other contributing skills are satisfactorily developed and are functioning correctly. As Bond [2] correctly points out, "The way to make the majority of students *rapid* readers is to make them *effective* readers."

Word Meaning. Another reading skill which reveals the growth nature of reading is that of understanding word meaning. While it is usually recognized that vocabulary should be taught and not caught, it is undeniably true that children catch and share the enthusiasm an able teacher shows for the selection of the right words. A good teacher in any subject teaches the meaning of words in many ways as he continually whets young appetites with new approaches. The routine study of formal lists of words out of context is being replaced by the study of words as they occur in material being read [23]. This second method calls for more preparation on the part of the teacher; and, as is often true, the change from a formal to an informal approach increases the risk that study will be minimized. Many teachers will want to use both approaches to teaching vocabulary.

Children should be given experiences in using words both orally and in writing. The development of understanding word meanings goes through three phases: ability to recognize the word in print; knowledge of extensions of meaning or the shift of meaning often referred to as semantics; and an appreciation of the depth or vividness of impression conjured up by the proper selection of words. All phases depend on ever-increasing experience with words. The growth function becomes more obvious when we recall that comprehension of word meaning is measured in all group and individual intelligence tests.

Reading Interest. Perhaps nowhere else do we see the developmental nature of reading so well as in the growth of interest. There appears to be a definite connection between interest and reading ability—the better readers having widespread interests [2]. Several devices are on the market for stimulating and recording spheres of interest and drawing attention to neglected areas. The S.R.A. Inventory [18] and My Reading Design [21] are two of them.

The cultivation of interest in reading is not the job of one teacher or even one department. If the school is to counteract the passive attitude toward reading unfortunately found in some children, the cooperation of all departments is essential. Radio programs, moving pictures, and television are used by the skillful teacher to stimulate reading. Scholastic Magazines now publish advanced listings of radio and television offerings which may be employed to advantage by giving boys and girls a choice of programs to follow outside of school.

Interest is often the unknown factor. When a reader is interested in a certain topic, he usually brings to his reading a background knowledge of concepts and a technical vocabulary which enable him to comprehend materials of greater and greater difficulty. In other words, interest may provide many of the techniques and attitudes necessary to readiness for reading.

Interest may be deepened and broadened by starting with students' current interests at the reading level appropriate for each individual. But the book-report systems used by many English departments leave much to be desired. A book report a month from a prescribed list, often ungraded and heavily weighted in favor of the classics, is standard practice in many schools. The report a month from such a list is too much to expect of the poorer readers, who often are not interested in a single book from such a list and are unable to read them. At the same time, the better readers should be able to double or treble the quota. However, the formalized written report frequently dampens whatever interest the better readers may have in actual reading. Two alternatives are suggested as being better from a developmental reading point of view.

The first suggestion is to incorporate the reading as a supplement to classroom work. This enables the student to gather ideas from several sources, evaluate and combine them in his own mind, and, in short, to do creative reading. Informal reports on this reading, which at times may replace text assignments for certain units and certain students, may thus be made a vitalized part of the instruction in every subject.

The second improvement is the establishment of a guided free reading period once a week for the entire class period. This is usually done under the direction of the English department, although a school could well allocate different grades to various departments. A 3- by 5-inch card, a different color for each school year, records pertinent data and is kept on file. A fuller explanation of this reading period is to be found in Dunn [5]. While good readers usually plan their own reading from book reviews, the teacher and the librarian give careful attention to the retarded readers by employing such reading lists as the Durrell-Sullivan *High Interest–Low Vocabulary Booklist* [7], or, in the case of those who have interests other than reading, a list similar to *Fare for the Reluctant Reader* [5]. This reading period has the added advantage of giving the teacher an opportunity to work individually with retarded readers in the class.

Differentiated Attack. The young reader learns how to select appropriate reading techniques by wide reading of many different types of material. *Differentiated attack* is the term applied to skill of varying reading approach in accordance with the difficulty of the material and the purpose for which it is being read [2]. Skimming a magazine article to determine whether it has suitable information for a report calls for a different approach than does reading the directions for performing a science experiment. If a student is called upon to do little reading except the day-to-day assignment

in a textbook, he will have little chance to develop this highly refined skill which so many of our high school and college students
fail to possess. Here, as in other phases of reading, the individual
learns through his own experience. In other words, he actively
participates in the learning process [23].

Independence in Reading. Finally, the goal of all reading instruction is to produce independent readers, able to continue on their
own after formal schooling has terminated. This reading must be
of high enough quality—both in the nature of the material and in
comprehension of it—to be stimulating and rapid enough to be
functional. If reading is slow, laborious, and lacking in comprehension, the reader will soon cease to read. That this has been true
in the past is attested to by the relatively little reading done by a
vast segment of our adult population.

One of the principal ways to gain independence in reading is to
set up in all subjects situations in which students have to locate and
use materials for the purpose of meeting a goal [2]. The important
requirement is that the reading be utilized to make a report, oral or
written, to illustrate a statement in a textbook, or to write a summary. True learning takes place as the reader *reacts* to what is
being read by doing something with the information he has obtained. In order to have this occur, students must be released from
page-by-page textbook assignments. They need to be freed from
the deadly necessity of throwing back facts read from a book. To
achieve this, teachers will investigate the possibilities of unitary
teaching on different levels of reading difficulty. Classrooms will
become learning and discovery laboratories rather than question-
and-answer recitation rooms. Examinations will need to be changed
radically, for information will be valued not of and for itself alone
but only in so far as it is employed to illustrate and clarify concepts.

READINESS FOR READING

Good teachers have always recognized the necessity of taking
time to get their classes prepared or in the right frame of mind,
as some say, for a new reading selection. This preparation takes on
added significance in the light of what is known about the developmental nature of reading.

Much confusion has been caused by the rather loose use of the term *reading readiness*. Originally the term referred to that period in the primary grades, before reading instruction commenced; which at first consisted primarily of workbook teaching and readiness tests, and later included school activities designed to develop the emotional and social, the physical and mental, and the vocabulary and general language growth of children. Then teachers became aware that preparedness was essential to success in every reading situation encountered in school and adult life. However, the same term was applied to both sets of circumstances. In the interest of clarity, the term *readiness for reading* will be used when reference is made to this later preparedness.

Components of Readiness for Reading. Readiness for reading is a complex pattern of attitudes and abilities, both physical and mental, which a reader should possess in order to achieve the maximum from a forthcoming reading situation. Getting ready to read includes such widely different components as interest, technical and general vocabulary, basic knowledge of concepts involved, a purpose for reading, and, of course, those particular reading and study skills necessary for reading the selection in question with adequate comprehension.

Vocabulary. Most teachers think that preparedness in connection with readiness for reading lies in the vocabulary area. Science particularly lends itself to the development of a technical vocabulary. However, most subject-matter teachers acknowledge responsibility for teaching the particular vocabulary of the subject. But a teacher sometimes forgets this teaching area, or takes too much for granted, and neglects to draw attention to an author's method of defining technical terms. Harris [13] lists eight ways that are commonly employed. They are italics, definition of the word in parenthesis or footnote, an explanatory phrase or clause, a synonym, a simile or metaphor, a pictorial illustration, an explanatory sentence, and writing the sentence so that only one meaning can be attached to the word in question. Of course, dictionaries are essential to word study, but in the last analysis it is the author's use of the word in context that determines meaning. Good readers are skilled in deducing meanings from context. They become skilled by being challenged and shown how to develop this study technique.

Teachers are prone to take for granted matters of general vocabulary which they are responsible for developing. Often knowledge of common words is assumed, yet these common words are frequently used in a technical sense. A freshman girl, absent when the assignment was made, was told by her high school teacher to prepare a Civil War paper. Taking the assignment literally, she prepared a newspaper appropriate to the Civil War period. The teacher needs to be aware of the semantic shift in meaning of common words and to clarify meaning through example.

Concepts. A knowledge of the meaning of individual words is important, but so is an understanding of the basic concepts of the course being studied or the book being read. In so-called "sequential subjects," this is not so much of a problem. However, in subjects like science, English, and social studies taught by a problems approach, succeeding units of work are often not correlated, so that new groups of concepts keep appearing. Each new set of concepts is likely to require a new series of technical words which may not be mastered before another new subject introduces another series of words.

One way of simplifying the curriculum for slow learners is to reduce the number of concepts studied, automatically simplifying the vocabulary load, and to spend more time developing a few important ideas. A good example may be found in such social studies courses as those dealing with world history. Here, a reduction in the number of civilizations studied and the use of books of suitable difficulty are at least part of the answer.

Purposive Reading. A third way in which to facilitate readiness for reading is to give pupils an overview of what is to be accomplished. Human beings are purposive; they react to certain definite goals. Boys and girls outside of school usually have a reason for doing what they are doing, although possibly not a good reason from an adult's point of view. Children frequently see no purpose for things they are asked to do in school. The teacher should take the time to inform them or, better still, to work out with them the objective of their activities. Assignments should have one or more purposes for each individual. Page-to-page assignments, while they may occasionally be necessary, usually fail to give the reader a reason for his reading. One of the better ways of establishing purpose in reading is to allow the reader to have his own individual and specific reason for reading.

Interest. Much has been said of the importance of the interest factor in the reading situation. Sometimes, despite the efforts of the teacher, individuals or entire classes fail to respond. Lack of interest on the part of individual students may be due to physical, mental, emotional, or social causes. In this respect, upper-grade readiness for reading resembles primary grade reading readiness, but there are some major differences. The spontaneous enthusiasm of the earlier grades has very largely disappeared, so that if a child is ignorant about a subject he is quite likely to say he is not interested. At other times, a social veneer of pseudosophistication precludes showing true feelings. A child who has previously failed because the task given him was beyond his ability will frequently reveal no enthusiasm—in this way he adopts a protective mechanism.

When an entire class lacks interest, the teacher may well suspect the material being used. Either it is too difficult, or it has not been chosen wisely. Norvell [16, 17] has discovered the interest potentials of many of the literary selections customarily taught in school. He suggests that it is better to choose materials that possess an inherent interest for boys and girls than to take a selection that is more or less devoid of interest and attempt by sheer brilliance of teaching to attract them to it. Whatever the cause of lack of interest, the experienced teacher will seek to locate the reason and break down the barrier.

SQ3R Technique. An approach to readiness for reading that is worth developing, since it has much of value to contribute toward reading situations in senior high school and college, is Robinson's [20] SQ3R technique. Adaptations may also be made for the earlier grades.

The S of Robinson's study technique stands for survey. The individual reader or class finds out what is already known about the subject. Since, in one sense, reading may be thought of as adding new ideas to previously acquired knowledge, in effect the reader is marshaling his forces. Pooling information in the classroom arouses interest. The survey also includes looking over pictures, charts, graphs, paragraph leads, chapter headings, and summaries.

The S precedes the Q which stands for questions that the individual or class thinks should be answered. This has the effect of establishing a purpose for the first R, which is the reading of the material under consideration. The second R stands for recitation. With individual readers, the process becomes an ongoing reaction to the material being read. The third R refers to the review of selected parts which have not been fully understood, as shown by the recitation. This second attack on the material calls for two very different types of reading: first, a rapid skimming to locate pertinent paragraphs; second, a somewhat slower, more careful reading of the passages not comprehended.

The Robinson technique is really a study process through which the reader is able to become interested in the forthcoming assignment and is forced to formulate goals which he tests as he reacts to the material read. It is very different from the far too common study technique of opening the book at the correct page, plunging into the assignment with no previous thought at all, and hoping to pick out and remember important ideas. The Robinson plan may be expanded to provide a whole teaching cycle.

Teaching Reading Skills. Readiness for reading includes other study skills such as outlining, the locational skills, and dictionary reference. The time to teach and review reading skills is when they are needed. Review should be combined with the assignment and the first steps may be started in class. When this is done, sufficient time should be allowed to make the experience significantly worthwhile. The contrast between a bewildered class hearing a teacher's assignment, "For next time read pages . . . ," and a group of interested boys and girls who have reviewed the necessary reading skills and have definite purposes for doing the assignment, is illustrative of the need for continued and continuing instruction in reading.

DISTINCTIVE FEATURES OF DEVELOPMENTAL READING

It would be a mistake to imply that developmental reading is an easily obtainable educational panacea. To continue reading instruction in all subjects through the upper elementary and secondary school imposes many problems [8].

Increased Library Resources. Wider reading in various associated areas at different levels of difficulty demands more books and more carefully selected books. Much of the reading material should be organized in classroom libraries to be readily usable by both students and teacher.

Elimination of Single Textbook. A developmental reading program requires reading material at different levels of difficulty. Therefore a number of partial sets of textbooks are needed instead of a complete class set of one book. The provision of partial sets sometimes means more money. For example, when a small school loses a teacher who has been using several texts, the replacement may want to order a complete set of one textbook.

A teacher reported that during an interview, the hiring official was quite enthusiastic about the provision for several reading levels until the new teacher suggested buying five copies of one text, ten of another, and seven or eight of a third. The principal replied that it could not be done. The reason given was that the new teacher was obviously going places; and the principal was afraid that, when the young teacher left to take a better position, the replacement would probably want a single text, with the result that the school would be left with several incomplete sets of books on its hands. Obviously neither the school nor the principal was ready for this teacher.

Misunderstanding of Purpose. A third point involves a misunderstanding of the purpose of developmental reading. Mention has already been made of the need for a good public relations program. Both parents and the general public are apt to seize on the curriculum and materials prepared for the below average rather than the work laid out for the able. As a result, teachers are often accused of watering down the school's offering.

It is true that many schools attempt to meet the demands of a widely heterogeneous school population with varying levels of reading ability without understanding the developmental reading philosophy and merely achieve a course that fails to challenge the better students. It is also true that a school making provision for individual reading ability actually *steps up* its offering for the able learners while providing the slow learners with easier materials at their learning levels. It is unfortunate that many good school systems are wrongfully criticized because of incomplete information on the part of the taxpayer.

More Difficult Teaching. The final consideration is that, in providing for differences in reading ability, teaching becomes more difficult. This appears to be most pronounced at the secondary level where securing materials on many levels of reading difficulty is complicated. Although the guidance department assists in determining the proficiency of each student, the teacher must keep groups elastic and guard against unduly forcing the slow learners while challenging the more able. Since concepts generally do not lend themselves to simplification, the alert teacher must be ready to interpret, give examples, and clarify difficult concepts through discussion, analogy, and identification with students' own experiences.

FURTHERING A DEVELOPMENTAL READING PROGRAM

Before considering ways in which a developmental reading program can be furthered, one misconception regarding the outcomes of such a program needs to be corrected. A dynamic reading program will not equalize reading levels. On the contrary, as such a program becomes established, the spread of reading abilities will tend to become larger rather than smaller. The mentally slow will be limited to comparatively small gains, while the able learners will make relatively larger improvement. Thus, the aim of developmental reading instruction is not to bring all up to a certain standard but to enable each individual to achieve all he is capable of achieving [19].

Training Colleges. Our teacher training institutions can help by carrying their philosophy of providing for individual differences in learning and reading ability out of the theory stage and into actual practice. This includes identifying the poor reader in the classroom, learning what materials are available at different levels of difficulty, developing units to meet varying reading abilities and interests, and affording first-hand experiences to several groups within one classroom.

Help for Beginning Teachers. Many beginning teachers accept positions in smaller communities where heterogeneous classes tend to be the rule and are faced with most difficult teaching assignments at the precise time when they lack experience. Many supervisors and department heads assign a faculty member who is acquainted with local problems to assist the beginning teacher in matters pertaining to the curriculum, cumulative folders, the register, grouping, and instructional materials.

Unit materials, which have been developed by teachers and which fit the local situation and are adjusted to the resources of the library, should remain the property of the school. A new teacher coming to a school would thus have something on which to build instead of starting with an empty file cabinet. A businessman would not expect the firm's bookkeeper to walk off with the company's books when leaving for another position, retirement, or marriage. Yet practically every teacher walks away with the units he has prepared. Very few teachers would want to use another teacher's material exactly, but much drudgery could be avoided by a businesslike approach to this problem.

Help for Experienced Teachers. Beginning teachers may feel the need for the sense of security afforded by using a single textbook. However, experienced teachers soon realize the desirability of providing materials of varying degrees of difficulty to challenge young readers. As subject-matter specialists, they know reference books, shorter articles, and the textbooks available in their own fields. They do not always know the difficulty of these materials. Thus, a knowledge of various difficulty formulas, together with an understanding of the limitations implied in the use of them, becomes an effective tool as teachers seek to provide reading materials for both slow and able learners in their classrooms.

Difficulty Studies. Many attempts have been made to discover methods of determining the difficulty of reading materials. In 1935 Gray and Leary [12] made a comprehensive study of more than eighty elements influencing reading difficulty for adults. Since that time, numerous difficulty formulas have appeared. Some of the better known formulas are those by Dale and Chall [4], Flesch [11], Lorge [14], Spache [22], and Yoakam [24]. Figure 3 gives the factors of difficulty used by each and the effective grade range.

The typical difficulty study is based on a sampling of the entire work, except in the case of relatively short articles. These samples,

FIGURE 3. REPRESENTATIVE DIFFICULTY FORMULAS SHOWING FACTORS
OF DIFFICULTY AND POSSIBLE USE

Name	Factors of Difficulty	Possible Use
Dale-Chall	Average sentence length. Per cent of words not on Dale list of 3,000 words.	Grade 4–College
Flesch Reading Ease	Average sentence length. Average word length in syllables.	Grade 5–College
Flesch Human Interest	Percentage of "personal words." Percentage of "personal sentences."	Grade 5–College
Lorge	Average sentence length. Relative number of prepositional phrases. Words not on Dale list of 796 words.	Below Grade 7
Spache	Average sentence length. Words not on Dale list of 796 words.	Grades 1–3
Yoakam	Words having difficulty index of 4 or above as determined by Thorndike *Teacher's Word Book of 20,000 Words.*	Grades 4–6

which may vary from ten pages per book to a hundred-word passage every tenth page, are analyzed for such factors as sentence length, word length, vocabulary difficulty, and others.

Difficulty studies are open to several criticisms. The first concerns sampling itself and is based on the need to economize on the time required to make the study. Obviously, the greater the number of samples, the more closely they tend to represent the whole article or book. Despite the care taken to ensure random sampling (i.e., the selection of every tenth page), one can never be sure that he has actually obtained a representative sampling.

A second objection to difficulty studies concerns those employing special word lists. Here, the procedure is to classify as difficult any words not appearing on a specified list. However, scientific research and invention are constantly introducing new words to our language and today's mass media are popularizing them. "Sputnik," "atomic," "nuclear reactor," "jet propulsion," and "electronic" are specialized words entering common usage because of an aroused interest in scientific progress. They might well appear in an article selected for a difficulty study. These words, although frequently well known to young children, do not appear on lists of familiar words. Their absence would seem to indicate that the selection is difficult, whereas this is actually not the case.

A third objection also centers about vocabulary. Word difficulty may be effectively measured by word length or omission from a list of familiar words at the earlier grade levels of elementary school; but at the secondary and adult reading levels a more important factor is the difficulty of the ideas presented [15]. Closely connected to this is the rate of intake of ideas with their supporting factual information.

Fourth, reading-difficulty formulas can take no account of various kinds of reading done for different purposes—at least existing formulas make no provision for this. For example each subject-matter area has its own particular set of technical terms which tend to form a basic vocabulary for that particular area although the words may be most difficult. These terms depend upon concepts which are being developed in the subject-matter area, but they correlate with vocabulary in other subjects and areas and become part of an individual's general vocabulary.

Fifth, with the exception of the Flesch [11] human-interest formula, no difficulty study takes account of the interest factor. Human interest is only part of the picture, yet interest—the reader's personal interest in the selection—and the interest inherent in the reading material appears to be one of the more important considerations in attempts to determine readability.

A final criticism concerns the amount of time required to make a difficulty study. The number of samplings to be made is a determining factor which is controlled by the length of the book being tested and the requirements specified by the author of the formula. Familiarity with the content of word lists and practice in computing mechanical details cut down the working time. It is probably correct to say that the time required to evaluate a book of 400 pages is somewhere between a minimum of two to five hours and a maximum of ten to fifteen hours. Articles, which are tested either in their entirety or by sampling, take substantially less time.

Use of Difficulty Formulas. In all probability, teachers will continue to employ appropriate difficulty formulas on magazine and newspaper articles which are of sufficient importance to warrant repeated use in unitary teaching. Materials of passing value should be given to several students whose reading abilities are known. Since they will read at varying levels, their oral or written reports will indicate what reading ability the material requires. For the time being, teachers may find it necessary to check the difficulty of textbooks. This can well be the undertaking of a subject department.

Once the demand has become apparent, publishing companies can furnish the teaching profession with accurate information on the difficulty of books to be used as texts. A starting point might be made with required subjects such as social studies, English, and general science. Later, the elective subjects could be included. The actual grade or grade range of difficulty should be given rather than descriptions such as "Suitable for Slow Learners in Grade 10." This would eliminate the teacher's time-consuming tasks of determining the grade placement of reading materials and making individual difficulty studies.

The philosophy underlying a developmental reading program would indicate that a single text cannot be suitable for use in a given grade. In fact, the use of a single text does not meet the requirements of such a program. Several texts—at least three—of varying degrees of difficulty are needed. If these texts, written for heterogeneous classes, are to be of optimum use, the general organization of topics or units should be parallel. This will not result in the same book written at different levels of difficulty. Rather, the result will be separate, independent texts which may be used in the appropriate sections of homogeneously grouped classes. Obviously, publishing companies will issue such texts only if teachers, department heads, and administrators indicate a need for them. From the point of view of the publishing companies, the fulfillment of this request for parallel content on various levels is difficult but not impossible.

Many of the objections to difficulty formulas may be avoided if material is checked for difficulty at the time of writing. Errors introduced by sampling and by using fixed word lists would be eliminated. Sentence length and the number of polysyllabic words (exclusive of technical terms) can be more effectively controlled at the time of writing than later. The density of factual information or fact packing can be reduced in books which are being prepared for easier reading levels. Teachers interested in writing their own material will find Flesch [10] helpful.

Need for Cooperation. Developmental reading is obviously a cooperative effort on the part of all members of the staff, assisted by outside agencies. Parents, the general public, teacher training institutions, and publishing companies are involved. A child's continuous progress in reading depends on the teachers he will have later on as well as on his present instructors. Only by a concerted effort can a developmental reading program become really effective.

REMEDIAL READING

Just what is the place of remedial reading in a developmental reading program? Is it necessary? Should it come before or after a developmental program? These and other questions confront teachers and administrators as each in his own way seeks to evaluate reading instruction in upper elementary and secondary grades.

What Is Remedial Reading? Many answers to this question are possible. All teachers at times give instruction which is remedial, but the term is usually applied to a special program for selected cases. It is an adjunct to developmental reading and is itself developmental in the sense that instruction begins at the individual's own reading level. Diagnostic analysis is made before instruction begins, and special materials are usually employed. Instruction is usually individual or by small groups, with a specially trained reading teacher or, failing that, by a teacher who is interested in this type of instructional therapy.

Is a Remedial Program Necessary? If a developmental reading program were 100 per cent effective, there would still be a place for remedial reading. With transfer students, sickness, and crowded classrooms, remediation becomes a necessity if a school is to do effective work in reading. Approximately 15 per cent of any given school population is estimated to be in need of remedial instruction [3]. In schools where developmental reading programs have not been functioning, or where programs have limped along as programs in little more than name, the numbers may tend to be greater.

The principal advantages to be gained from a remedial program are two. First, there is more rapid improvement because of the intensive nature of the program. Gains of from two to three years in a single academic year are not unusual. Second, many boys and girls who, because of emotional or other causes, cannot be reached in the regular classroom program respond to more specialized remedial therapy. The quicker such individuals find success in reading, the easier is their adjustment to the classroom.

Who Are Remedial Reading Cases? Obviously, those who profit most from this specialized instruction are the reading-disability cases and others mentioned in Chapter 2. First, there are those in the high-intelligence–low-reading-ability group; second, those in the average-intelligence–low-reading-ability group; and, third, the low-intelligence–low-reading-ability group. This last group will make comparatively small progress and students are usually taken by the regular classroom teacher in slower homogeneous sections. One of the common mistakes in remedial programs is to load the reading teacher with students whose intelligence is such that progress is necessarily slow, thereby depriving the first two groups, whose gains can be more rapid. Where slow learners are taken, they should be taught in small groups.

Should Remedial Reading Come before Developmental Reading? A qualified "no" is the answer here. Unless the members of a school faculty are in general agreement regarding developmental reading and are actively engaged in doing what they can, setting up a remedial reading program actually may do harm. Unless there is a keen sense of the importance of reading instruction in the regular classroom, the teachers are likely to sit back, and "let George do it," with the result that the remedial reading teacher may be faced with the impossible task of supplying the reading instruction for the entire school. This is more true of the secondary school than it is of the elementary school. Within the elementary school itself, a similar situation is more likely to occur in the intermediate than in the primary grades. The reason for these statements is that the further away from the primary grades a teacher is, the more concerned he is with subject matter.

Bond [2], writing in 1941, pointed out that ". . . those interested in the reading problem in the high school have been unduly concerned with diagnostic and remedial work. . . . Consequently, there has been a failure to realize the need of the entire high school population for continued instruction in reading." [1] Many schools, almost twenty years later, are still trying to solve their reading problems through remedial means; yet a large number of retarded readers need the help of the classroom teacher in developing their reading skills. The preventive side of developmental reading instruction should also be stressed.

When a school staff is aware of the need for continuing reading instruction and challenged to do something about it, the addition of a remedial program is likely to be most rewarding. A well-qualified reading specialist or reading teacher can give much valuable assistance in setting up and extending a continuous and continuing instructional program in reading. The important consideration is that each and every member of a school staff recognize the contribution that he can make through developmental reading to the remedial reading program.

SUMMARY

The basic provision of developmental reading is that each individual be taken at his present level. To do this, both reading and intelligence tests are necessary. Skills such as comprehension in silent reading, fluency in oral reading, vocabulary, reading interest, differentiated attack, and independence in reading need to be refined. This is best done by the classroom teacher in each subject.

Just as reading readiness precedes beginning reading instruction, so readiness for reading precedes all later reading situations. Re-

[1] Guy L. Bond and Eva Bond, *Developmental Reading in High School,* The Macmillan Company, New York, 1941, p. 58. Used by permission.

duced to its simplest terms, readiness for reading includes knowledge of vocabulary and concepts, the establishment of a purpose for reading, and the awakening of interest. Robinson's SQ3R technique is suggested as one method which accomplishes much that is desirable from a readiness-for-reading point of view. The time to teach reading skills is when they are needed in each subject. By identifying and eliminating reading obstacles as early as possible, the teacher can make the reading experience significantly worthwhile.

The distinctive features of developmental reading include increased library resources, the use of partial sets of books rather than a single textbook, and more difficult teaching. Training colleges, supervisors and administrators, and publishing companies can all help, since developmental reading is essentially a cooperative effort.

Remedial reading is a part of developmental reading. It is a necessary adjunct, for about 15 per cent of the school population is likely to need specialized instruction which permits greater gains and helps many who cannot be reached in the regular classroom. Those who are not reading up to their capacity are potential candidates. Remedial reading should be introduced after a school staff is aware of its involvement in developmental reading; otherwise, there may be a tendency to let the reading teacher provide the reading instruction for the whole school.

REFERENCES

1. Betts, Emmett A.: *Foundations of Reading Instruction,* American Book Company, New York, 1957.

* 2. Bond, Guy L., and Eva Bond: *Developmental Reading in High School,* The Macmillan Company, New York, 1941.

3. Davis, L. R., and Jacqueline Davis: "What Principals Should Know about Remedial Reading," *Clearing House,* vol. 29, pp. 298–300, January, 1955.

4. Dale, Edgar, and Jeanne Chall: "Formula for Predicting Readability," *Educational Research Bulletin,* vol. 27, pp. 11–20, 37–45, Ohio State University, Columbus, Ohio, January, February, 1948.

* 5. Dunn, Anita, Mabel Jackman, and Bernice Bush: *Fare for the Reluctant Reader,* CASDA, The New York State College for Teachers, Albany, N.Y., 1953.

6. Durrell, Donald D.: *Improvement of Basic Reading Abilities,* World Book Company, Yonkers, N.Y., 1940.

* 7. Durrell, Donald D., and Helen Blair Sullivan: *High Interest–Low Vocabulary Booklist*, Boston University, Boston, 1952.

8. Early, Margaret J.: "About Successful Reading Programs," *English Journal*, vol. 46, no. 7, pp. 394–405, October, 1957.

9. Evans, N. D.: "An Individualized Reading Program for the Elementary School," *Elementary School Journal*, vol. 54, pp. 157–162, 1953.

10. Flesch, Rudolf: *The Art of Readable Writing*, Harper & Brothers, New York, 1949.

11. Flesch, Rudolf: *How to Test Readability*, Harper & Brothers, New York, 1951.

12. Gray, William S., and Bernice E. Leary: *What Makes a Book Readable*, University of Chicago Press, Chicago, 1935.

* 13. Harris, Albert J.: *How to Increase Reading Ability*, 3d ed., Longmans, Green & Co., Inc., New York, 1956.

14. Lorge, Irving: "Predicting Readability," *Teachers College Record*, vol. 45, pp. 404–419, March, 1944.

15. Newton, J. Roy: "A Technique for Determining the Difficulty of Reading Materials on the Secondary Level," unpublished doctoral dissertation, Boston University School of Education, Boston, 1948.

16. Norvell, George W.: *The Reading Interests of Young People*, D. C. Heath and Company, Boston, 1950.

17. Norvell, George W.: *What Boys and Girls Like to Read*, Silver Burdett Company, Morristown, N.J., 1958.

18. Remmers, H. H., and Robert H. Bauernfeind: *SRA Junior Inventory, Form S*, Science Research Associates, Inc., Chicago, 1955.

19. Rickover, Hyman G.: *Education and Freedom*, E. P. Dutton & Co., Inc., New York, 1959.

20. Robinson, Francis P.: *Effective Study*, Harper & Brothers, New York, 1946.

21. Simpson, G. O.: "My Reading Design," *The News Journal*, North Manchester, Ind., 1945.

22. Spache, George: "A New Readability Formula for Primary-grade Reading," *Elementary School Journal*, vol. 53, pp. 410–413, March, 1953.

* 23. Strang, Ruth, Constance M. McCullough, and Arthur E. Traxler: *Problems in the Improvement of Reading*, 2d ed., McGraw-Hill Book Company, Inc., New York, 1955.

* 24. Yoakam, Gerald A.: *Basal Reading Instruction*, McGraw-Hill Book Company, Inc., New York, 1955.

* See Appendix A for annotated list of books for the professional library in schools.

Chapter 6

TESTING PROGRAMS

The only professionally justifiable use of a testing program employing reading and intelligence tests is the improvement of instruction. This improvement may take several forms. By studying test results, a subject-matter teacher becomes conscious of the wide differences in reading ability in his classes, resulting from chronological promotion and a developmental approach to reading in the earlier grades. The reading-test scores of his own students will make him aware of these differences and the result will be better instruction. As instruction improves, he will look upon the results of reading tests as one measure of his teaching achievement. Again, the reading teacher needs the information acquired through such a testing program to decide who could profit from specialized work. The guidance department needs such information to direct students, particularly concerning special programs and college entrance courses. The formation of class sections in homogeneously grouped schools depends, in part, on ability as it is measured by tests. Finally, all teachers can profitably use the results of a testing program as one of the bases for selecting instructional materials. By experiments based on a knowledge of reading and mental abilities, the classroom teacher is in a position to add many valuable contributions to research in teaching and reading techniques.

Much harm may be done by establishing a testing program too rapidly, before definite plans for both developmental and corrective work—including provisions for staff, time, and materials—have been made. A testing program that does not benefit instruction is worse than useless, since both children and parents expect something from it. If nothing is done, parents are prone to consider the tests as the basis upon which the school judges the fitness of children for promotion.

The attitude of "Now, thank goodness, we can go back to teaching," on the part of the teaching staff, is difficult to condone in a modern school system. The fact that such a feeling does exist, happily rather rarely, is an indication that someone has moved too fast. A reading program cannot be built in a day, and careful preparation is required before a testing program can improve instruction.

THE READING SURVEY

There are many ways in which a school may be aroused to an awareness of the importance of reading. In some cases public criticism results in an increased awareness; in others, individuals and groups of teachers realize that the needs of the slow learner and the gifted are not being met. By whatever means criticism of a program manifests itself, there is apt to be an uneasy realization that something is wrong.

Before a school can determine what steps to take in improving reading instruction, it must ascertain by a reading survey the relative effectiveness of its program and discover where weaknesses exist. Two methods are generally available: the survey may be conducted by some outside organization, or it may be undertaken by the school system itself. Whichever course is decided upon, all members of the staff, including the administration, should be involved in its inception, planning, and the resulting corrective measures.

Outside Survey. A survey by an outside agency has the advantage of being objective. This may be the more desirable procedure in extreme cases where a school system is on the defensive. However, its very objectivity is a weakness in some respects. Far too frequently individual teachers are not consulted, or, if they are consulted, their attitude toward the survey is that they, rather than the reading program, are on trial. Any evaluation of a school must go far beyond testing and reporting test results. The uses made of materials, shortages of equipment, atmosphere of classrooms, particular contributions of individual members of the staff, and the whole philosophy of the faculty are significant items.

Sometimes the reading specialist of a nearby college may conduct the survey, employing students who are being trained as reading specialists. Such a practice usually results in a better attitude toward the survey, since some of the teachers probably know the college specialist. Whatever is lost in objectivity is more than made up for by greater sensitivity. By far the greatest problem to be faced is the feeling that the staff does not want the survey, or that it has been imposed from without or from above.

Internal Survey. The alternative to the survey made by an outside agency is one conducted by the school system itself. The Reading Improvement Committee, suggested in Chapter 1, may assume responsibility for organizing the survey.

By beginning with carefully selected tests, administered in a professional manner, objectivity is obtained at the start. With this as a point of departure, teachers are then ready to formulate answers to the question "Why are some pupils failing to make average growth in reading?" Each teacher lists names of boys and girls who are not making satisfactory progress [7]. From this point on, the staff survey has distinct advantages, since classroom teachers know —better than any outside agency—past school achievement, have ready access to cumulative folders, are aware of social and emotional behavior patterns, and are acquainted with the influence of the home and community.

Perhaps both the Reading Improvement Committee and the administration should be warned that there can be no halfway measures where a survey is concerned. During a survey, a school staff will almost inevitably become vocal regarding limitations of materials, deterrents to successful reading instruction in the community, and problems involving the promotion and reporting practices of the school. Teachers will be examining the philosophy underlying grouping, promotion, reporting, cumulative folders, examinations, and developmental reading. Under the skillful direction of the Reading Improvement Committee and the administration, this increasing awareness of the interrelationship of many of our perennial school problems ultimately leads to improvement of instruction.

Action research of the type indicated involves teachers as they try to find the causes of poor performance and work out corrective measures. Research of this kind is one of the most effective types of in-service training, since individual teachers are involved and no outside consultant is present to do their thinking or to make recommendations for them. Such research is sorely needed in every school for it "reaches and benefits the child, helps the teacher grow . . . and is operated on the ground floor of teacher-pupil interaction in the school" [7].

The point has been made that a staff survey is often superior to that of an outside agency because of the involvement of individual teachers and the learning that emerges from group thinking. The logical extension of the survey is to include parents and boys and girls. Community participation may be independent [9] or it may be a joint undertaking.

Chapter 1 suggests that young people, their parents, and other members of the community be included in the Reading Improvement Committee. While much of the survey must be limited to professional people because of the personal nature of intelligence-test results and other information contained in the cumulative folder, lay members should be included in planning the survey and implementing it. Later, in developing such areas as community resources, the lay members of the committee will become increasingly important. But to call them in only for a specific task is a weakness in survey design which should be avoided.

SETTING UP A TESTING PROGRAM

There are a number of important decisions to be made when setting up an intelligence-testing program. They will vary with each school, depending upon size, the training of staff, and the intelligence testing that has been done in the past. The entire teaching staff, together with the administration, will need to consider a number of topics.

Frequency. How often should intelligence tests be given? For a minimum testing program, it is desirable to have mental-age scores at the beginning of first grade, fourth grade, seventh grade, and, depending somewhat upon the curriculum, at either ninth or tenth grade. Secondary school students who are seeking college admission will probably take a further psychological examination and the results will be forwarded to the school. Terminal students should be tested by the school so that all profiles will be complete. As reading instruction is extended to junior and senior high school, the appropriate tests should be added. However, there appears to be little sense in building up a file of intelligence scores—as is sometimes done when such tests are administered annually—unless the school program utilizes the results.

Selection of Tests. Some teachers and guidance counselors prefer to use different batteries of the same test, feeling that the results may be compared. Others prefer to use the appropriate level battery of several tests throughout the span of elementary and secondary education. Much might be written about both plans, but probably the second course is superior—if only because this procedure enables the staff to become familiar with several measuring instruments. Good policy would indicate that the actual form of the test given at each of the testing levels should be changed from year to year. This practice removes the possibility of any well-meaning, but ill-advised, person rendering the results of such tests invalid.

Economy. In the interests of economy—in both time and money—tests which permit the use of machine-scored answer sheets should be selected. Test booklets can be used several times if they are collected and carefully examined for possible markings after each use. An exception may be made in early elementary grades where the use of separate answer sheets often introduces an unnecessary complication resulting in lower scores. While some tests have been accompanied by slightly lower norms for use with individual answer sheets, on the whole it is better to avoid the difficulty. Since test forms go out of print, a good supply of answer sheets and test booklets should be purchased. If the school does not have a test-scoring machine, two or more school systems may share the equipment, the machine may be operated on a county-wide basis, or the answer sheets may be forwarded to a nearby college. When this is done, the appropriate scoring stencils, clearly marked "Property of _____," should be sent with the answer sheets.

Reliability. Some intelligence tests are published in long and short forms. Other things being equal, the long form should be used where possible, as it tends to be more reliable.

Administration. A decision needs to be reached concerning who should administer the tests—the guidance department or the classroom teacher. For young children, administration by the classroom teacher is better. For the youngest children, groups smaller than the entire class should be formed. For older children, one has to balance several considerations: the number to be tested, the availability of large rooms, the lack of rapport in testing large groups, and possible disruption of the daily schedule. Obviously there can be no set answer to these testing problems. The main consideration is that test administration should provide optimum working conditions for those taking the test.

Methods of Reporting Intelligence Scores. Two of the more common ways of reporting intelligence-test results are by intelligence quotient (IQ) and by mental age (MA). Both have advantages and disadvantages. The IQ is probably the method known best to teachers and has the further advantage of remaining relatively stable. On the other hand, IQs are very easily remembered and a child's IQ is likely to be branded in the teacher's mind. For comparison with reading-test scores, mental-grade scores are most useful, but these are not always readily obtainable. Both mental-age and mental-grade scores are less meaningful since they go out of date, and for the same reason, students are not so easily labeled by them.

If an IQ score obtained some time ago is to be used in reading, a calculation must be made to estimate the present mental age [6]. This calculation is a simple one consisting of multiplying the present chronological age expressed as a decimal (i.e., 8 years 4 months = 8.33) by his obtained IQ also expressed as a decimal (i.e., 80 IQ = .80). To convert a mental age to a mental-grade score simply subtract five years and convert to a decimal. An easier procedure is to select a test which reports results in terms of mental grade, thus avoiding any calculation when current tests are employed. An even simpler method is to use the handy inexpensive conversion table supplied by the California Test Bureau.

The mental-grade method of reporting intelligence-test scores varies from year to year. Since tests are usually not given every year, a workable procedure is to record scores as IQs on the cumulative folder and convert them to mental-grade scores when making comparison with reading-test results.

GROUP AND INDIVIDUAL TESTS

The school setting up a reading program, or extending it to cover the secondary levels, will be concerned first with group intelligence tests. As work progresses and as individuals are to be selected for special work, individual intelligence tests will be needed to aid further diagnosis. A convenient alphabetical listing of many tests is to be found in Harris [6], while Buros [3] is the final authority.

Group Intelligence Tests. By far the most widely used test in many parts of the country is the Otis Quick-Scoring Mental Ability Test. It has the advantages of being easy to score and relatively inexpensive. A good test to use when no work is done in reading, the Otis becomes less effective when a school becomes reading-conscious, since it yields a single intelligence score. It becomes, in effect, a reading test as well as a measure of mental ability. This is an advantage when no special work is done in reading, but it may become a disadvantage, since for reading instruction we need language and nonlanguage or verbal and nonverbal subtest scores.

Another widely used group test is the California Test of Mental Maturity. This furnishes verbal and nonverbal quotients, enabling the reading specialist to obtain more useful information about the boys and girls with whom he is working. For example, a child whose language IQ is markedly higher than his nonlanguage IQ is not so likely to show as much improvement in reading as a person whose nonlanguage score is considerably higher than his language score. We might suspect that something has caused the verbal score to become artificially high in the first instance.

Of the many group intelligence tests available, there are some which give verbal and nonverbal subtest scores. Among this smaller group are the American Council Psychological Examination and the Differentiated Abilities Tests. The DAT, as it is called, is somewhat more expensive since it is composed of a number of separately bound subtests. This, of course, enables the guidance counselor to select the tests he wishes to administer. A relative newcomer, the School and College Ability Test, is published by the Cooperative Test Division of the Educational Testing Service. SCAT provides measures of language and numerical ability.

Individual Intelligence Tests. So far, no mention has been made of individual intelligence tests. The Revised Stanford-Binet is well known, but for certain age groups it is being replaced by the Wechsler Intelligence Scale for Children. The principal advantage of the WISC is that approximately one-half of the subtests are nonverbal, thus removing the necessity of administering a perform-ance test as is often done when the Binet is used.

Guidance counselors usually have little time for the administration of individual intelligence tests, yet for special cases they are admit-tedly much superior to group tests. Partly for this reason, many schools are now adding a psychologist to the staffs. Of course, there are many other special-purpose tests which supply additional in-formation affecting the learning situation, and they are also quite regularly administered by school psychologists.

READING INFORMATION

Before considering reading tests, certain information is very useful to teachers of grades 1 to 7. This material may or may not be con-tained in the cumulative folder. The Reading Improvement Com-mittee may wish to ascertain whether such information is being handed on and if teachers of succeeding grades are using it. (A form for rapid checking of this and other items pertaining to the school's reading climate is included in Appendix B.)

Basal Reading Level. Each teacher from the first grade through the sixth knows which groups her children are reading in and the level of their books. For example, she knows that in June the high reading group in the second grade has completed the second-grade basal readers and accompanying supplementary material and has read some third-grade supplementary books in addition. Her sec-ond group is halfway through the second book of the second-grade basal reader. Her slowest group has just completed the supplemen-tary material accompanying the first book of the second-grade basal reader. Two children are ready to start the second book of the first-grade basal reader. The teacher who has these children the following year will find this information more useful than the scores on a reading test alone.

The listing of actual materials read is of importance to the teacher of the following grade, the supervisor or reading specialist, and the principal. The teacher uses it in forming reading groups. Of course, this information will be checked informally after the teacher knows the children. The principal, supervisor, and reading teacher use this information in making up class sections for the following year. The school may not follow a strict homogeneous organization, but the two children reading at the first-grade level could advantageously be placed in a third-grade classroom where, with others reading at the same level, they will form a workable group. Finally, whoever is responsible for book orders will need this information for checking supplies for the next year. A businesslike handling of such information is a major step toward promoting the continuous progress of young readers.

Reading Achievement. Of course, not all boys and girls in each reading group will be achieving at the same level. This is one of the reasons why all such groupings should remain flexible. Some students may be good at word attack; others may excel in silent-reading comprehension. The teacher will learn the strengths and weaknesses of each student. Some publishing companies furnish achievement tests to accompany each reader. This may not be the case, or the teacher may prefer some other standardized test. Sometimes the teacher would rather use her own judgment based on observations of the child's whole school life plus her own informal diagnostic tests and evaluation. However obtained, this data is of great use to the teacher of the succeeding grade and every effort should be made to see that it is made available.

Reading Capacity Test. A special-purpose test that is helpful in certain cases is the Durrell-Sullivan Reading Capacity Test. Two levels are obtainable, the Primary for grades 2.5 to 4.5 and the Intermediate for grades 3 to 6. It is not a reading test in the usual sense, since the children being tested do no reading. As its name indicates, the test seeks to determine a child's capacity for reading or his reading intelligence by means of pictures. Its primary use is to supplement information obtained from intelligence tests in cases of individuals who do not seem to be reading as well as could be expected. A boy reading at the first-grade basal level in the third grade might be given this test to determine if he is a slow learner or if he has the capacity to improve his reading. In the latter case, his teacher or the reading specialist would give him individual or small-group work. The capacity test is not an individual test but may be given to groups of three to six children and rarely do more than this number need it at any one grade level. It should never be given to a whole class because there is only one form available, and our experience has been that children can remember the answers for a long period of time.

The Durrell-Sullivan Achievement Test, or an appropriate standardized silent-reading test, enables a teacher to compare achievement and capacity. In Figure 4, Henry and Bill show room for im-

FIGURE 4. COMPARATIVE SCORES ON *Durrell-Sullivan Reading Capacity* AND *Achievement Tests,* THIRD GRADE LEVEL

Pupil	Test	Reading Grade
Henry	Reading Capacity Reading Achievement	6.5 1.4
Bill	Reading Capacity Reading Achievement	3.9 2.6
Fred	Reading Capacity Reading Achievement	2.5 2.3

provement, while Fred is achieving all that should be expected of him.

The Reading Capacity Test is intended for children up to sixth grade and is therefore of particular interest to junior high school teachers and principals. Sixth-grade teachers should be encouraged to give this test to students who, in their estimation, are not achieving as they should. The test results will help them in working with these children for the balance of the year and will be invaluable in planning reading instruction at the beginning of the seventh grade. Perhaps this, more than any other single example, illustrates the necessity for cooperation between sixth- and seventh-grade teachers.

Cumulative Folder. The suggestions made concerning the kinds of reading information that may be obtained will indicate to elementary teachers and administrators that the cumulative folder used in many elementary schools probably needs to be changed to include the following items: basal reader, title and pages completed; titles of supplementary books read; achievement at basal level, including strengths and weaknesses; reading capacity, where test has been indicated, date administered, and results; corrective work done. All this is in addition to data concerning reading readiness, group and individual reading- and intelligence-test scores, vision, hearing, and general health data. No attempt is made here to design a cumulative folder embracing all this information, but a sample report page to be included in the folder is suggested in Appendix C.

Many educators feel it is good practice at the junior high level to abstract pertinent information previously collected. A child will normally have had several intelligence tests, plus many more reading tests. His reading progress each year should be recorded, as well as any special instruction that he may have had. Health records, including the results of screening tests, should be preserved. The usual information regarding school achievement, attendance, and parent conferences should also be included. Some junior high schools find it advantageous to set up their own personal data sheet, especially when they enroll children from several elementary schools. An even better procedure is to have teachers and principals of all schools concerned work together in drawing up an appropriate cumulative folder. If they can also agree on a minimal testing program which would have particular advantages for grouping and educational guidance beyond sixth grade, an important step in bridging the gap between the elementary and junior high schools will have been made.

SELECTION OF READING TESTS

Considerations of answer sheets, reusable booklets, the length of a test and its effect on reliability closely parallel the information included earlier in this chapter under the heading Setting up a Testing Program. Some other factors need to be considered before the reading tests themselves are enumerated.

Types of Reading Tests. Two of the more common kinds of standardized silent-reading tests are the survey-type test and the analytic test which is sometimes called diagnostic. The survey test, as its name indicates, is constructed to give an over-all estimate of reading ability. Usually the survey-type test contains, in addition to items on word meaning, paragraphs selected from different types of material such as might be found in the sciences, social studies, and English. These paragraphs are usually arranged in order of difficulty. These tests yield scores which are measures of vocabulary and comprehension, and there is a total score which is a composite of the others. Survey-type tests are usually administered to all the pupils of a given grade.

The analytic reading test can be readily distinguished from the survey-type test because it has a larger number of subtests, frequently six or more. Those who do poorly on the survey test should be given the analytic test. This does not mean all children who fall below the norm for the grade, but those whose reading falls substantially below what might be expected of boys and girls of their mental ability. Harris [6] suggests that in the first three grades the difference should be at least six months; for fourth and fifth grades, the difference should be at least nine months; and for grades above the fifth, there should be at least a year's difference between reading and intelligence scores. Normally, the analytic tests will be given to children having the greatest difference between scores.

A word of caution is necessary regarding the reliability of individual subtest scores in analytic tests. Provided the subtest items are well chosen, the longer the test, the more reliable it tends to be. A comparison of the two types of reading tests may be made on one item they both contain—vocabulary. The survey-type test will have from fifty to sixty items, while the analytic test may have only twenty to thirty. Obviously the vocabulary subtest scores of the analytic test tend to be less reliable than the scores for the longer vocabulary subtest of the survey reading test. The same thing is true of other subtest scores, which are derived from as few as ten items in some analytic tests. This does not mean that the analytic test results are worthless, but that they should be regarded as indications of possible weakness which should be further checked by drills in specially prepared materials. This is, of course, a normal working procedure in remediation. The total score on analytic tests is usually fully as reliable as that obtained from survey-type tests.

Purpose and Time of Testing. The purpose for which a reading test is given determines both the type of test selected and the time in the school year at which it is administered. Thus, a test to be used in helping set up homogeneous sections must be given toward the end of the previous school year. Since achievement tests are given at about the same time, the two may be combined by giving a survey-type test in May.

Classroom teachers, seeking to adjust instruction and improve reading abilities, would give an analytic test at the beginning of the year or semester. Very often a test which covers many of the reading study skills necessary to the reading of subject matter is chosen. There are many such tests, but the teacher should examine them carefully to see whether the subtest items deal with the particular reading skills demanded by his subject.

Special-purpose tests are administered at any time during the school year. The common practice is to give them just prior to special instruction.

Norms. When work is being initiated at any grade level, teachers, the guidance department, the reading specialist, and the administrator want to know who the good, average, and poor readers are. At first, the comparisons will have to be made with representative children, using norms furnished by the test publishers. As a school system continues testing year by year, it may develop its own norms. Statistical evidence of this sort is one of the most effective answers to public criticism of reading instruction. School districts that are somewhat removed by geographic location, cultural or economic background, the presence of large numbers of foreign-born children—or any factors which tend to make them atypical—should investigate the practicality of developing their own norms.

Validity of Reading Tests. There is no reading test comparable to the Revised Stanford-Binet test of intelligence which can serve as a yardstick to determine the validity of reading tests. Thus it is not possible to find reported in Buros [3], or in the literature accompanying reading tests, a coefficient of validity. Instead of a numerical coefficient of validity, two alternative measures of validity are used for reading tests. These are psychological validity and the judgment of experts. The former is based on the reasoning that there are certain skills which go to make up proficiency in reading.

The test in question is constructed with items covering these skills, therefore the test is a reading test. In the second measure of validity, a group of several experts on reading state that in their opinion the test in question is a test of reading. Both these measures of validity are more or less subjective—a limitation which probably accounts for the rather wide variation in reading tests. This variation, in turn, enables teachers to say, "I like test X, but I don't like test Y." Teachers should be encouraged to be critical, but they should seek to evaluate the basis for their criticism. Sometimes, unfortunately, they do not like any test that reveals weakness in the reading of their boys and girls.

Examination of Tests. Before a decision is made as to which test to purchase, there are a number of specific points to be considered. (1) The grade range of the test is important. It is poor policy to choose a test with a wide range if it is to be used at either extreme of the range. To ask tenth graders to take a test covering the grade range 3 to 10 means that they will have to answer an inordinately large number of easy items before reaching those which challenge their reading ability, to ask seventh graders to take a test for the range 7 to 12 means that they will find relatively few items they can answer. Another way of expressing this is to say that the proposed test should bracket the grade to be tested. Thus a test with a range of grades 3 to 10 might be a wiser choice for fifth, sixth, seventh, or eighth grade than it would be for third and fourth, or ninth and tenth grades. (2) While survey-type tests are simple to administer, some analytic tests have tricky subtest directions, timing, and scoring. (3) Answer sheets and scoring keys are sometimes confusing. (4) Reading scores for both survey and analytic tests are reported by grade and month up to approximately the eighth grade. Tests covering the higher ranges of reading ability report scores by percentiles since the amount of change per month at these higher levels is too small to be significant. Hence, it is better for junior high purposes to choose a test which is specifically designed for the junior high school than to use a test which covers the whole range of the secondary school. Using a junior high test will facilitate a comparison of reading-grade and mental-grade scores. For these reasons, examination copies of all tests being considered should be purchased. An even better procedure is to administer the test to one individual or to take the test personally before arriving at any decision.

Test selection as it applies to both elementary and secondary schools is discussed at greater length in Greene, Jorgenson, and Gerberich [4, 5]. Those desiring a single reference will find that Jordan [8] gives much the same information.

READING TESTS

The following consideration of reading tests—survey, analytic, and oral—is by no means complete. Many good tests have been omitted. Both Strang [11] and Harris [6] provide the names of additional tests. For those wishing a more complete evaluation, Buros [3] is the best source.

Reading Survey—Elementary Grades. Common practice is to give an achievement test toward the end of each school year in every grade. This battery of tests includes a reading test which may be given separately. Two of the better known tests are the Metropolitan Achievement Test and the Stanford Achievement Test. Similar to these is the California Reading Test, part of the California Achievement Tests.

Other survey-type tests which are not parts of achievement batteries are the Gates Primary Reading Test (1–2, 2–3), the Detroit Reading Tests (all levels), and the Nelson Silent Reading Test (3–8).

Reading Survey—Junior High. For teachers and guidance personnel seeking a survey-type reading test for use at the junior high level, there are many from which to choose. In addition to the reading parts of achievement batteries mentioned above, the reading test included in the Iowa Every-pupil Test of Basic Skills meets the needs of junior high testing programs, since the series covers achievement tests in English usage, arithmetic, and social studies. The test, Silent Reading Comprehension, Test A, Advanced, covers grades 6 to 8. Test B is a useful study-skills test. Where an extreme range of reading abilities is expected, the Gates Reading Survey, covering grades 3 to 10, is probably a better instrument. Two other well-known tests at this level are the California

Reading Test (7–9), which some teachers feel yields higher scores than other tests, and the Traxler Silent Reading Test (7–10).

Reading Survey—Senior High. The Cooperative English Test, Test C1, Reading Comprehension, Lower Level, has an indicated grade coverage of 7 to 12. However, it is best suited for use in senior high school, especially where poor readers in the upper grades are concerned. Also available are the California Reading Test (9–14), the Nelson-Denny Reading Test (10–12 and college), and the survey section of the Diagnostic Reading Tests (7–13).

Analytic Reading Tests. An analytic reading test should be selected to suit the level of reading abilities determined by the survey test. Occasionally the survey test is omitted where work in reading has been done previously. In such cases, testing starts with the analytic test.

The Sangren-Woody Reading Test (4–8) has subtests covering word meaning, rate, factual material, total meaning, central thought, following directions, and organization. Two forms are available. The Iowa Silent Reading Test is the most comprehensive as far as grade coverage is concerned. The three batteries are Primary (3–6), Elementary (4–9), and Advanced (9–12). The elementary test furnishes measures of rate, comprehension, paragraph meaning, sentence meaning, word meaning, following directions, outlining, and use of the index. There are four forms at each level. The SRA Reading Record is one of the most ambitious tests in so far as the amount of ground covered in thirty minutes is concerned. Ten subtests cover rate, comprehension, paragraph meaning, directory reading, map, table, and graph reading, advertisement reading, index usage, sentence meaning, and technical and general vocabulary. One form is available. Finally there are the Diagnostic Reading Tests, which are by far the most elaborate on the market. Eight separate booklets cover vocabulary, silent comprehension, auditory comprehension, general rate in social studies, rate in science, oral word attack, and silent word attack. The best use of these tests is probably as a very thorough and worthwhile addition to an established testing program rather than as a basis for use in setting up a new one.

Mention should also be made here of the Sequential Tests of

Educational Progress (STEP). These tests, published in separate booklets by the Educational Testing Service, cover listening, writing, reading, science, mathematics, and social studies. They are available as parts of batteries at intermediate, junior high, senior high, and college levels. The student is asked questions on a number of paragraphs of reading material in science, mathematics, and social studies. Thus, his ability to handle materials of different difficulty in these areas rather than his actual achievement is measured. The information obtained from these tests should be useful in placing boys and girls at various levels of homogeneous groups.

Oral Reading. For a complete diagnosis of reading disability, a test or tests of oral reading must be included. Such tests, time-consuming because they must be individually administered, are usually included when definite remedial instruction is being planned. The method of recording errors, indicated in the manual of instructions, should be followed implicitly so that other teachers can refer to the results.

A very useful introduction to oral-reading diagnosis is Gray's Standardized Oral Reading Paragraphs. This test consists of relatively short paragraphs at each grade level from first to twelfth. The Gray Check Tests comprise slightly longer paragraphs of five levels of difficulty. Four comparable forms at each level make these tests useful for periodic checking of progress. Another test of similar form is the Gilmore Oral Reading Test which consists of ten paragraphs ranging in difficulty from first through eighth grade. It has the added advantages of having comprehension questions and two forms of the test. The Bond-Clymer-Hoyt Reading Diagnostic Tests, published by Lyons & Carnahan, attempt to get some of the information obtained through oral-reading tests.

Another type of test of oral reading is the *informal reading inventory.* This is not a published test but a booklet, compiled by the reading teacher, of passages from basal readers of known difficulty [2]. It is frequently used as an intermediate step between the tests mentioned above and those mentioned below. Errors are recorded substantially the same way as is done with the Gray reading tests. For all practical purposes, informal reading analysis continues whenever a child reads aloud from material of known difficulty. Betts [1], in his *Handbook on Corrective Reading,* which accompanies the

American Adventure Series, gives an example of the informal reading inventory. Teachers might wish to examine this and use it before making their own. A somewhat similar provision for informal diagnostic testing is included in the Sheldon Readers, published by Allyn and Bacon, Inc. [10].

Finally, there are two tests which seek to do for reading what the Revised Stanford-Binet and the Wechsler-Bellevue tests do for intelligence testing. The first of these, the Durrell Analysis of Reading Difficulty, is intended for a grade range of 1 to 6 and covers many aspects of both oral and silent reading and word analysis. The second test, the Gates Reading Diagnostic Test, is for grades 1 to 5 and contains several tests of phonics in addition to oral and other reading skills. Both tests call for a highly trained examiner and take upwards of one hour to administer.

USE OF TEST RESULTS

Even though the teachers of a school have advanced in their concepts of developmental reading to the point of realizing the need for adequate measurement, many of them will need help in using test scores. Summer school students in professional courses continually ask, "Now that we have given the reading test, what do we do with the results?" This question is raised not by student teachers, but by experienced teachers. The circulation of reading and intelligence scores to teachers is far too frequently the end of the testing program.

Reading Habits. The teacher can learn a great deal about the reading habits of his boys and girls from their responses in test booklets or on answer sheets. When answers are machine-scored, it is advantageous to have hand-scoring stencils available for teachers to use in checking individual papers. Does the child work slowly but correctly? Or does he complete everything, obviously guessing madly? An affirmative answer to the first question may be checked by allowing the child additional time to complete the unfinished items of the test. If he raises his score substantially, work on rate of comprehension is indicated. Of course, for comparative purposes, his score should not be changed. If, however, the answer to the second question is in the affirmative, he needs to build up his comprehension and to learn how to adjust his rate to the difficulty of the material being read.

Survey Test Results. The subtest scores on survey tests show, in addition to the general reading level of individuals, whether whole classes, or groups within the class, could profit from work in vocabulary or comprehension, or both. The subject-matter teacher will be guided by the results in selecting reading materials on different levels of difficulty, in adjusting instruction, and in providing differentiated assignments.

Frequently teachers will say, "I am working with all the boys and girls whose reading scores fall below the grade norm. I hope to get them all up to the norm by the end of the year." Implied here are two rather serious misconceptions. First, such a statement hints strongly that the teacher still adheres to the grade-standard concept and feels he should be turning out a uniform product. Second, he is entertaining an erroneous idea of the relationship between intelligence and reading. He forgets that in a normal distribution there should be as many below the norm as there are above it. In working with all below the norm, he is working with slow learners as well as those whose capacity permits marked improvement in reading. At the same time, he may be neglecting the able learners who, while they may be doing average reading for their grade, are in reality reading far below their capacity. By a comparison of their reading achievement with their intelligence- or reading-capacity test results, the teacher should be able to adjust his instruction so that all boys and girls make the progress of which they are capable.

Meaning of Test Scores. What do test results in reading mean? Or more specifically, if a boy has a total reading (grade) score of 7.8, does that mean he can read seventh-grade materials? The answer to this question is usually "no." While he may read materials of seventh-grade difficulty along lines of his own interests (indicating that he has readiness for reading in that technical vocabulary and that the necessary basic concepts are known to him) his test level is what Betts [1] has termed the *frustration level.* Presumably, when taking the test, he was performing at his best. He cannot work at frustration level day in and day out. His workaday or *instructional level* is apt to be about one grade lower, or in the neighborhood of 6.8 in this case. This is the level of difficulty at which he can

function with the teacher's help in questions, explanations, and vocabulary and assisted by the momentum of the class situation in discussion and in group projects. A third level, about a grade lower or
5.8, is termed the *independent reading level*. Here unassisted reading or reading for fun is carried on. An understanding of the three
reading levels, and a realization that they are not exactly a grade
apart, helps teachers interpret and use test results. Many a teacher,
having found through classwork that a child cannot function at the
test level, proceeds to say the test was wrong. A little consideration
of how reading-test scores were obtained and the difficulty of the
reading expected in the classroom will show that Betts's principle
of differing reading levels contains much of significance for the
classroom teacher.

A SANE TESTING PROGRAM

A little thought will reveal that while a great deal may be accomplished by means of a well-organized testing program, some
dangers need to be avoided. Furthermore, a testing program which
does not pave the way toward better instruction often tends to be a
justification of low achievement and a warrant to continue the *status
quo.*

Undue Reliance upon Tests. The practice of administering reading-achievement tests toward the end of each school year may lead
to using test results as the sole basis for promotion or nonpromotion.
Probably no one thing can do more harm—both to a testing program
and to public relations—than such a misuse of tests. Certainly
nothing could be farther from the philosophy of developmental
learning.

No matter how well-constructed an intelligence test may be, there
is always a certain margin of error within the test itself so that inac-
curacies of from two to six months are by no means impossible.
Despite the criticism of standardized tests from some quarters and
the suggestion that guessing may result in unduly high scores, it
is probably correct to say that the individual's intelligence is rarely
lower than that indicated by the test and true capacity may be,
and frequently is, much higher. Performance at any specific time
may be markedly less than that indicated by test results.

Part of the discrepancy between potential capacity and actual achievement is brought about by the use of group tests for individual prognosis. Many children will score up to 20 points higher on an individual test of intelligence than they do on group tests. There is a danger that cut-off points, such as admission to a special class or remedial instruction, may be arbitrarily decided on the basis of group tests.

Overtesting. Another danger is that children will be subject to an undue number of standardized tests, thus cutting down instruction time. Here informal reading analysis is of particular value together with what might be called ongoing evaluation through instruction. This evaluation through instruction is possible in reading when the teacher and groups of boys and girls are working at the appropriate levels.

Labeling. The branding of children as too dumb to learn has already been mentioned as a possible danger resulting from testing. The use of mental-grade scores rather than IQs minimizes this difficulty. Reading levels do not hurt family pride to the same degree as does limited intelligence, but even these reading scores must be handled circumspectly. Some reading teachers believe that when special instruction has been undertaken and initial improvement shows that remediation is effective, the individual should be told in general terms the level at which he is reading as an incentive to further improvement.

Grouping. The use of intelligence-test scores as a basis for the formation of homogeneous groups has largely been replaced by a combination of school achievement, teacher judgment, and reading-ability scores. The reason for discarding the mental scores as a basis for grouping was the relatively low correlation found between latent ability as measured by intelligence tests and actual classroom performance.

Conclusion. A functional testing program is one of the basic requirements of every developmental reading program, since the measurement of intelligence and reading ability facilitates continuous and continuing instruction. Periodic testing with carefully selected instruments will enable teachers to stress the preventive aspects of reading by making possible the identification of individuals who are not making satisfactory progress before they become severely retarded. At the same time such a testing program will indicate those who could profit from specialized instruction.

SUMMARY

The justification of any testing program is the betterment of instruction. Decisions that need to be made regarding intelligence testing include frequency, selection, economy, reliability, administration, and methods of reporting scores.

For use in conjunction with reading tests, group intelligence tests yielding both verbal and nonverbal scores are required. As individuals are selected for special work in reading, individual measures of mental ability are desirable.

Before considering reading tests, valuable information concerning basal reading levels and reading achievement can be obtained from the previous teacher. A reading-capacity test aids in the selection of those who are not reading up to their ability. All this information should be included in the cumulative folder which accompanies each child through school.

Two common types of reading test are the survey-type test and the analytic test. The purpose for giving a test determines both the time in the school year at which it is administered and the type of test used. Careful examination of tests should be made before any are purchased. Diagnosis for special instruction necessitates the use of oral-reading tests.

The teacher can obtain from answer sheets information useful in planning classroom instruction, selecting the materials of instruction, and making differentiated assignments. The three reading levels are the frustration level, the instructional level, and the independent reading level.

A sane testing program seeks to avoid the dangers of undue reliance upon tests for promotion, overtesting, and the labeling of boys and girls. Homogeneous groups are formed on the basis of teacher judgment, school achievement, and reading ability rather than on the results of intelligence tests.

REFERENCES

1. Betts, Emmett A.: *Handbook on Corrective Reading,* Wheeler Publishing Company, Chicago, 1956.

* 2. Bond, Guy L., and Eva Bond: *Developmental Reading in High School,* The Macmillan Company, New York, 1941.

3. Buros, Oscar K. (ed.): *The Fourth Mental Measurements Yearbook,* The Gryphon Press, Highland Park, N.J., 1953.

4. Greene, Harry A., A. N. Jorgenson, and J. R. Gerberich: *Measurement and Evaluation in the Elementary School,* 2d ed., Longmans, Green & Co., Inc., New York, 1953.

5. Greene, Harry A., A. N. Jorgenson, and J. R. Gerberich: *Measurement and Evaluation in the Secondary School,* 2d ed., Longmans, Green & Co., Inc., New York, 1954.

* 6. Harris, Albert J.: *How to Increase Reading Ability,* 3d ed., Longmans, Green & Co., Inc., New York, 1956.

7. Hicks, Vernon: "A School Staff Surveys Its Reading Problems," in *Reading for Today's Children,* The National Elementary Principal, vol. 35, no. 1, September, 1955, pp. 208–212.

* 8. Jordan, A. M.: *Measurement in Education,* McGraw-Hill Book Company, Inc., New York, 1953.

9. "Scarsdale Finds Flaws in School—Citizens Group's Report Says Graduates Fall Short of Expectations at College." *New York Times,* Mar. 15, 1959.

10. Sheldon, William D.: Sheldon Readers, Allyn and Bacon, Inc., Englewood Cliffs, N.J., 1957.

* 11. Strang, Ruth, Constance M. McCullough, and Arthur E. Traxler: *Problems in the Improvement of Reading,* 2d ed., McGraw-Hill Book Company, Inc., New York, 1955.

* See Appendix A for annotated list of books for the professional library in schools.

Chapter 7

THE STAFF AND READING

Achievement in subject-matter areas tends to improve both in quantity and quality as members of a school staff incorporate elements of reading instruction in their everyday teaching. To separate reading, a thought-gaining process, from the study of a subject is well-nigh impossible. Good teachers habitually employ many practices which are sound reading theory without always realizing the efficacy of what they are doing from a reading point of view. In other words, in any school there are present the foundations of a good developmental reading program. These practices should be fostered and stimulated. One of the most useful booklets for awakening a faculty is a publication of the New Jersey Teachers' Association entitled *All Teachers Can Teach Reading* [25]. In brief form, under such headings as "It Seems to Be True That . . ." and "In Your Subject, Can You . . . ," teachers are attracted to the reading potentials inherent in their subject-matter teaching.

A developmental reading program is essentially an intensification of good teaching procedures and techniques. Every member of the staff is, or should be, involved since reading cannot be divorced from learning. Reading instruction must be cooperative. As Strang [31] points out, "Every member of the school staff should realize that helping students read more efficiently is part of his professional job, not an extra task. If each focuses attention on essentials and makes his special contribution, the success of the school-wide reading program is assured." [1]

This chapter spells out the particular contributions of the guidance department, the librarian, the school nurse, and the classroom

[1] Ruth Strang, Constance M. McCullough, and Arthur E. Traxler, *Problems in the Improvement of Reading*, 2d ed., McGraw-Hill Book Company, Inc., New York, 1955, pp. 29–30. Used by permission.

117

teacher. The Reading Improvement Committee should expect to find mentioned many things which are already being done. This is an encouraging sign, but the committee should also expect to discover other practices which need planning and organizing to increase the effectiveness of staff members.

GUIDANCE DEPARTMENT AND READING

The guidance department functions in five areas in developing a reading program: testing, curriculum, scheduling, recordkeeping, and advisement through conferences and reporting.

Testing. Placing a school on a firm footing as far as reading is concerned will necessitate some additional testing in most cases. At the beginning, this will consist largely of group silent-reading tests of the survey type and possibly some changes in the type of intelligence tests administered. Details of the testing program are given in Chapter 6. Individual teachers and the instructors of reading classes will profit from the use of additional analytic tests. Many schools will rightly wish to start with a minimal program and add to it as weaknesses in reading become evident and as qualified teachers are obtainable to do further remedial work.

The guidance department may suggest two or three suitable tests to the teachers concerned for their examination, or the initial suggestion may come from the teachers themselves. The important thing is that both teachers and guidance department should know the reasons for giving the tests selected and the use which can be made of their results.

As we have seen, the reason for giving tests is always the betterment of instruction; the use to be made of test findings should be specifically in mind when the tests are selected, since the purpose of a test governs the type chosen. Subject-matter teachers will need to take the results of survey and even analytic tests as general indications of strengths and weaknesses, since these tests are not intended to be measures of reading ability in subject-matter fields such as science, social studies, or mathematics [11]. Practically the only exception to this statement is the battery known as the Diagnostic Reading Tests, which include tests yielding measures of reading ability in specific subject-matter areas. Measures of rate and comprehension in science and social studies materials are available.

The Sequential Tests of Educational Progress, published by the Cooperative Test Division of the Educational Testing Service, also seek to measure understandings, skills, and abilities in the areas of mathematics, science, and social studies. The general format consists of a paragraph, chart, table, or map similar to those found in textbook material. A series of questions which test the student's ability to handle these materials through reading is asked. Teachers of the subjects indicated should find these tests instructive. On the other hand, the content teacher will learn how to use survey tests as measures of general reading ability in selecting multilevel reading materials. He will also learn how to use analytic tests to detect weaknesses in work-study reading skills which may be corrected by drill in specific content material at the appropriate level of difficulty.

Curriculum. Larger schools may be able to afford a curriculum coordinator, but many schools will have to make use of committees of teachers and guidance counselors in planning new courses. The guidance counselor has the advantage of having a comprehensive picture obtained from dealing with individual students of greatly differing interests and aptitudes. Also, he knows which areas are trouble spots as far as students are concerned. The need for new courses and for changes in existing offerings should become apparent as the testing program develops. The desirability of including materials of instruction on both easier and more difficult reading levels will also certainly be recognized.

The Reading Improvement Committee plays an important part in curriculum revision. Either through this group or the Curriculum Committee itself, lay persons from the community may be brought into the discussion to add their viewpoint to that of the teachers. At the same time, of course, they are improving community understanding of the school's problems. A second contribution of the reading group to curriculum revision is in the provision of continuing reading experiences.

Curriculum provisions at the secondary level will vary all the way from a single heterogeneous program to a multilevel organization of homogeneous groups. In the elementary grades, the most common form of organization is heterogeneous classes, although the strength of particular staff members, plus local conditions, may make it desirable to employ some form of homogeneous grouping. The basic principles to keep in mind are that reading materials should be adjusted to the group's range of abilities, and the number of concepts studied should be carefully controlled for the slower groups. The use of homogeneous grouping is an administrative device to reduce the range of abilities within classes. However, such grouping does not remove the necessity of the teacher's providing for individual differences.

Frequently a faculty in an elementary school is called upon to select a basal or cobasal reading series. Such selection frequently serves as valuable in-service training, not the least of which evolves from setting up criteria for judging the reading series. Guidance personnel faced with a like problem will find much useful information in *Reading for Today's Children* [26]. The same publication furnishes suggestions for the organization and distribution of reading materials [6].

Scheduling of Special Work. The third function of the guidance department which will be affected by an increased emphasis upon reading is the assignment of students to special courses and remedial work. The nature of these courses is indicated in Chapter 12. The purpose of work in reading needs to be kept in mind. When it is, such pitfalls as placing fifty seventh graders in a class called Remedial, meeting five days per week, will be avoided. Assignment of half the group two days per week and the remainder three days per week, with the stigma removed by calling the course simply Seventh Grade Reading, may complicate the scheduling difficulties of the guidance department, but it is one of the better ways of ensuring the success of the program. Under such a plan the two groups would alternate the second semester. If boys and girls are assigned to certain sections on the basis of survey tests administered the previous spring and the judgment of their sixth-grade teachers, the range of abilities within any one group will be curtailed, making the assembling of materials and the teaching somewhat easier.

As may be seen from the previous illustration, scheduling depends largely on the type of organization chosen for reading instruction. At elementary levels the work in reading is done by the classroom teacher or, where classes are large, by the reading teacher, who takes reading-disability cases directly from the class-room. When the latter plan is followed, care should be taken that the boys and girls continue regular reading periods in the class-room. At the junior high level, the simplest provision for special instruction is the reading home room, since such a period is already scheduled, although it may need to be lengthened. Reading instruc-tion by home rooms is most effective when the guidance personnel are trained in reading instruction and where activities for the home-room period should be developed. Scheduling other ways of pro-viding for instruction in reading—seventh-grade reading classes meeting two to five times per week, special English sections, and released time for instruction in the reading laboratory—tends to be much more complicated since such arrangements are scattered throughout the day.

Reading instruction is usually not successful if boys and girls are deprived of something that interests them deeply in order to attend reading classes. Some authorities [14] see no objection to giving reading instruction at the end of the regular school day; others [29] feel that the student is not likely to do his best work at that time. In many schools, extraclass activities or the school-bus sched-ule, make remedial work impractical at this hour. Each school will work out its own scheduling problem, but instruction for thirty to fifty minutes, depending on the age of the child, at least two or three times per week is desirable.

Cumulative Folder. In embarking upon an enlarged testing pro-gram, the guidance department may require more space to record pertinent data [23]. In addition to recording information as sug-gested in Chapter 6, the exact form of each test and the date ad-ministered (rather than the date corrected) are important. Subtest scores should be recorded for both survey and analytic tests since they often make total scores more meaningful. The use of specially prepared rubber stamps for commonly administered tests cuts down the time required to transcribe scores. The anecdotal record, while time-consuming to compose, is certainly informative and should be employed where remedial instruction is offered on an individual or small-group basis.

Reporting. The guidance department, teachers, and the adminis-tration require a system of reporting on students selected for special instruction. It is important that the staff concerned, especially the guidance counselor, know who is being worked with, for how long, and with what success. A series of forms is more effective than informal notes and reduces the tendency toward procrastination in writing reports. A specimen set of reporting blanks, which will need to be changed slightly to fit individual situations, is included in Appendix D.

Conferences. The fifth function of the guidance department concerns the holding of conferences. Meetings may be initiated by the guidance department, which may also act as a clearinghouse for subsequent reports and conferences. Once again, the *modus operandi* will vary from school to school. The reading teacher will want to be free to schedule some conferences with students, parents, teachers, special members of the staff, and outside agencies preferably with the prior knowledge of the guidance department.

In this way, the guidance department acts as the control center for the reading program [19]. Its responsibility for testing, test results, school marks, cumulative records, and student and teacher conferences make this logical. Obviously, the guidance counselor must be aware of present and future status of curriculum, courses, and staff; he must also be acquainted with and sympathetic toward the principles of developmental and remedial reading. If one or more of the guidance counselors is trained in the psychology of reading, cooperation is made easier. Records should be easily accessible so that those engaged in specialized reading instruction do not have to duplicate the records kept in the guidance department office. Since the reading teacher and the reading specialist are frequently not available because of instruction, supervision, visitation, or demonstration, the guidance department should serve as liaison between pupils and teachers, teachers and parents.

Perhaps a word of caution is necessary here. The practice of employing students to help in the guidance office is dangerous because of the intensely personal nature of much of the information contained in the cumulative folder. If the school is large enough to warrant it, and most schools are, a dependable adult should be employed. Nothing will offset the service function of a guidance department so much as malicious gossip.

Increasing Importance of Guidance. A basic principle of developmental reading underlies all that has been said regarding the functions of the guidance department. If boys and girls differ in reading ability, mental ability, and interest in and aptitude for the various curriculum subjects, block scheduling of students must give way to individual advisement. This would suggest that the fairly common practice of naming various subject-matter offerings—College English, Business English, and General English—should be discontinued. For the same reason, naming of various branches of the curriculum and publishing curriculum booklets describing such courses would be questionable. Each boy or girl should be placed in the section of a subject that will enable him to achieve to the maximum of his ability [8]. Thus, a student may be in the top section in science and social studies, the second section in mathematics, and the third section in English. Of course, this presumes a school large enough to provide several offerings at each level. In smaller school systems, the individual classroom teacher must provide both adjusted work for the slow learner and enrichment for the more able.

Such individual scheduling places increased emphasis on measurement of the individual's abilities and aptitudes. In turn, attention is focused upon prior achievement, the cumulative folder, and standardized tests. At the same time, increased importance must be given to the advisement of parents. This is absolutely necessary to overcome the tendency on the part of students and parents to select the easy course rather than the more difficult one that challenges the individual [27].

Parents need help in seeing that they are doing their children a disservice when they undervalue or overestimate ability. A more realistic reporting of reading abilities, physical handicaps, and mental limitations—at least to some extent—at the elementary level will make this increasingly possible at the secondary level. With the system of marking now employed by many schools, parents do have a point in preferring an A in an easy section to a C in a more difficult one. This suggests that schools have a long way to go in equating marks and reporting them to parents.

The Reading Improvement Committee will have to wrestle with this perennial problem of developing improved reporting practices. Some schools are experimenting with a statistical method known as *stanines* [16]. This method, which is basically a division of the normal curve into nine parts, was developed during World War II. All grades, both those assigned by the teacher and those derived from standardized tests, may be compared. In addition, a student's achievement in school subjects may be shown in relation to his intelligence. He may be achieving below, equal with, or above his established capacity. The stanine picture of actual achievement and potential ability may be used as a report to parents. Naturally a certain amount of statistical computation is involved.

Other schools use a system of exponents to indicate grade level and subscripts to show reading ability. Thus, A_6^9 represents a student in the ninth grade with sixth-grade reading ability who is doing, for him, very satisfactory work. While this method does present some advantages, its two prime disadvantages are that parents are likely to be confused and the grade of A does not give an estimate of the student's work suitable for comparative purposes.

The above consideration leads to several generalizations about reporting practices. (1) Whatever system of marking is decided upon, it must be intelligible to both students and parents. (2) If the selected method of reporting increases the work of classroom teachers, as in the case of stanines, suitable clerical help should be forthcoming. (3) The method of reporting should afford a measure of performance by which students of varying abilities may be compared without discouraging those of limited abilities. (4) The system selected should yield a mark which is satisfactory for the cumulative record and for college entrance purposes.

The problems of marking are serious, involving parents, students, colleges, and the school itself. Brackenbury [3] gives some useful advice on this topic. Certainly it is about time school personnel evolved a sane, simple, and fair way of marking students of differing abilities.

THE LIBRARIAN AND READING

Like the guidance department, the librarian has an increasingly important role to play in developmental reading. As Blair [1] has said—

The backbone of a good . . . developmental reading program is a good reading library. It is the *sine qua non* of a successful program. A school which purports to be carrying on an adequate reading program should have available for pupil use thousands of books dealing with a tremendous range of subjects and of all levels of difficulty.[2]

Furthermore, the books must be accessible and library facilities must be used. Indeed, a good measure of the success of a reading program is to be found in the use of the library. Few schools get as much use out of their libraries as they have a right to expect, partly because teachers adhere to stereotyped lessons with daily textbook assignments and partly because of the limitations of the library itself. Such teachers are ignoring the fact that self-reliance is itself developmental in nature and may not be achieved by teacher selection of materials. Bond [2] points out that "an individual's independence in reading is his ability to rely upon his own resources to locate and use printed materials for the purpose of meeting a goal." [3] In a reading-centered school, the librarian becomes a key figure. Her duties tend to divide themselves into three main parts: work with boys and girls, work with teachers, and the somewhat more impersonal job of organizing and running the library.

Student Use of Reference Materials. One of the primary concerns of the librarian is the students' use of reference materials. This includes the Dewey decimal system, the card catalogue, the standard books of reference, and periodical and fiction guides. The initial instruction in these reference materials should come from the classroom teacher. Each subject-matter teacher should assume the responsibility for giving instruction in using the references appropriate to his subject. Obviously, careful planning and cooperation among the several faculty members teaching the same boys and girls are required to ensure ample coverage. A visit to the library or a mimeographed plan of the library helps students learn the location of reference materials. The librarian and teacher frequently

[2] Glenn Myers Blair, *Diagnostic and Remedial Teaching*, rev. ed., The Macmillan Company, New York, 1956, p. 174. Used by permission.

[3] Guy L. Bond, and Eva Bond, *Developmental Reading in High School*, The Macmillan Company, New York, 1941, p. 202. Used by permission.

cooperate to produce a series of practical exercises in using library facilities. By starting at different places in the exercise, or by working in groups, undue bottlenecks may be avoided. After initial instruction has been given by the classroom teacher, the librarian assumes responsibility for supervising students using reference materials and reports any gross examples of poor habits or incomplete learning to the teacher. Late transfers and children who have been absent are not forgotten in this procedure.

Boys and girls are released from formal classwork as they demonstrate their ability to locate pertinent material on their own or with a minimum of guidance from the librarian. Neither the teacher nor the librarian will expect all children to do this at the same time or equally well. This phase of the librarian's work is very different from the traditional job of providing books for recreational reading.

Student Book Selection. Instead of supplying books at random for personal reading, the librarian now seeks to build progressive reading experiences, knowing that what boys and girls learn to like in free reading is quite likely to mold their reading habits after they have left school [9]. Use is made of book lists built on well-known favorites. "If you have read and liked ___, try ___, ___, and ___." Such a listing takes into account both interest and reading ability since books are of the same general subject matter and are arranged in ladder form, from easy to more difficult. The librarian is also aware of the therapeutic effects of reading as young people seek to understand themselves and others by employing such listings as Heaton's *Reading Ladders for Human Relations* [17].

The librarian also encourages boys and girls to become self-sufficient in locating books for use in the content subjects by introducing them to *Gateways to Readable Books* by Strang [30], *Looking at Life through American Literature* by Lombard [21], and *Gateways to American History* by Carpenter [5]. Strang [31] gives the names of many other references of this type for use with the content subjects.

Another increasingly important part of the librarian's work is whetting interest by book talks and displays. Book recommendations deeply affect reading patterns, particularly those of two groups of poorer readers who, at first, may not have the interest or ability to choose books for themselves. The first group is composed of retarded readers who may be reading from two to four or more grades below their actual grade placement. However, they are not interested in "baby" books. For them, the *High Interest–Low Vocabulary Booklist* [10], mentioned in an earlier chapter, supplies titles of books within their capacity. The second group might be called lazy readers, for they will do almost anything to avoid reading. For them, the previously mentioned book list, *Fare for the Reluctant Reader* [9], contains titles that have tempted other unenthusiastic readers away from comics and television. Other lists of books for retarded readers are to be found in Blair [1] and Carter and McGinnis [7].

Special Groups. In addition to encouraging growth and providing guidance in reading, the librarian at times may be called upon to assist one or the other of two widely separated groups of readers, the able and the slow learners. Such help is usually more in demand in schools not having homogeneous grouping, although a librarian may be asked to help under this arrangement also. The able learners in the upper grades of elementary school or in junior high school form a club or literary group and meet in the library. Such literary clubs depend in large measure upon the interests and training of the librarian. Gifted boys and girls welcome the opportunity to follow their own interests, plan their own reading, and share the ideas discovered in books through clubs of this kind [31].

Sometimes the librarian's interest and training tends toward work with the slow learners. Smith [28] reports a waiting list for such a group, in which teachers recommend children for participation and student teachers assist the librarian in remedial instruction. The first part of each period is devoted to free reading in easy materials, while the last part of each session finds children working individually with student teachers.

Classroom Teachers. The second part of the librarian's work concerns classroom teachers. As a teacher becomes more adept at breaking away from a single-text approach to his subject, he needs assistance in several ways. The librarian acts as a resource person to teachers constructing multilevel units. Once the reading lists for these units are compiled, the librarian selects the volumes for the classroom libraries. Obviously, advance notice of from two to three weeks facilitates this. In many school systems, librarians are asking teachers to assist in book selection so that teachers interested in their students' supplementary reading can build up weak areas in the library. In such a scheme the librarian supplies the teachers with book reviews and lists and has the final say on what is to be bought. To avoid disappointment, the budget for new books is subdivided among the various departments and levels of a school. The administrator can obtain a fairly clear idea of the type of teaching being done by the use teachers make of the librarian's services.

Classroom Libraries. In order that the library be used to the fullest extent possible, books must be readily available. There are three ways of accomplishing this. The most effective is the classroom library. Because setting up classroom libraries removes books from general circulation, a few librarians tend to discourage this practice. Usually this is an indication that the library is insufficient for the school's reading needs. If teachers are businesslike in administering classroom libraries and return books promptly, the only possible problem is that different teachers may be teaching similar or overlapping courses.

The second alternative—not quite as good because books are not as readily accessible—is the special shelf in the library itself. Both the provision of classroom libraries and special shelves are intermediate steps between teacher selection or a single-text approach on the one hand and complete freedom of choice on the other. At all times students should be encouraged to discover books for themselves.

The third possibility is for the class, or a part of it, to meet in the library. This method is particularly effective with elementary children. A regularly scheduled half-hour period enables children to borrow books for out-of-school reading and thus get the library habit, or to listen to a story from the librarian, her assistant, or an older student. At the same time the teacher, while supervising the book selection of the poorer readers, may be choosing books for the classroom library and future units of work.

Library Organization. The third phase of the librarian's work in a reading-orientated school is organizational. This area is the least changed of the three originally mentioned, and no attempt is made here to indicate in detail how the library should be operated. However, the relatively few changes will be mentioned briefly.

1. *Scheduling classes.* Both the administrator and the librarian should be alert to the possibilities of increasing the uses of the library. In elementary schools where there are visiting special teachers, one possibility is to put the children of two sections of the same grade together. The boys might then have music, shop, or gym while the girls, accompanied by their teachers, go to the library for either recreational reading or work on supplementary materials.

At the secondary level some scheduling of free reading periods is desirable to prevent an undue rush to borrow books. The simplest and most effective solution is for the teachers to arrange to hold their reading periods on different days. Some overlapping of book selection from one grade to the next will be inevitable, but usually library or study periods will not coincide, so that the demand for books tends to equalize itself.

2. *Design of the library.* Where libraries are being built in conjunction with new school buildings, the library should be constructed with glass partitions so that the reading room, the shelves, the reference room, and two or more committee rooms may be supervised from the main desk. Wherever possible the study hall should not be held in the library; where lack of space makes this necessary, the librarian should certainly not be in charge of this study hall. Holding the traditional study hall in the library gets boys and girls to the library under the wrong conditions, and placing the librarian in charge of such a study hall renders her ineffective for her primary purpose.

3. *Book purchase.* Books make increasingly heavy demands on the budget. One elementary school [15] has set a goal of five books per child as a minimum for its reading library. Once this goal has been reached, it can be maintained and gradually expanded on a budget allotment of 60 cents per child per year. By increasing the appropriation, new school libraries can be stocked in about four years. Of course, costs are proportionally higher for secondary school libraries.

Small schools should be aware of the possibilities of augmenting funds earmarked for book purchase. Art exhibitions, musical and dramatic entertainments, and book fairs afford possible ways of raising money where budgets are inadequate. Civic groups and PTA organizations are frequently willing to contribute to classroom and school libraries.

Another method of increasing the number of books available is to make greater use of state, county, and community public libraries. Books for special units and for recreational reading may be borrowed. In many schools the weekly visit of the bookmobile is a red-letter day.

Then, too, there are many "fugitive" materials such as reprints, newspaper and magazine articles, and free material put out by commercial concerns. Government pamphlets, either free or at nominal cost, often provide reading material of a practical nature. In some school systems [18] committees of teachers and librarians are using the Dale, Flesch, or Dale-Chall formulas for determining the reading difficulty of these materials (see Chapter 5).

4. *Location of books.* As purchases are made from special-purpose book lists for retarded readers, the question frequently arises as to where such books should be kept. In general, librarians are interested in making books available to the greatest possible number of readers, but there is some danger that poor readers will select books which are too difficult. The division of the library into sections, or the use of a color code to indicate books of different reading levels, are possible ways of handling the problem. The danger here is that a stigma will be attached to reading books from certain sections or marked by a certain color. Some schools keep all the books on open shelves on the theory that it does little harm for a good reader to read an easy book occasionally. Unfortunately, the reverse is not equally true. Other schools keep these special-purpose books, such as the American Adventure Series, in the reading classroom or laboratory, so that when boys and girls who should be reading this type of material go to the library they are referred to the reading teacher. This method offers two distinct advantages. It enables the reading teacher to check on the reading habits of poor readers and it permits the teacher to follow up those who are, or have been, special reading problems. Workbooks, special-purpose readers, and adjusted materials are kept in the reading laboratory.

THE SCHOOL NURSE AND READING

General health, as we have already seen, directly affects the learning processes. A large part of the duties of the school nurse is what might properly be called preventive medicine.

Duties Shared with Guidance Department. The school nurse should share with the guidance department the responsibility for checking on excessive absence from school and, after consultation with teachers and the administration, for calling in special services where they are deemed necessary.

Screening of Hearing and Vision. The other area where the school nurse can effectively assist the reading program is in screening for hearing and vision handicaps. Partly because of the fact that school medical facilities are usually under the control of the various state departments of education and not the medical associations, and partly because of the interpretation school nurses tend to place on the ethics of their profession, the screening of children for vision defects is a delicate problem. It should be unnecessary to state that it seems ridiculous to penalize boys and girls by using outmoded screening methods because of an overlapping of jurisdiction and because of a misunderstanding regarding the purpose of such screening. The situation warrants the consideration of the Reading Improvement Committee to ensure good working relationships with the ophthalmologist and the optometrist. Medical associations and departments of education should work together more closely on this matter of screening.

THE CLASSROOM TEACHER AND READING

In a cooperative attack upon the reading problems of a school, each member of the staff is important, but the backbone of the movement is the classroom teacher. The teacher knows the boys and girls in his classes better than anyone else in the school system; and, if he is alerted to the reading possibilities of his subject, he is in the best position to improve their reading in the content area. In order to do this effectively, there are certain basic principles with which he should be familiar.

Administrative Grouping. In forming class sections the administration may have employed homogeneous, heterogeneous, or (in a
two-track program) a form of interest grouping partly based on
college aspirations of students. Yet another form of administrative
grouping is the core or block program. Here, children may be
selected on the basis of ability or assigned at random. Finally, certain boys and girls, usually the extremely retarded, are kept with
the same teacher for a period of two or three years to ensure their
continuous progress. From the reading point of view, these last two
methods of grouping have the advantage of reducing the number of
individuals with whom the teacher comes in contact, thus enabling
him to learn more about their reading disabilities. In these days of
increased class size, this is no small advantage.

The teacher should have a clear understanding of the basis by
which his class was formed, since this will affect the grouping he
uses within the class, the range of materials he should be prepared
to use, and the techniques of teaching he will employ. He should
realize that, apart from a few scheduling changes made by the
guidance department, this administrative grouping usually continues
for the year.

The purpose of most administrative grouping is to facilitate teaching, usually by reducing the extreme range of abilities within any
one class. Teachers realize at the beginning of the year, or shortly
thereafter, the necessity for providing for differences in reading
ability in heterogeneous classes, some core or block programs, and
in college and terminal classes in a two-track program. But far too
frequently teachers assume that the administrative practice of setting up homogeneous class sections frees them from the necessity of
providing for differences in reading abilities. Often such teachers,
talking about reading levels, will say, ". . . but I have a homogeneous group . . . ," as if that ended the matter.

The facts are that two identical total reading scores may identify
two completely different reading problems. One student may be
slow, accurate in vocabulary, and good at grasping details; the
other may be fast, inaccurate, poor in vocabulary, and able to get
only the main ideas. Two such individuals will need different materials, different teaching methods, and the development of different
skills. Certainly homogeneous grouping increases the possibility that

a teacher may neglect individual differences in reading ability simply because the range of differences is reduced.

The Reading Improvement Committee can help new teachers by explaining the method of determining class sections and can help all teachers by seeing that full information concerning past reading achievement is made available to and used by the entire staff.

Classroom Grouping. One of the basic provisions for differences in learning abilities and interests is the grouping procedure which the teacher uses within his own classroom. In fact, he may employ several types of grouping in the same class at the same time, or he may use one kind for part of a lesson and then change to another for the remainder of the period. At times the teacher may also make use of a committee of the whole when introducing a new topic or concluding a unit of work. Flexibility of grouping is thus assured.

1. *Achievement or ability grouping.* In matching the difficulty of reading material to the reading ability of a student, we have the common grouping used in basal reading instruction in elementary school. It is frequently employed when recreational reading is done from reading-ladder lists and may likewise find application in an English class where three novels are selected according to the reading abilities of the class. The poorer readers are assigned the easier novel; the average readers, the one of medium difficulty; and the good readers, the most difficult one. If three novels dealing with different aspects of the same general problem are selected, very rewarding discussions may be developed. Strang [31] indicates how the teacher may schedule the work so that each group receives the benefit of discussion of their own novel within their group, plus the ideas derived by the other two groups from their books. A similar procedure can be used in content subjects with textbooks of differing degrees of difficulty.

2. *Research or interest grouping.* Some authorities [31] separate these categories into research grouping, where several members of the class elect to find out more about a certain subject, and interest grouping, in which class members pursue a hobby or other interest. However, since there is a great deal of overlapping, the two will be considered concurrently.

Research or interest grouping lends itself to unit teaching in the content subjects. For example, a social studies class in the seventh or eighth grade might be studying the westward movement in American history. As part of the introduction to such a topic, the class would have discussed what they should know and what they should get out of such a unit. This discussion acts as an interest arouser, and the class might decide to study (a) territorial acquisitions (map work), (b) life on the various frontiers (reading novels and biographies), (c) particulars regarding the acquisition of each territory (work-study reading), (d) contributions of other countries and individuals (creative reading), (e) present economic worth of the territory acquired (reading for details), and (f) present frontiers (main idea and creative reading). As the teacher knows the reading weaknesses of individual students, he can frequently give them practice by differentiated assignments.

3. *Special-needs grouping.* Some boys and girls in a class may need additional practice in work-study reading through outlining; others may need to build up self-reliance and word-recognition skills by relatively large amounts of easy reading; and still others may need specific attention to vocabulary development through various means, including dictionary usage. Special-needs grouping would provide for all these in the reading material of the content subject itself. Frequently this type of grouping may be combined with research grouping by selecting a research topic involving the special skill needed. Of course this cannot be done at all times. A common use of special-needs grouping is also to be found in special-class reading instruction.

4. *Team grouping.* The term applies to grouping two or more class members together because of mutual interest or need. In order to facilitate such grouping the teacher often finds the information obtained from a sociogram of the class helpful [12]. By this means latent leadership may be developed.

5. *Tutorial grouping.* Occasionally a few boys and girls may need extra practice. To obtain this while leaving the teacher free to work with other groups, the assignment of a competent student who has finished his own work is often effective. Use may again be made of the sociogram to help eliminate personality clashes. Frequently the better student learns a deeper appreciation of others' problems in giving this assistance. The work should be short, instructions spe-

cific, and it should not necessitate the grading of the pupils being helped.

Approaches to Instruction. The classroom teacher, making plans for instruction in either elementary or secondary school, has three main approaches to the reading of his subject: (1) single textbook, (2) two or three texts of differing degrees of difficulty, or (3) a multilevel approach.

1. *Single textbook.* In the primary grades, with groups formed as children become ready to read, the newness of a single basal reading series has worn off by the time the second and third groups are ready to read. This is true both for the teacher and the pupils. A sense of boredom is hard to avoid when the teacher is forced by paucity of material to cover the same ground three times or more a year; pupils overhear other reading groups, with the result that all novelty is lost, and the fact that other children are ahead of them is emphasized. For this reason many schools are adopting a second and even a third cobasal reader.

In the intermediate grades—usually beginning with the fourth grade where basal, cobasal, and supplementary readers are used for reading instruction—a single text is frequently employed for content subjects. This is one of the primary causes of reading failure in the elementary school. For those who cannot read the text it means that reading instruction is confined to the basal reading series so that they get no instruction in work-study reading.

In the junior and senior high school, many beginning teachers tend to rely on a single-textbook approach because they are not sufficiently well acquainted with methods, materials, and subject matter to do otherwise. This procedure possibly does less harm in homogeneously grouped classes, provided the text used is chosen in the light of the known range of reading abilities in each section. Far too frequently, however, the same text is given to several homogeneous sections of widely different ability where it cannot be of the right difficulty for all of them. Instances of using an easier text with college-bound students and the harder text with terminal students are not unknown. Going more slowly by giving shorter assignments is not the way to adapt a too difficult text for slower sections.

Many teachers begin their teaching in small schools where, because of the limited number of sections, students are heterogeneously grouped. It is a difficult teaching situation for anyone, particularly for the inexperienced teacher. Consequently, administrators, guidance counselors, and reading specialists, in addition to giving such teachers all possible help, should be on the watch for students who are unable to handle the single textbook.

Within limits, much can be done to atone for the inadequacies of the one-book approach. Careful attention to vocabulary *before* the reading assignment is undertaken is useful. Asking for ideas in the individual's own words rather than in those of the book is another helpful technique. The teacher may ask different types of questions—factual questions for the poorer readers and more difficult questions involving deduction, implication, and comparison for the better readers. Differentiated questioning will enable the teacher to provide several different purposes for reading the same assignment, but none of these procedures removes the fact that some members of the class will not be able to read the book at all.

Once the ineffectiveness of the single-text approach has been revealed [22], alternatives will need to be examined. The teacher unfamiliar with grouping practices should not rush into grouping too quickly, for the results are likely to be unsatisfactory and he may hesitate to try again. Where possible, he should observe a class in which grouping is practiced. Then he may begin by freeing some boys and girls from the regular assignment. Usually they do more work than the assignment would have entailed. The teacher will want to check informally on their progress and to help them provide a short, effective way of reporting. Nothing kills an initial attempt at grouping more quickly than does a lengthy series of individual oral reports. By starting with a splinter of the class, the teacher will gain confidence before working his students into the appropriate grouping for any particular activity.

2. *Two- or three-text approach.* Having gained experience and confidence, the teacher is ready for a two- or three-track reading program. This is usually accomplished by achievement or reading-ability grouping in heterogeneous classes. Even in homogeneous classes, provision for differences will usually result in better learning situations. An alert instructor may well find that the exigencies of

scheduling may have forced the guidance department to place a few superior students and some who are not as able as the rest of the class in the same section. Needless to say, teachers should always be informed of such actions.

It is difficult to find two or three textbooks that approximate the required reading levels and at the same time have somewhat the same organization or sequence of topics. Of course, this is the result of having to use texts by different authors rather than material prepared by one author.

At the elementary level this concept of parallel material has been worked out by Lyons & Carnahan in their Classmate edition. At the secondary level teachers will find that Scott, Foresman and Company has published two world history textbooks for use in tenth-grade classes. *Living World History* [32] is approximately eighth-grade difficulty, and *Man's Story* [33] is about tenth-grade difficulty. Both books are by the same author and parallel each other closely. The publisher reports that school systems are using these books principally to provide materials of different difficulty for homogeneously grouped classes. But apparently teachers have not yet realized the possibilities inherent in this provision for differences in reading ability within a single class.

Usually the easier text will tend to give a more factual approach while the harder text goes into greater detail, often involves greater use of comparison, inductive and deductive thinking, the interpretation of figures of speech, and more complex sentence structure. With a detailed knowledge of what is to be found in each text, the teacher can call on the readers of the easier text for information contained in their books and then build on this with the contributions of those reading the harder text.

In American history it is often possible to find a new text, written for the fifth grade but having no grade designation on it, which will be about the correct difficulty for retarded readers in the seventh or eighth grade. Textbooks used in earlier grades should not be employed, as they will be familiar to the class. Even if two or three completely parallel texts cannot be found, a number of units will usually approximate each other. Even if only half of the year's topics can be studied in this way, the poorer readers are getting more practice than they would if given the harder text, which they are unable to read. Differences of opinion and even of fact which result from using more than one text will be healthy. Every care should be taken to bring the retarded readers into the class discussion and procedures; if they are praised for their contributions, they usually read with a will.

3. *Multilevel unit approach.* Certain broad bodies of subject matter lend themselves to a multiple-level unitary teaching procedure. Reading materials consist of textbooks of varying degrees of difficulty, trade books, newspaper and magazine articles, pamphlets, and reference materials. Since there must be adequate reading material available for a successful unit, certain specific subjects are ruled out. In English, a unit on short stories might be more desirable than a unit on one of Shakespeare's plays; while in science, a unit on the weather might be preferred to a unit on photosynthesis or osmosis.

If the class shares the exploring stage and develops what might come out of a unit and the appropriate activities for it, students will be eager to participate. The class, as individuals or small groups, studies various aspects of the topic under consideration. Much of the work is done in the classroom and library; and the teacher, moving from group to group, is ready to help with reading problems, including the selection and organization of materials. During this laboratory period the teacher may call everyone together for certain learning that all should have, write the material in simple language for all students, or distribute an easy text. As groups and individuals finish their assignments, they contribute their reports in a pooling and sharing period. The exchange of information may be by tape recording, panel of experts, quiz games, bulletin-board displays, debates, and the more formal committee report.

Unitary teaching is based on several psychological principles. Children and young people react better to activities when they have shared in the planning and when work is done for the group rather than for the teacher. Use is thus made of the gang instinct, since each member is contributing to the group effort. Goals are specific and, with suggestions from the teacher, tend to be within the scope of students' interests and reading abilities. Finally, the various members of the class are discovering how to learn in a controlled situation, yet they are free to experiment.

Unit teaching is more popular in the intermediate grades than it is in many junior and senior high schools. Many teachers feel that the existence of factual examinations necessitates requiring every student to read the same material. Apparently, the hardest thing for a secondary school teacher to comprehend is the fact that not everyone has to do the same thing for learning to take place. In summing up the 1956 conference of the International Reading Association, a group of teachers on the secondary level under the leadership of LaBrant decided that "work built around units or special topics seems to be the approach suggested by the reading situation" [20].

Unitary teaching is not easy. The teacher needs carefully worked out objectives which the student goals—brought out in the exploratory stages of the unit—will tend to approach. The introduction may be a film, visiting speaker, or any suitable interest arouser, and it is followed by a planning discussion. The teacher will have already developed a skeleton list of group and individual activities, a minimum vocabulary list, common-learnings reading materials, and extensive reading lists. A mimeographed list of activities suggested by the class, augmented by the teacher if necessary, enables the various groups to see where their contributions fit into the general plan. The pooling and sharing periods are instructive and interesting, and give practice in oral reading, speaking, and writing. Many teachers, having worked with the groups during the laboratory period and having observed how reporting was done, feel that no formal evaluation is necessary. If a test is given, it should be less specific than when everyone has read the same material. Apart from the changes in teaching techniques, the unit approach calls for careful organization both within and without the classroom.

The rewards of unitary teaching are many; boys and girls, working independently and at their own levels, tend to accomplish more than they do with formal instructional methods. Many who have not participated when a single text was used find that—given materials of proper difficulty and a special task in which they are interested—they can make worth-while contributions. The reason for this is partly that they are not competing against the entire class, but are carrying out their specific part of a larger group plan. Furthermore, the teacher has class time to assist them, which is not possible when assignments are prepared outside. From the teacher's point of view, the unit itself can be used from year to year with minor changes.

The pitfalls of unitary teaching are rather obvious. Time may be wasted on activities which cannot be justified from an educational viewpoint. The teacher must be continually aware that certain individuals may not be working up to their capacity. Confusion results if the unit is not carefully structured and if sufficient time is not allowed for developing objectives and activities. At the same time, too much structuring in spelling out group and individual activities deprives young people of the chance to develop initiative.

The unit approach to teaching is applicable to any grade level from second or third up to and including graduate school. It works well in English, social studies, some science courses, especially general science, and in certain business courses such as law, office practice, and office management. In foreign languages it comes into its own in the study of geographical areas and the habits and customs of a foreign people. Here it is a welcome change from the more usual routines of language instruction.

Teachers who remain skeptical should try the unit approach in the lower sections of homogeneous groups and in the general sections of a two-track program. However, its principal effectiveness is in the higher sections in homogeneous groups and in the college preparatory sections in a two-track curriculum, for here it stimulates individual initiative and independent research. In many ways, the unit approach seems particularly effective for use with able learners.

Reading in Content Subjects. The main reason for expecting teachers to give reading instruction in the content subjects is that each subject calls for its own particular combination of reading skills [2]. All have problems of technical vocabulary, and in some, too many facts are crammed into relatively few words [31]. This fact packing is prevalent in social studies. In subjects such as biology, concepts follow each other so quickly that the student fails to master one with its specialized vocabulary before going on to another with totally different technical terms [13]. The author's purpose is important in subjects like English, where it is often necessary to read between the lines; in other subjects, the sequence of events and the ability to outline are important [31].

Some content areas call for slow, careful reading as in science, or even three and four rereadings as in word problems in mathematics [2]. But in other areas the student should be prepared to read rather quickly for the main idea or skim an article first and then read selected parts more slowly. All these differences are caused by variations in the nature of the material and the purpose for which it is being read. Obviously the only person who can do justice to the reading of a content subject is the teacher.

Two methods are commonly employed to help boys and girls understand the types of reading encountered in content subjects. In one, suggestions of how to read the materials are given at the beginning of each course. The other and better procedure is to take up different techniques as they are needed. This can often be done as the teacher works with whatever grouping arrangement fits the situation.

The different approaches to instruction have been considered separately, but no teacher should feel constrained to follow any one of them for the entire year. In almost every course certain topics will lend themselves to the unit method. Other topics may be covered by a two- or three-track plan because the teacher knows that, while it is a difficult part of his subject, not enough reading material has been assembled to permit using the multiple-level method. At the beginning of the year, the single text may be used as the teacher gets to know his class, and he may fall back on this approach at any time. By a judicious selection of method based on interests, abilities, and materials available, the teacher can go a long way toward furthering reading instruction within his own subject. Mursell feels that teachers are neglecting an opportunity to improve instruction [24].

> Reading ability above the primary grades could most certainly be improved but not by tricks or devices, or narrow courses on how to study, or by more drastic testing. It can be improved by a transformation of the teaching done in all fields along developmental lines, so that all the reading done in school becomes what it ought to be—a purposeful adventure and not a drudge task.[4]

Teachers who remain skeptical of the possibilities of reading instruction within subject-matter areas will find Bullock [4] informa-

---

[4] James L. Mursell, *Developmental Teaching*, McGraw-Hill Book Company, Inc., New York, 1949, p. 164. Used by permission.

tive. Several different ways by which teachers may help the non-reading boy or girl in the secondary school are described in detail. Introspective teachers will see themselves in some of the practices described.

The topic of reading instruction in the content fields is a large one, fully justifying a workshop type of in-service training course. Both beginning and experienced teachers will find that Bond [2] is a good starting point. Strang [31], while covering much the same ground, goes further in suggesting a large number of activities and exercises which clarify the demands each subject makes on children's reading abilities. Strang and Bracken [29] do substantially the same thing for the classroom teacher. Gray [13] furnishes additional information arranged according to primary, intermediate, junior, and senior levels.

SUMMARY

Reading instruction is part of each classroom teacher's professional job, and he is aided by the guidance department, the librarian, and the school nurse.

The guidance department assists the reading program by (1) testing, so that all teachers may be informed of various abilities; (2) curriculum changes, providing instruction to meet wide ranges of ability; (3) scheduling, not only of reading classes and remedial periods, but also individual rather than block scheduling of students' course selections; (4) expanding the cumulative folder to furnish additional data; and (5) acting as a control center to coordinate conferences and provide for the ready flow of information.

The librarian's role increases in importance as a school embarks on a developmental reading program. Reference materials and book lists, including those for content areas, leisure reading, and special-purpose books—all of these play an important part as the librarian seeks to provide for growth and self-guidance in reading. The second part of her work consists of helping classroom teachers in working out multiple-level units, preparing bibliographies, ordering books, and furnishing classroom libraries. The third part of the librarian's work concerns the library organization, scheduling library periods, purchasing books, and arranging special-purpose materials.

The school nurse shares with the guidance department responsibility for checking on absences and calling in special services. Screening to detect physical defects, including abnormalities of vision and hearing, should be by up-to-date methods and equipment acceptable to both the medical profession and state educational authorities.

The classroom teacher is the backbone of any developmental reading program. He should know the basis used in forming class sections and realize that homogeneous grouping does not obviate the need for provision for individual differences. He will use various forms of grouping, including achievement, research or interest, special needs, team, and tutorial instruction. Various approaches to teaching, such as the use of a single textbook, the two- or three-track plan, and the multiple-level unit method, will help him meet varying interests and abilities in his classes. Finally, he will make himself an authority on the reading skills demanded by his subject so that boys and girls will become better readers and thus better students of his subject.

REFERENCES

* 1. Blair, Glenn Myers: *Diagnosis and Remedial Teaching,* rev. ed., The Macmillan Company, New York, 1956.

* 2. Bond, Guy L., and Eva Bond: *Developmental Reading in High School,* The Macmillan Company, New York, 1941.

3. Brackenbury, Robert L.: *Getting Down to Cases,* G. P. Putnam's Sons, New York, 1959.

* 4. Bullock, Harrison: *Helping the Non-reading Pupil in the Secondary School,* Bureau of Publications, Teachers College, Columbia University, New York, 1956.

5. Carpenter, Helen: *Gateways to American History,* The H. W. Wilson Company, New York, 1942.

6. Carson, Louise G.: "Making Materials Accessible," in *Reading for Today's Children,* The National Elementary Principal, vol. 35, no. 1, September, 1955, pp. 168–171.

7. Carter, Homer L. J., and Dorothy J. McGinnis: *Learning to Read,* McGraw-Hill Book Company, Inc., New York, 1953.

8. Conant, James Bryant: *The American High School Today,* McGraw-Hill Book Company, Inc., New York, 1959.

* 9. Dunn, Anita, Mabel Jackman, and Bernice Bush: *Fare for the Reluctant Reader,* CASDA, The New York State College for Teachers, Albany, N.Y., 1953.

* 10. Durrell, Donald D., and Helen Blair Sullivan: *High Interest–Low Vocabulary Booklist,* Boston University School of Education, Boston, 1952.

11. Fay, Leo: "How Can We Develop Reading Study Skills for the Different Curriculum Areas?" *The Reading Teacher,* vol. 6, pp. 12–18, March, 1953.

12. Glock, Marvin D.: "Discussion: Classroom Techniques of Identifying and Diagnosing the Needs of Retarded Readers in High School and College," in William S. Gray and Nancy Larrick (eds.), *Better Readers for Our Times,* International Reading Association Conference Proceedings, vol. 1, Scholastic Magazines, New York, 1956, pp. 132–133.

13. Gray, William S. (ed.): *Improving Reading in All Curriculum Areas,* Supplementary Educational Monographs, no. 76, University of Chicago Press, Chicago, November, 1952.

* 14. Harris, Albert J.: *How to Increase Reading Ability,* 3d ed., Longmans, Green & Co., Inc., New York, 1956.

15. Harris, Emily, and D. Richard Bowles: "Our Library Is a Center for Recreational Reading," in *Reading for Today's Children,* The National Elementary Principal, vol. 35, no. 1, September, 1955, pp. 140–144.

16. Hart, Irene: *Using Stanines to Obtain Composite Scores Based on Test Data and Teacher's Ranks,* Test Service Bulletin No. 86, World Book Company, Yonkers, N.Y., 1957.

17. Heaton, Margaret M., and Helen B. Lewis: *Reading Ladders for Human Relations,* American Council on Education, Washington, 1955.

18. Hinds, Lillian R.: "Discussion: Providing Reading Materials Appropriate to Interest and Maturity Levels," in William S. Gray and Nancy Larrick (eds.), *Better Readers for Our Times,* International Reading Association Conference Proceedings, vol. 1, Scholastic Magazines, New York, 1956, pp. 86–87.

* 19. Kawin, Ethel: "Guidance Specialists as Resource Persons," in *Guidance in the Curriculum,* 1955 Yearbook of the Association for Supervision and Curriculum Development, National Education Association, Washington, 1955, pp. 101–113.

20. LaBrant, Lou: "How the Conference Proposals Can Be Implemented in Secondary Schools," in William S. Gray and Nancy Larrick (eds.), *Better Readers for Our Times,* International Reading Association Conference Proceedings, vol. 1, Scholastic Magazines, New York, 1956, pp. 173–174.

21. Lombard, Carol: *Looking at Life through American Literature,* Stanford University Press, Stanford, Calif., 1951.

* 22. Low, Camilla M.: "Setting Our Sights," in *Guidance in the Curriculum,* 1955 Yearbook of the Association for Supervision and Curriculum Development. National Education Association, Washington, 1955, pp. 12–25

23. Marzolf, Stanley S.: *Psychological Diagnosis and Counselling in Schools,* Henry Holt and Company, Inc., New York, 1956.

24. Mursell, James L.: *Developmental Teaching,* McGraw-Hill Book Company, Inc., New York, 1949.

25. New Jersey Secondary School Teachers' Association: *All Teachers Can Teach Reading,* 1035 Kenyon Avenue, Plainfield, N.J., 1951.

26. Patterson, Charlotte E.: "Choosing a Reading Series," in *Reading for Today's Children,* The National Elementary Principal, vol. 35, no. 1, September, 1955, pp. 164–167.

27. Rickover, Hyman G.: *Education and Freedom,* E. P. Dutton & Co., Inc., New York, 1959.

28. Smith, Linda C.: "Retarded Readers Flock to This Club," *New York State Education,* vol. 30, pp. 186–187, December, 1950.

* 29. Strang, Ruth, and Dorothy Kendall Bracken: *Making Better Readers,* D. C. Heath and Company, Boston, 1957.

30. Strang, Ruth, Alice Checovitz, Christine Gilbert, and Margaret Scoggin: *Gateways to Readable Books,* 3d ed., The H. W. Wilson Company, New York, 1959.

* 31. Strang, Ruth, Constance M. McCullough, and Arthur E. Traxler: *Problems in the Improvement of Reading,* 2d ed., McGraw-Hill Book Company, Inc., New York, 1955.

32. Wallbank, T. Walter: *Living World History,* Scott, Foresman and Company, Chicago, 1951.

33. Wallbank, T. Walter: *Man's Story,* Scott, Foresman and Company, Chicago, 1956.

* See Appendix A for annotated list of books for the professional library in schools.

Chapter 8

THE READING SPECIALIST

The establishment of an effective reading program is essentially a cooperative effort, necessitating careful planning. The continued improvement of reading instruction, involving teachers at all grade levels, calls for purposeful administration. The appointment to the staff of a reading specialist, or specialists, is a concrete indication that a school is serious about its interest in reading.

If reading is deemed important in all learning situations, and if the duties of the reading specialist indicated here are significant, opposition to the introduction of yet another specialist will be replaced by understanding support. More and more schools are moving in the direction of placing the over-all responsibility for the reading program in the hands of the reading specialist.

DUTIES OF THE READING SPECIALIST

The position of reading specialist is a relatively new one in our schools. As a result, there is no set pattern to follow when planning the program for this additional staff member. Many accounts of the duties of reading specialists are based on the results of questionnaires [8, 16, 17]. The responsibilities of the specialist—be he reading consultant, reading coordinator, reading supervisor, or reading teacher—tend to overlap each other and to change as teachers or additional reading staff become involved in reading instruction.

Appraisal of School Resources. One of the first duties of the reading specialist—whether the school has had a reading program for some time or whether a new one is being set up—is that of appraisal [5].

1. *Materials.* Many reading specialists prefer to begin by evaluating the physical or material side of the program. This would

146

normally include the supply of reading materials; basal, cobasal, supplementary readers, and resource materials; the availability and use of classroom libraries; the quality, recency, difficulty, and suitability of textbooks employed by content teachers; and the use made of workbooks and teacher's manuals.

There are several valid reasons for this approach to the situation. By starting with the materials side, the reading specialist has something that is impersonal, yet concrete and constructive, to talk about with teachers. At the same time, he is becoming acquainted both with the teachers and the school's philosophy of reading instruction. While ostensibly interested in books, the specialist is observing how these books are being used and the reaction of boys and girls to them. He is analyzing the particular qualifications of every staff member considering where each can be of greatest help in the program, and he is also evaluating the quality of the reading being done.

The survey of reading materials should be completed as quickly as possible, although other matters will be competing for attention. Frequently assistance may be obtained from the librarian, supervisors, and individual teachers, with the building principal helping with the delegation of duties.

2. *Testing program.* The appraisal of the existing testing sequence is one of the next considerations; through it the specialist can obtain a comprehensive idea of the effectiveness of reading instruction [18]. If a survey of the reading achievement of boys and girls is not a part of the testing program, such a survey should be undertaken. Whether it is to be school-wide or limited to the grades where work in reading is to be concentrated is a decision to be arrived at by the teachers involved, the reading specialist, the guidance department, and the administration. If there is any uncertainty about this, the reading survey should be used to obtain information which may be useful in deciding at what levels special corrective instruction should be introduced.

Usually special work in reading will be started with reading-disability cases at the earliest possible grade level. For example, if there is a choice among fourth, fifth, and sixth grades and only one can be taken, fourth grade is the logical one in which to begin unless there are factors peculiar to the individual school. At the secondary level, logical starting places are seventh, ninth, and tenth grades, depending on the vertical organization of the school [10]. Giving either the sixth or twelfth grade an emergency treatment comes close to being a shot in the arm. Such a procedure is likely to be rather unrewarding, since there is the added difficulty of following up stubborn cases which will probably take more than a year to correct. One exception which should be noted is the program for college-bound seniors in the twelfth grade.

3. *Staff.* The reading specialist will already be thinking of another area in which appraisal should be made—the training staff members have had in reading. Since much of the specialist's work will be advisory, he should learn about the special interests and abilities of the teachers with whom and through whom he will be working. Frequently such an appraisal will locate several teachers who are willing and fitted by training or prior experience to assume specific responsibilities; such information will also be useful in planning future in-service training programs.

While each school system will have its own methods of securing the desired data, much may be said for permitting the reading specialist to obtain the information through informal means. Then, at a later conference, the building principal and the specialist may pool their findings. As Bond [5] says, "In the ultimate analysis the reading program in no small measure depends upon the quality of the reading instruction that is done by the individual members of the staff. Hence, the co-ordinator must know the quality of instruction that can be expected and consider means of improving it when need for improvement is indicated." [1]

4. *Other school resources.* Other school resources which should be appraised are certain services performed by the school health department, the speech department, and the guidance department.

The school health department assumes responsibility for screening for vision and hearing defects and for the more general function of following up extended absences. Appraisal should be made of the type of equipment employed, frequency and thoroughness of screening, the practices employed in reporting to parents, and the check-

[1] Guy L. Bond and Eva Bond, *Developmental Reading in High School,* The Macmillan Company, New York, 1941, p. 332. Used by permission.

ing of referrals to medical authorities together with suggestions to the teachers of the children concerned.

The speech department, adding to its regular program, can assist in kindergarten and first-grade speech screening and provide necessary corrective work in speech classes, speech clinic, or through the classroom teachers.

The guidance department is frequently the first to become aware of students' social and emotional problems. The guidance office has long been the clearinghouse for students, teachers, and parents; as far as possible, this should be continued to avoid needless duplication. The yearly testing program in reading should be worked out jointly by the guidance personnel and the reading specialist.

Close cooperation with existing departments can best be achieved by appraisal and analysis of their function. The reading specialist can then make use of existing facilities, supplementing them only when it is necessary for the efficient operation of the reading program. No two schools will be found to be exactly alike.

Appraisal of Community Resources. The modern school cannot and should not exist apart from its community. The reading specialist will want to investigate fully the professional and general resources of the community.

The professional resources include several branches of the medical profession, such as eye and ear specialists, pediatricians, general practitioners, psychologists, and psychiatrists. The reading specialist will want to meet with them to explain the purpose of the reading program and to make sure that they are in sympathy with screening, reading therapy, and the general objectives of the program. In smaller communities, the names of specialists to whom patients are usually referred may be learned from a local general practitioner. All this takes time, but it should be systematically undertaken in the early stages of community appraisal. Gathering information should not be left until an acute case precipitates action.

The other professional area involved in this survey of community resources is more closely connected with reading. It includes clinics for children with emotional problems, various diseases, and reading and other learning disabilities. These may be private foundations or they may be operated in conjunction with a hospital, medical college, teachers college, or university. While the reading specialist will be able to handle the majority of reading problems, inevitably there will be a few cases which require special diagnosis and therapy. With these, the reading specialist should be able to continue the therapy once diagnosis has been made and remedial measures suggested.

Both of these professional groups may serve another function for the school interested in reading. Both are possible sources of speakers on topics concerning teachers engaged in developmental reading.

The general community resources to be appraised include both people and places. The attitude of taxpayers toward the school is important to the reading program and so is the opinion parents have of methods of reading instruction. But the survey of community attitudes must go deeper than this. The socioeconomic backgrounds of parents, the college and vocational choices of their sons and daughters, the presence of foreign-born groups, the number of books in home libraries, and the avocational use of reading in the community—all of these affect the school's reading program.

Places are secondary to people in importance; but museums, libraries, farms, industries, and historical sites give meaning to learning, since learning is based on experience. Most reading series start with the home and move out into the community, so that each class trip adds new words and reality to a reading lesson. The specialist will want to investigate these resources in order to suggest further ways of enriching the reading program.

A survey of community resources is too big a task for one individual. The reading specialist will welcome assistance from teachers, librarians, guidance counselors, the principal, and the PTA.

The specialist will look upon the PTA as a means of community evaluation. He will also see in it one of the more effective ways of judging the community itself and of evaluating the school's public relations program. At the same time the PTA can bring a wealth of assistance as individual parents show their willingness to share their knowledge in specialized fields.

Appraisals of school and community resources should not be limited to the start of a reading program or the addition of a reading specialist. Each school that is desirous of maintaining an effective reading program must be continually prepared to assess the community, the school itself, the reading program, and the curriculum.

Periodic self-examination is necessary because of changes in staff, shifts in population, improvements in reading techniques, the introduction of new books, and new demands placed on adult reading— to say nothing of changes in boys and girls themselves and in the community where they live. A school may discover that some or all of the above factors have contributed to the weakening of what was once a good reading program. The idea that once a good reading program has been set up it will continue indefinitely of itself is a dangerous assumption built on complacency.

Reporting. Since the reading program is essentially a cooperative effort on the part of the staff and all departments, an important phase, which is the reading specialist's responsibility, is that of record keeping and reporting [5]. For his own use in working with reading-disability cases, the reading specialist will keep detailed records of the types of errors made in both oral and silent reading. Such information is an essential part of diagnosis and remediation and is usually on file in the reading classroom or laboratory. However, it should be made available to elementary teachers who will be continuing instruction, to teachers of junior high reading classes, and to others interested.

The classroom teachers of students selected for special instruction should be kept informed throughout the instruction period. The attitude "Now the reading teacher is working with him, he is out of my hands," should be avoided at all costs. Indeed, there is much that the elementary classroom teacher and the secondary subject-matter teacher can do to complement remedial instruction.

The suggestion has been made that the guidance department be used as a clearinghouse for reporting to teachers. Where the customary procedure is to make constant use of the guidance department, it is both easier and wiser to continue the practice than to set up a separate information center. Granted that the size of the school and the attitude of the guidance counselors affect this procedure to some extent, yet reading data carried in cumulative folders in the guidance office has been found to be most accessible.

At times the reading specialist will want to report the outcomes of instruction to specific groups of teachers. These may be all the teachers of a particular grade in elementary school or the teachers of certain students in the secondary school. The employment of grade meetings is an efficient way of conveying this information and one that permits discussion, thus leading to yet another form of in-service training.

At other times the specialist reports outcomes of instruction to the whole faculty or to the general public. Such reporting is essential to the advancement of the reading program and underlines the desirability of yearly measurement of reading progress.

Research. From this measurement and from experimentation comes yet another duty of the reading specialist. The improvement of reading teaching depends to a large degree on the amount and quality of the research done by individual teachers and individual school systems. Bond [5], writing in 1941, pointed out that reading instruction in the secondary school was in its infancy. In many respects, this statement is still true. It is important that teachers be acquainted with the results of experimentation and that they be encouraged to try out new practices in their own classrooms. To this end, accounts of successful reading activities should be carefully reported in professional journals by reading specialists and others.

Remedial Instruction. Yet another responsibility of the newly appointed reading specialist is to provide remedial instruction. As soon as possible he will begin work with individuals and small groups of boys and girls who are not working up to their ability. These reading-disability cases give the reading specialist an additional opportunity to evaluate reading instruction by working with individuals for whom the program has proved not wholly satisfactory. While he is doing this, the specialist is showing teachers what may be accomplished by this phase of reading instruction— an important opportunity, for frequently both the specialist and the new program are on trial until their efficacy has been demonstrated.

Improvement of Classroom Instruction. A major part of the reading specialist's time should be devoted to the improvement of instruction through supervision, demonstration, visitation, the selection of reading materials, and the organization of instruction. These aspects of the work will tend to enlarge as teachers come to know the reading specialist and become more deeply involved in the reading program.

1. *Supervision.* Provided the reading specialist is well trained, has practical teaching experience, and is tactful, classroom teachers will welcome his visits. He will assist classroom teachers in planning work adjusted for slow learners, including the compilation, collection, and sometimes the preparation of suitable materials. Classroom teachers might request help in determining the reading skills that should be taught in their subject-matter area or grade. They might also welcome suggestions and help in grouping.

2. *Demonstration and visitation.* One of the in-service training duties of the reading specialist is providing for demonstrations and visitations. He may give some of the demonstrations himself, or he may arrange for a teacher who has had considerable success with a particular technique to demonstrate it before the group. Visitation days, both within the school system and on a reciprocal basis with neighboring schools, enable teachers to observe techniques in class situations. When such visits are planned, provision should always be made for teachers to discuss their observations with the demonstration teacher.

3. *Selection of reading materials.* Next to the teaching staff, the factor contributing most to the success of a reading program is the quantity and quality of reading materials available. The survey will have shown what areas and grade levels are insufficiently or poorly equipped; one of the more effective ways of breaking down reticence of teachers toward the new reading specialist is to have him work with them in selecting reading materials. The provision of additional money when needed will give concrete proof of the administration's attitude toward reading.

The specialist should seek to build up and maintain a collection of newer reading materials, including basal series and supplementary readers, workbooks of all kinds, teacher's manuals, special-purpose materials at various levels and appealing to different age groups, games [9], and devices to arouse interest and provide necessary drill. These should be available for teacher examination and use. No published listing of materials is ever complete, so the reading specialist must be continually on the lookout for new materials. However, for help in setting up such a collection, Blair [4] and Simpson [18] will be found useful, and Spache [19] notes many aids and devices.

4. *Allocation of materials.* Closely connected with the problem of the selection of reading materials is that of deciding at what levels certain books should be used. Nothing undermines a seventh grader's ego quite as much as being given a book which he has previously seen in the hands of classmates in the third, fourth, or fifth grade.

At present—and this is likely to be true for some time to come—there is a dearth of material of first- and second-grade reading difficulty which can be used with nonreading pupils aged ten years and upward. If they can be obtained, materials prepared for the armed forces [20, 21], are of some help, but naturally they are narrow in scope and increase in difficulty very rapidly, since they are designed for adults. The Cowboy Sam Series [7] and the Aviation Readers [3] are probably among the best for slightly older boys. The American Adventure Series [1] and the Reader's Digest Reading Skillbuilder [15], starting at second-grade difficulty, are two others preferred by boys. If we could be sure that no child would pass through the primary grades without learning to read, the above books and others like them could be used at the levels designated. But the discovery of nonreading pupils and even nonreaders in the upper grades—transfers and those who are slow to mature are two of the possible groups—makes it imperative to designate certain books for upper levels. For example, the Cowboy Sam Series might be used for the retarded reader in the intermediate grades and the Digest series could be reserved for remedial use in the junior high school. The reading specialist will have to work out with the classroom teachers the grade allocation of these and other special-purpose books. Two other useful additions to these reading materials are the Elementary Reading Laboratory [13], grades 2 to 9, and the Secondary Reading Laboratory [14], grades 3 to 12. There are enough basal and supplementary readers so that primary and intermediate teachers do not have to rely on the limited supply of special-purpose materials for their normal instruction.

A source of graded reading selections which many teachers employ to increase interest in supplementary reading without infringing upon special-purpose materials, is to be found in *My Weekly Reader* [12] and similar publications. Boys and girls look forward to having their own newspaper with its games and special features; moreover, summer issues help carry reading into the home and serve to reduce forgetting during the holidays. A third-grade teacher will often order 25 copies of a weekly newspaper for her 25 young readers. A better procedure would be to order according to individual reading needs, possibly 2 first-grade, 5 second-grade, 15 third-grade, and 3 fourth-grade editions. A certain element of skillful prophecy is required as the orders are placed twice a year.

Even basal reading series enter into the allocation of books, since they vary a great deal in the difficulty of concepts presented and in vocabulary load. Some are more mature than others in content, control of repetition, and illustrations. A series should probably not be selected unless all the books are available for examination. A certain series may fit faster groups in some communities, while those of another publishing company may be better suited to slower reading groups.

5. *Coordination of the reading program.* Closely paralleling the selection of materials is the coordination of reading instruction. The basal, cobasal, and supplementary readers, together with the teacher's manual, to a large extent govern reading instruction in the elementary school except for the content lessons. Here the reading specialist will be helpful in suggesting supplementary materials and in working out with the teachers units of common interest on many reading levels.

Of almost equal importance in the elementary school is the provision to be made for individual growth as indicated in Chapter 4 and detailed in Chapter 12. These changes in primary instruction should be prepared for in the testing program, book orders, allocation of teachers according to their special interests and abilities, and, last but not least, by helping parents become aware of the reading, promotion, and marking philosophy of the school.

At the junior high level, the principal problem of coordination concerns the steps required to further developmental reading in all content subjects. This is complicated because of the number of teachers involved and the wide variety of subject-matter offerings.

However, this part of the reading program is best thought of in terms of in-service training with individual and small group conferences as logical starting points.

The setting up of special reading classes—if this course is decided upon to complement developmental reading instruction in content areas—calls for adequate testing, formation and scheduling of classes, and securing, training, and supervising teachers selected to teach them.

The remedial phase of the reading program is also the concern of the reading specialist. Problems of organization include the selection of reading-disability cases from certain grades in the school, the administration of additional individual tests, and the diagnosis and preparation of case studies. In some instances referral will be made to nearby clinics or medical specialists. Finally, the remedial work will be planned in the light of all the known facts; and the specialist, or some qualified teacher, will undertake instruction. Group work is usually tried first in order to conserve the teacher's time, but individual remediation may be substituted if progress is unduly slow.

One of the criticisms of secondary reading programs [5] in the past has been that remedial reading has been overstressed to the detriment of the preventive aspects of reading instruction. However, the fact that the remedial program has been overemphasized in the past does not mean that it should be eliminated now. Provided all members of the staff are mindful of their contributions to reading instruction, specialized small group and individual work will yield gratifying results.

The actual number of reading-disability cases varies with the size of the school; between 5 and 10 per cent is a fair average [10]. Of course some of these students could be provided for in regular content classes, but classroom teachers generally do not have the special-purpose materials, the time, or the highly technical knowledge required for therapy. Special work in reading class will help the less severely retarded, but remedial instruction is the answer for the 5 to 10 per cent mentioned above. From the point of view of the boys and girls involved, the most urgent need is rapid improvement so that they may function in regular classroom reading activities.

Teachers are prone to suggest more children than the specialist can work with efficiently; there is a danger that teachers will tend to overload the remedial program in their interest in children. Among those recommended for remedial instruction will be some who are already reading up to their capacity, although not at their grade level. The fact that Jack is well-behaved and Mary is eager to help in the classroom does not mean that they are necessarily the ones to be selected for special instruction. A waiting list is sometimes necessary if a carefully organized remedial program is to work effectively.

THE READING CLASSROOM OR LABORATORY

Remedial instruction may be carried on anywhere—in the back of classrooms, in corridors, or in the principal's outer office. However, the fact that instruction can be given in all sorts of inconvenient places does not mean that this practice is desirable or efficient.

Location of Reading Classroom. New schools and many old ones are providing a reading classroom or laboratory on the same floor as the school library and as close to it as possible. An alternative location—sometimes a better one in many respects—is close to the guidance department. Either location usually ensures a central position. This is an advantage if boys and girls are to be dismissed from study hall and the library for reading instruction, if special-purpose books for slower readers are to be shelved here, and if teachers are to be encouraged to make use of the room as a resource center.

Plan of Reading Classroom. The room itself may be adapted from any average-sized classroom having one or two entrance doors. Figure 5 indicates the suggested arrangement, which may be modified. The room should contain two glass-partitioned offices, one for the reading specialist and the other for testing purposes. There should also be low bookshelves for elementary children and somewhat higher shelves for secondary students; a reading corner with easy chairs and carpet, which is separated from the rest of the room by a screen doubling as a two-faced bulletin board; flat-topped movable desks and chairs; and the required office furniture.

If the office partitions do not extend to the ceiling, ventilation will

FIGURE 5. PLAN OF READING CLASSROOM OR LABORATORY

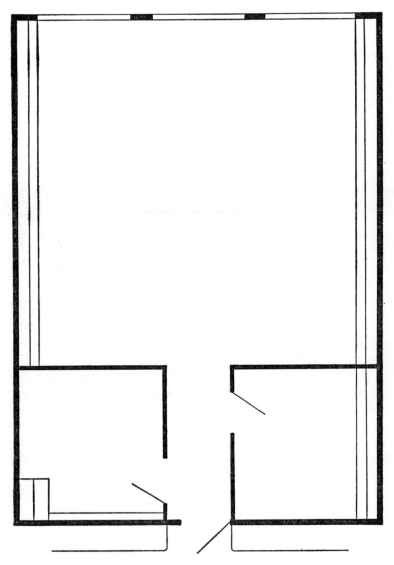

usually be good, but some arrangement for heating the offices is essential. The use of one-way glass is a possibility, but plain glass permits supervision from both offices. The necessary privacy is obtained if glass starts at about 4½ feet from the floor so that occupants of the room are not visible when seated. Opaque glass in the sections of the partitions forming the corridor into the room will also help.

Other provisions which add to the usability of the room are slanting shelves for book and magazine display purposes, with cabinets beneath for storage of bulky equipment; space for exhibiting hobby collections; and an aquarium or vivarium to add interest and counteract any feeling of clinical atmosphere. Soundproofing the ceiling will permit pupils and teachers to use testing room, office, and laboratory at the same time with some degree of quiet.

Lighting. Adequate lighting is essential, not only in the reading classroom, but in all classrooms and working areas of the school. Older concepts of what constituted good lighting included windows extending from a few inches from the ceiling to the eye height of someone sitting in a chair. Artificial illumination consisted of two or three rows of incandescent fixtures. The intensity of the light was measured in foot-candles at the working surface. For reading tasks, 30 foot-candles was usually agreed upon; and, if light was found to be inadequate by this standard, additional fixtures were added.

Newer concepts of adequate lighting tend to be much more complicated. In addition to the intensity of light, illuminating engineers and school architects are concerned with brightness, the amount of light emitted by the fixtures themselves and that reflected from visible surfaces inside and outside the room. While the human eye can readily adjust to differences in the intensity of light, it is relatively less able to accommodate itself to contrasting areas of brightness. This brightness is measured in foot-lamberts. Attempts are made to control the amount of contrast so that the brightness of any surface "should not exceed ten times the foot-lambert brightness of the poorest lighted task" [2].

In order to reduce the contrast between light and dark surfaces, the following points merit attention. The ceiling should be white in order to reflect as much light as possible both from the lighting fixtures themselves and from the outside. Pastel shades are indicated for the walls although for maintenance purposes the wainscot area may be slightly darker. Even the floors should be relatively light in color, and contrasting squares and borders are to be avoided. The traditional blackboard should be replaced by green chalk boards. Desk tops and other surfaces should be free from glare. Some method of controlling light admitted through glass areas is necessary. Venetian blinds, curtains, tinted and opaque glass all have possibilities but frequently create further problems [11]. Finally, the lighting fixtures themselves should be selected to provide as uniform as possible a source of artificial light. Since excessive bright spots are to be avoided, indirect lighting using the ceiling as a reflector is a possibility, although this method may prove inadequate for rooms to be used at night.

Maintenance is important if conditions of maximum efficiency are to prevail. This includes keeping shades in good repair, washing globes and reflectors, and replacing burned-out fluorescent tubes and incandescent bulbs.

Justification for Reading Laboratory. The administration may question the economic desirability of devoting one or more classrooms to a reading laboratory. However, in view of the number of children to be tested and provided with corrective instruction, the need for a central clearinghouse for special materials, and the requirement of economizing on the time of the specialist, the reading room is a virtual necessity. Furthermore, the existence of such a room goes a long way toward establishing the reading program in so far as boys and girls, parents, and the teaching staff are concerned.

QUALIFICATIONS OF THE READING SPECIALIST

The position of reading specialist is a comparatively difficult one to fill because it necessitates advisement to the staff, all of whom will probably not be equally advanced in their thinking. In fact, some will be opposed to any changes in teaching procedures. Since the duties of the reading specialist include making suggestions regarding skills in many subject-matter areas, the position calls for a knowledge of materials in many different fields at all grade levels, plus a good general appreciation of the curriculum. At times the reading specialist will be called upon to do demonstration teaching. At other times such a specialist will be involved in individual and small-group remediation. Some of the difficulties faced by the reading specialist will become apparent to the administrator and to the Reading Improvement Committee as they consider staff members and individual students known to need assistance in reading.

Personality. In the light of these difficulties, it is obvious that the reading specialist should be a person who is kindly, sympathetic, patient, and, above all, tactful. He must be able to exhibit confidence in working with boys and girls and be both dynamic and resourceful in relationships with adults. In this latter regard, the reading specialist needs to be well-equipped professionally with a sound philosophy of learning in general and reading in particular. Such a person should have knowledge of reading instruction and perspective sufficient to enable him to avoid fads in reading, and yet he should be able to experiment in areas where experimentation is desirable.

Training. From the above demands, the Reading Improvement Committee will see the dangers attendant upon hiring a partly or poorly trained individual. Rather than risking this, many schools are selecting experienced teachers who are interested in the psychology of reading and are advising them to take courses leading to specialization in reading. Since they are able teachers, respected by the staff and the community, they are likely to be far more effective in helping the committee set up a reading program than is a teacher who is new both to the field of reading and to the system. Of course, this procedure may result in some delay in achieving the full effectiveness of the reading program, but the time can usually be well spent in developing staff and community attitudes.

The qualifications of a reading specialist should consist of actual and successful teaching experience in one or more subject-matter fields or grades. Professional courses leading to a master's degree or its equivalent, with specialization in reading, are also desirable. Many young men are entering the field by gaining teaching experience in the primary grades. A sixth year of professional study or a doctorate is usually a prerequisite for positions in larger school systems.

Minimum Standards for Reading Specialists. The Membership Standards Committee of the International Reading Association is recommending certain standards for specialists in the field of reading. The committee recognizes that many positions involving added responsibilities will necessitate training and experience beyond the following minimum standards:

A. A minimum of three years of successful teaching and/or clinical experience
B. A master's degree, or its equivalent of thirty graduate hours, in reading and related areas as indicated below:
  1. A minimum of twelve semester hours in graduate-level reading courses, with at least one course in each of the following areas of reading:
    a. Foundations or survey course
    b. Diagnosis and correction of reading difficulties
    c. Clinical or laboratory practicum
  2. At least one graduate-level course in each of the following content areas:
    a. Measurement and/or evaluation
    b. Personality and/or mental hygiene
    c. Educational psychology
  3. The remainder of the semester hours to be in reading and/or related areas

Upon application, persons holding certain positions for a stated period may be accepted under a so-called grandfather clause.

The adoption by the International Reading Association of such a set of minimum standards should provide leadership in several vital areas: (1) Teachers planning to enter the reading field will be helped in the selection of professional work. (2) School administrators will find these provisions a guide in determining the professional preparation of reading personnel. (3) Colleges and universities will find in them criteria for setting up or revising professional programs. Enough latitude exists to permit local adaptations. (4) Reading programs in those states not having certification of reading specialists will be strengthened. (5) The existence of minimum standards should be of assistance to states contemplating the setting up of certification requirements.

State Certification of Reading Specialists. One of the reasons for a lag in the attention paid to reading in our schools is that state education departments have largely failed to provide the necessary leadership in establishing requirements for reading specialists. Whether such failure is because of a feeling that reading is the province of primary and intermediate grade classroom teachers or because of reluctance to issue certificates in another field is uncertain. Whatever the reason for hesitation in the past, state departments of education have the possibility of asserting their leadership function in this matter. There can be no doubt that certification requirements would strengthen reading instruction in public elementary and secondary schools throughout the United States.

Figure 6 indicates states currently specifying certification requirements for reading specialists and states considering such a move in the near future.

Six states—Connecticut, Delaware, Massachusetts, Oregon, Pennsylvania, and Wisconsin—now issue certificates for both elementary and secondary reading specialists. One state, New Jersey, makes provision for a secondary certificate and plans shortly to expand it to cover kindergarten through twelfth grade.

Eight states indicate that they are contemplating certification on both the elementary and secondary levels and two additional states are considering it at the elementary level.

By far the most encouraging sign is that thirty of the fifty states showed that they were interested in finding out what the other states were contemplating in this area of certification.

Certification requirements vary considerably, but enough similarities exist to form a general pattern. The first requirement is from one to three years of successful teaching experience. Obviously, the more successful classroom experience the prospective reading specialist has had, the better able he should be to work with teachers in classroom situations.

The second requirement is clinical experience. Before a reading specialist can advise other teachers on the remediation for individuals, he should have had actual practice in working with reading-disability cases as well as with retarded readers. From the viewpoint of colleges engaged in training reading specialists this requirement may present a bottleneck. Despite this limitation, the

FIGURE 6. STATE CERTIFICATION OF READING SPECIALISTS

State	Special Certificate		Certificate Contemplated		Certificate Requirements		
	El.	Sec.	El.	Sec.	1*	2*	3*
Alabama	No	No	No	No	—	—	—
Alaska	No	No	No	No	—	—	—
Arizona	No	No	Yes	Yes	—	—	—
Arkansas	No	No	No	No	—	—	—
California	No	No	No	No	—	—	—
Colorado	No	No	No	No	—	—	—
Connecticut	Yes	Yes	—	—	3	Yes	15
Delaware	Yes	Yes	—	—	3	Yes	21
District of Columbia	No	No	No	No	—	—	—
Florida	No	No	No	No	—	—	—
Georgia	No	No	No	No	—	—	—
Hawaii	No	No	No	No	—	—	—
Idaho	No	No	No	No	—	—	—
Illinois	No	No	No	No	—	—	—
Indiana	No	No	Yes	No	—	—	—
Iowa	No	No	No	No	—	—	—
Kansas	No	No	No	No	—	—	—
Kentucky	No	No	No	No	—	—	—
Louisiana	No	No	No	No	—	—	—
Maine	No	No	Yes	Yes	—	—	—
Maryland	No	No	No	No	—	—	—
Massachusetts	Yes	Yes	—	—	No	Yes	18
Michigan	No	No	No	No	—	—	—
Minnesota	No	No	Yes	Yes	—	—	—
Mississippi	No	No	No	No	—	—	—
Missouri	No	No	No	No	—	—	—
Montana	No	No	No	No	—	—	—
Nebraska	No	No	No	No	—	—	—
Nevada	No	No	No	No	—	—	—
New Hampshire	No	No	Yes	Yes	—	—	—
New Jersey	No	Yes	Yes	Yes	3	No	18
New Mexico	No	No	Yes	Yes	—	—	—
New York	No	No	No	No	—	—	—
North Carolina	No	No	No	No	—	—	—
North Dakota	No	No	No	No	—	—	—

FIGURE 6. STATE CERTIFICATION OF READING SPECIALISTS (CONT.)

State	Special Certificate		Certificate Contemplated		Certificate Requirements		
	El.	Sec.	El.	Sec.	1*	2*	3*
Ohio	No	No	No	No	—	—	—
Oklahoma	No	No	No	No	—	—	—
Oregon	Yes	Yes	—	—	1	Yes	36 †
Pennsylvania	Yes	Yes	—	—	3	3	24
Rhode Island	No	No	No	No	—	—	—
South Carolina	No	No	No	No	—	—	—
South Dakota	No	No	Yes	No	—	—	—
Tennessee	No	No	No	No	—	—	—
Texas	No	No	No	No	—	—	—
Utah	No	No	No	No	—	—	—
Vermont	No	No	Yes	Yes	—	—	—
Virginia	No	No	Yes	Yes	—	—	—
Washington	No	No	No	No	—	—	—
West Virginia	No	No	No	No	—	—	—
Wisconsin	Yes	Yes	—	—	—	Yes	12
Wyoming	No	No	No	No	—	—	—

1* Number of years teaching experience.
2* Clinic experience (semester hours).
3* Courses in psychology of reading and allied fields (semester hours).
† Expressed in quarter hours.

clinical practicum or laboratory experience in working with poor readers appears indicated.

The third requirement consists of courses in the teaching of reading, psychology, and allied fields. Both course content and the number of semester hours vary considerably from state to state. This variation depends, in part, upon the interpretation placed on the phrase "allied fields." Complete uniformity is neither desirable nor practical.

Most states do not differentiate among the positions of reading teacher, reading consultant, reading coordinator, and reading supervisor. However, the reading supervisor must usually hold a supervisory certificate in addition to the one in reading.

The advantages of certification appear obvious. While the existence of requirements and taking prescribed courses do not of themselves ensure better teaching, the professionalization of teachers of reading will tend to encourage more and better qualified people to enter this branch of teaching.

ELEMENTARY READING SPECIALIST

A decision will have to be reached on the scope of the activities of the elementary reading specialist if such an addition to the staff is being considered. A brief summary of the more important duties of such a specialist will aid the Reading Improvement Committee and the administration in deciding which functions are particularly called for by local school conditions.

Primary Grade Area. In kindergarten and through third grade, the reading specialist works largely with and through the regular teachers. Assistance should be given in the selection and carrying out of the reading readiness program together with the administration of such intelligence and reading readiness tests as may be mutually agreed upon. The formation of reading groups and the determination of techniques of teaching reading—within the limits of general method imposed by the basal reading series—are other important functions of the specialist.

The reading specialist will also work with classroom teachers in explaining to parents, individually and in groups, the aims of reading instruction at each grade level, what they may do to help, and what should be avoided. If these meetings follow physical examinations and screening tests, parents may be informed of findings which should be reported to them.

Another contribution of the specialist is acting as a resource person when a new basal series and accompanying workbooks are to be selected. Having a thorough working knowledge of different reading systems, the reading specialist will seek to introduce new ideas and improve the general level of instruction by tactful suggestion and demonstration.

In the primary grades the school reading specialist frequently assists the teacher in diagnosing special reading difficulties and in carrying on part of the remedial instruction. In this way, the efficacy of remediation may be determined.

The reading specialist advises the principal and the primary grade supervisor of the possible formation of class groups for the ensuing year. Information for the next year's teacher is collected and made available through the guidance department. Suggested changes in the school curriculum are advanced to the proper authorities.

One other important aspect of the specialist's position is working with the elementary supervisor to help new primary teachers form reading groups. Schedules are planned so that each group reads each day and so that the oral reading and seat work reinforce each other wherever possible [10].

While not precisely parts of the reading program, areas which often need to be considered for curriculum purposes are language, handwriting, spelling, and speech. School policy determines what methods are to be employed, the grade level where manuscript is replaced by cursive writing and formal spelling is introduced, and the emphasis placed upon language. At times there may also be the need for a writing supervisor to help make a school system conscious of legible writing. Correct spelling, legible penmanship, and correct English in written and spoken work are just as much the responsibility of every teacher as is reading.

Intermediate Grade Area. The duties of the reading specialist in the intermediate grades 4 to 6 include many of those listed in the preceding paragraphs. Many authorities believe that there is no such thing as a remedial-reading case prior to fourth grade. What they really mean is that in grades 1 to 3 it is the classroom teacher's responsibility to take boys and girls where they are in reading with the possible exceptions already noted. In grades 4 to 6, special instruction is given to small groups and occasionally to individuals. The spread of abilities in any one grade increases the farther the grade is removed from first grade. These special groups simplify teaching in intermediate grades and become increasingly necessary as larger classes are encountered. Before special instruction is undertaken, there is a large amount of testing to be done in addition to that arranged through and by the guidance department. This testing seeks to diagnose, by standardized and informal oral-reading tests, the types of errors made. As in the primary grade area, the specialist should either do a part of the remediation himself to check the reliability of the diagnosis or, alternatively, he should follow the case very carefully. A willingness to help here will pave the way toward another phase of the work—assisting the classroom teacher in planning adjusted work for retarded readers who are slow learners and who belong in the regular classroom. In smaller schools, provision for slow learners will be made by setting up subgroups within the regular class; in larger schools, homogeneous grouping will usually result in a class, smaller than other sections, composed of slow learners [10].

Finally, the reading specialist who is responsible for the reading work of the intermediate grades must coordinate the elementary reading program with that of the junior high school [6]. This coordination includes transmitting all pertinent information, working on curriculum committees, and through the guidance department, setting up the homogeneous sections for seventh grade. This task becomes more complicated in situations where several elementary schools funnel pupils into a junior high school.

Wide variations in reading preparation will frequently be noted among the several elementary schools of a large system. Contributing factors may be any or all of the following: differences in training and professional attitude of the staffs of the schools concerned, the socioeconomic backgrounds of the parents, the presence or absence of adequate materials, and the general responsiveness of the teachers. The efficient administrator would expect a reading specialist to assist him in raising the level of the poorer schools while continuing to improve the standards of the better ones.

SECONDARY READING SPECIALIST

The reading specialist who is attached to a secondary school has duties which fall into three main categories: (1) the developmental side of the program, including work with content teachers in improving reading instruction—his most important function, in the long run; (2) the continuation of formal reading instruction in special reading classes in junior high school; and (3) the provision of remedial instruction for reading-disability cases who have not yet reached their expected reading capacity.

Content Teaching. The program of the secondary school reading specialist should be planned so that he can work effectively with

FIGURE 7. WEEKLY SCHEDULE OF SECONDARY READING SPECIALIST

Period	Monday	Tuesday	Wednesday	Thursday	Friday
1		R-1	R-1	R-1	
2	C	C	C	C	C
3	R-x	R-y	R-x	R-y	
4	R-2		R-2		
Lunch					
5	R-y	R-y		R-y	R-y
6					
7			R-y		

C indicates subject-matter class.
R-1 and R-2 indicate seventh-grade reading classes.
R-x indicates group work with upperclassmen from library or study hall.
R-y represents small group work with individuals from other reading classes.
Remainder of periods for conferences on developmental reading, testing, reports, and case studies.

content teachers. Figure 7 indicates a proposed weekly schedule. Taking at least one subject-matter class of average ability in a content field in which he has had experience gives him a direct contact with classroom instruction and enables him to share the problems encountered in classroom situations.

The beginning specialist should not be expected to suggest, or even show by demonstration, how reading skills may be worked into subject-matter teaching before he has had the opportunity to appraise the situation thoroughly; but he may work with other faculty members to solve common problems. Through in-service training of the kinds mentioned earlier in this chapter, teachers will be prepared to incorporate better reading practices in their daily teaching.

Reading Class Teaching. Another means of bringing the reading specialist into direct contact with boys and girls is through a class, or classes, in reading which meet from two or three to five times a week. This specific reading-class situation strengthens the reading program in that the specialist will be in a better position to coordinate and supervise the work of the regular teachers who may be asked to teach one or more reading classes. At the same time, the danger of the reading specialist becoming an armchair authority is minimized. Provision should be made in this program for planning, organization, and supervision. The fact that the specialist may not be free to observe all the other reading classes is not as serious an objection as might at first be supposed, since often more may be accomplished by pre- and post-teaching conferences than by actual observation.

Remedial Teaching. A large part of the remainder of the school day should be devoted to small groups and individual students from other seventh-grade reading classes and upperclassmen who have not yet made all possible improvement in reading. Several periods are left for oral-reading testing, conferences, case studies, and reports. Students may be assigned to the reading classroom from study hall, other seventh-grade reading classes, or library periods and are allowed to return when suitable gains have been achieved.

An alternative arrangement, which lacks the flexibility of the program suggested, is to assign the specialist to a section of English or social studies composed of reading-disability cases. Where this is done, students are given credit for the course. When individual instruction is given for the period necessary to raise reading ability to meet mental capacity, usually no credit is given.

ORGANIZATION OF READING SPECIALISTS

The title "reading specialist" has been employed throughout this chapter since no attempt could be made to differentiate among various possible assignments. The work, rather than the title, is the important consideration [8]. Figure 8 shows the approximate range of various types of reading specialists. Each school will have its own ideas and will decide what plan of organization best fits the local situation.

Reading Consultant. The reading consultant is a specialist in reading who is frequently attached to some state or county organ-

FIGURE 8. RANGE OF READING SPECIALISTS

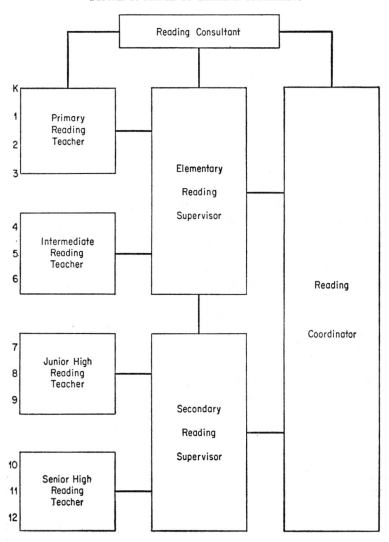

ization, although he may be found in large city school systems. The consultant tends to be a trouble shooter, a resource person who may be turned to for advice on perplexing problems. He usually works with reading teachers and supervisors through the local reading coordinator. His duties are largely advisory.

Reading Coordinator. The reading coordinator tends to be furthest removed from actual reading situations in a school simply because he covers a greater area. The coordinator is usually found only in the large school systems. In smaller systems, his duties are performed by the reading supervisor. In some cases the necessary coordination is accomplished by an assistant superintendent in charge of instruction, or alternatively, by a curriculum coordinator.

Reading Supervisor. Very frequently the specialist holds the position of reading supervisor. The emphasis is on working with teachers to improve the reading program of the school. In addition to supervisory duties, the specialist will also do a considerable amount of work with boys and girls, though not as much as the reading teacher normally does. The size of the system and the number of reading-disability cases determine his duties. The position of reading supervisor is often combined with that of elementary supervisor in smaller school systems. When this is done, in all but the very smallest schools, reading teachers are employed to assist with the actual remediation. The reading supervisor will often plan, implement, and direct experimental programs. In this phase of the work he may receive assistance from the reading coordinator, aided at times by a reading consultant.

Reading Teacher. Of utmost importance in the reading program is the position held by the reading teacher whose principal contribution is in actual remedial instruction of reading-disability cases. Better results are obtained if the reading teacher's schedule is kept flexible so that he may work with students when the testing program and the classroom teachers' suggestions indicate their need. Some schools attempt to achieve results by giving the elementary school reading teacher a class of retarded readers for the whole day. This tends to defeat the purpose for which the reading teacher was originally hired; it succeeds only in making a special-class teacher of the reading specialist, adding disciplinary, curriculum, and scheduling problems to the specialized problems of reading. A further objection to this program is that only fifteen or twenty pupils receive help in reading.

In the secondary school, the reading teacher will sometimes be a member of the English department. This may be a necessity in very small schools, but such a practice usually is not successful from a developmental point of view, since other subject-matter teachers tend to think of reading as a one-department responsibility.

Finally, where only one position can be provided, the specialist combines the duties of reading teacher with some supervisory work and coordinates the program. In such a situation, there is a tendency to concentrate on the intermediate and junior high grades.

SUMMARY

One of the first duties of the newly appointed reading specialist is the *appraisal* of resources which will aid the reading program. School resources include the materials of reading, the testing program, the training of the staff in reading, and the guidance, health, and speech departments, with whom the specialist will be working. Community resources include professional groups, such as medical specialists and clinics, and general resources, which comprise both people and places. Periodic self-examination is necessary if a school is to maintain an effective reading program.

Other duties of the reading specialist are *reporting* to the administration, teachers, and parents through the guidance department and the encouragement of *research* by which teachers keep abreast of new practices and acquaint others with their own findings. The *remedial instruction* of reading-disability cases will also concern the specialist.

At the same time the experienced reading specialist will be occupied with the *improvement of classroom instruction* by such means as supervision, demonstration and visitation, the selection and allocation of reading materials, and the organization and coordination of reading instruction. A reading classroom or laboratory facilitates these functions.

The qualifications of the reading specialist include tact, plus adequate experience and professional training. Minimum standards for the training of reading specialists, as proposed by a subcommittee of the International Reading Association, should simplify hiring reading specialists by administrators in states which do not yet specify certification requirements.

The actual responsibilities vary with the level at which the specialist is working, which may be primary, intermediate, or secondary school level. The presence of other reading specialists in the school system also determines responsibilities.

The duties performed and the size of the school govern the organization of the reading department. The various positions include those of reading consultant, reading coordinator, reading supervisor, and reading teacher.

REFERENCES

1. American Adventure Series, Wheeler Publishing Company, Chicago, Illinois.

2. American Association of School Administrators, *Common Sense in School Lighting*, National Education Association, Washington, 1956.

3. Aviation Readers, 1, 2, and 3, The Macmillan Company, New York.

* 4. Blair, Glenn Myers: *Diagnostic and Remedial Teaching*, rev. ed., The Macmillan Company, New York, 1956.

* 5. Bond, Guy L., and Eva Bond: *Developmental Reading in High School*, The Macmillan Company, New York, 1941.

6. Cooke, Dorothy E.: "How Conference Proposals Can Be Implemented throughout School Systems by Administrators and Supervisors," in William S. Gray and Nancy Larrick (eds.), *Better Readers for Our Times*, International Reading Association Conference Proceedings, vol. 1, Scholastic Magazines, New York, 1956, pp. 175–176.

7. Cowboy Sam Series, Beckley Cardy Company, Chicago, Ill.

8. Dever, K. I.: *Positions in the Field of Reading*, Bureau of Publications, Teachers College, Columbia University, New York, 1956.

9. Dolch, E. W.: *The Dolch Games*, Garrard Press, Champaign, Ill.

* 10. Harris, Albert J.: *How to Increase Reading Ability*, 3d ed., Longmans, Green & Co., Inc., New York, 1956.

11. Herrick, John H., Ralph D. McLeary, Wilfred F. Clapp,

and Walter F. Bogner: *From School Program to School Plant*, Henry Holt and Company, Inc., New York, 1956.

12. *My Weekly Reader*, American Education Press, Inc., Columbus, Ohio.

13. Parker, Don H. (ed.): *Reading Laboratory: Elementary*, Science Research Associates, Inc., Chicago, 1957.

14. Parker, Don H. (ed.): *Reading Laboratory: Secondary*, Science Research Associates, Inc., Chicago, 1958.

15. Reader's Digest Reading Skillbuilder, The Reader's Digest Educational Service, Inc., Pleasantville, N.Y.

16. Robinson, H. A.: "An Occupational Survey of Reading Specialists in Junior and Senior High Schools," unpublished doctoral dissertation, New York University, New York, 1956.

17. Robinson, H. M.: "Qualifications for Teachers of Remedial Reading," *School Review*, vol. 63, no. 6, pp. 334–337, September, 1955.

18. Simpson, Elizabeth A.: *Helping High-school Students Read Better*, Science Research Associates, Inc., Chicago, 1954.

19. Spache, George: *Resources in Teaching Reading*, University of Florida, Gainesville, Fla., 1955.

20. U.S. Bureau of Naval Personnel, *Navy Life Reader, Book One*, NAVPERS 16180, 1945.

21. U.S. Department of Defense: *Meet Private Pete: A Soldier's Reader*, Educational Manual, EM160, USAFI, Madison, Wis., 1944.

* See Appendix A for annotated list of books for the professional library in schools.

Chapter 9

SCHOOL PSYCHOLOGIST AND SPECIAL SERVICES

Of the many possible services that a school psychologist can render boys and girls, some are particularly appropriate for consideration in connection with a school reading program.

THE SCHOOL PSYCHOLOGIST

No attempt will be made here to define the various duties of the school psychologist or, for that matter, to list all the tests that might be used. Instead, the areas where the psychologist has a direct relationship to the reading program will be indicated. The desirability of obtaining additional information by psychometric tests is readily seen when we consider the problems which are likely to exist in any school system and which are apt to contribute to learning difficulties.

The Slow Learner. The slow learner is frequently so handicapped by poor reading ability that the reported intelligence quotient, as usually obtained by means of a group mental test, is an inexact measure of his mental ability. In extreme cases, this is true even when a verbal and nonverbal group test, such as the California Test of Mental Maturity, is used. When the services of a school psychologist are not available, the Durrell-Sullivan Reading Capacity Test affords insight into vocabulary and comprehension abilities. However, this test does not reveal as much information about the factors which are thought to make up intelligence as does an individual test, such as the appropriate form of either the Revised Stanford-Binet or the Wechsler-Bellevue. Frequently a slow learner's intelligence is revealed to be as much as 20 IQ points higher when measured by an individual test [5].

A school may be doing the child a grave injustice when it rates him as a slow learner on the basis of group intelligence-test results alone. In addition, the interpretation of the individual intelligence test may reveal much useful information about the kinds of instruction and types of reading drills required, and the reasoning abilities he needs to develop. In other cases, where an individual's subtest scores on a group test vary a great deal, the use of the individual test promotes a better understanding of the subject.

Maladjusted Students. A second group which the psychologist wants to help is composed of average students and even able learners who, while making fair progress in school, are obviously maladjusted. Because of this maladjustment they are not progressing as well as they and their parents have a right to expect. A personality handicap often goes unnoticed by those close to the individual, such as parents and classroom teachers, and remains to be spotted when instruction becomes departmentalized or when a special teacher is called in. Sometimes the presence of such personality maladjustments is indicated by the findings of a class sociogram revealing students who tend to be isolates.

The guidance department may have given these boys and girls one of the well-known group personality tests such as the California Test of Personality. However, the findings of the psychologist, who may have administered the Thematic Apperception Test, the Bender Gestalt, or the Rorschach, are much more informative and illuminating, since the individual has often learned to conceal his true feelings in common situations by outwardly conforming to pattern. Projective techniques confront the individual with amorphous stimuli such as ink blots or indefinite pictures, forcing him to respond in his own way, thus revealing his true feelings [9]. Wechsler has suggested that [11], "personality traits enter into the effectiveness of intelligent behavior, and hence, into any global concept of intelligence itself."

The Emotionally Upset. An individual who has been emotionally upset for any considerable period of time usually adjusts by changing or modifying his personality [7]. Sometimes, however, it is possible to spot these individuals before their personality patterns have been seriously affected. A skillful psychologist, especially one who has had considerable experience with children, is often effective in finding the reason for the upset. Once the cause is located, appropriate steps can be taken to improve the situation. Unless the emotional problem stems from relatively simple causes which the school can remove, the psychologist may decide that the child should be referred to a child-guidance clinic. However, if the origin of the emotional problem is lack of success in school, the psychologist will frequently refer the child to the reading specialist. Usually carefully planned instruction in materials of appropriate difficulty and interest will enable the child to overcome his emotional frustration by building up confidence in his own ability.

Blocks to Learning. Some children, while appearing normal in the social activities of the classroom, will be found to have more or less serious blocks to learning. Among the several causes of this difficulty may be found brain injury or the existence of a foreign-language background. Other children, though capable of mastering the mechanics of reading, have a poor comprehension of what is being read; or they are able to copy material in legible handwriting but lack comprehension of what has been written. Some of the performance tests yield useful information to add to the picture of their learning processes. Among these tests are the Arthur Point Scale, the Cornell-Cox Performance Test, Kohs Block Design, the Mosaics Tests, and Pintner-Patterson Performance Scale.

Where the services of a school psychologist are available, any behavior which limits, or tends to limit, learning (after proper adjustment to individual abilities has been made) deserves investigation. However, as Robinson [8] says, tests should "be administered only when it is anticipated that the results will supply specific information needed by the examiner."

Case Studies. Usually all available information is assembled into a case study. Classroom and special teachers, the school nurse and physician, parents, and the guidance department contribute [3]. Normally the reading specialist will assume responsibility for initiating the case study, collecting information, and preparing the record. However, local conditions, including personal interests, will affect this somewhat; and it is not at all unusual for the school psychologist to prepare the case study. Additional tests are given as the reading specialist and the school psychologist need the additional information such tests will reveal. Commonly included are such areas as health, home, school achievement, reading achievement, intelligence, and some measures of personality and emotional adjustment. Thus the case study presents all available information concerning the subject's physical, mental, and emotional characteristics [4].

From this assembled data a diagnosis is prepared. This may be done by the reading specialist, the school psychologist, or the two working together. If work in reading is indicated, the reading specialist plans remedial therapy in detail so that everyone involved in remediation will know specifically what is to be accomplished. The effectiveness of the remedial work is checked periodically; should changes be necessary to improve the therapy, prior warning is given to all concerned.

The use of case histories in reading therapy is amply illustrated by Woolf and Woolf [12]. Members of the reading committee, seeking a more detailed account of the case study technique as applied to remedial reading situations, will find this a most useful reference.

Reports made to teachers, parents, and cooperating agencies will differ in some respects. Those going to parents state general recommendations, while those going to professional personnel give specific information obtained through tests and are often accompanied by detailed technical analysis. The importance of periodic reports to all concerned, including those most involved—the subject and his parents—cannot be overstressed.

Making case studies is a time-consuming process, but it is a necessity where a number of individuals, within and without a school system, contribute data which must be carefully organized before the significance of individual observations becomes apparent. The school administrator should function as a resource person "to insure that all of the other resources of the system actually become fully available" [10]. In this way cooperative teamwork will be facilitated. The administrator will become familiar with staff needs and better able to report accurately to the community. Because the preparation of case studies is a lengthy but necessary process, individuals about whom a study is to be made should be carefully selected.

SPECIAL SERVICES

The shortage of properly qualified school psychologists with the necessary school experience is at least as great as that of reading specialists. Fortunately for the smaller school, however, there are ways of obtaining the services of a psychologist even though he may not be a member of the school staff.

Smaller Schools. One possibility is to employ a reading specialist qualified to administer individual intelligence tests and perhaps some of the apperception tests.

A second and, in many ways, a better alternative, is to use outside agencies. The school counseling services, the guidance department, the school medical personnel, and the reading specialist should know what clinical facilities are available in adjacent communities. A listing of clinics in the United States, such as that prepared by Barbe [1], is useful but not necessarily complete. Individual children can be transported to nearby clinics provided there is someone in the local school system who has time and qualifications to carry out the suggested remediation. Sometimes it is possible to find married women who have left teaching but who are willing to take a limited number of reading cases on a part-time basis. In this way a school can augment its staff as the occasion arises.

Cooperative Services Board. Another method by which the smaller school can enjoy the services of special teachers is through a cooperative services board. Such an organization may be at the state or county level, or two or more school systems may unite to provide the necessary personnel [6]. Usually a school nurse, guidance director, school psychologist, and a reading specialist form a team, although local needs and the presence of full- or part-time members on the local staff make changes desirable. Whether the unit is operated on a local, county, or state basis, each cooperating school should have definite plans for utilizing the visiting specialists.

The need for constructive leadership in employing the cooperative services board is illustrated in the case of three school systems. The first school asked for and obtained the services of the specialist for the first third of the school year. The other two systems shared the specialist for the remaining two-thirds of the year. The first school had no definite plans and, because of their time preference, found that they had no continuing program so that little or nothing could be carried to a successful conclusion. The other two schools continued the plan until they could each secure the services of a specialist.

The contributions of the board of cooperative services to the improvement of instruction are detailed by Bogdan [2]. The plan, sponsored by the New York State Education Department, involved five central and five rural schools. A shared staff was provided, consisting of a guidance director, a doctor, a dental hygienist, school nurses, agriculture and driver-education teachers, and a reading consultant. Among the many accomplishments of the program were summer reading classes for both pupils and teachers.

Professional Services Board. A larger system might well consider the advantages of a centrally located professional services board working in the district's elementary, junior high, and senior high schools. One school system employs a team of specialists to work within its own framework but calls on outside agencies, both medical and educational, in certain cases. The board in question consists of a psychologist, social service worker, and a reading teacher under the direction of a reading consultant. One of the special features of the board is the frequent scheduling of staff meetings at which case studies are planned, duties apportioned, data examined, and, once a case study has been made, therapy discussed. Close contact is maintained with other school services such as guidance departments and school nurses, but—and this is a most significant fact—the principals are the main channel of communication between the professional services board and the staffs of the respective schools.

Whatever the exact composition of such a board of professional services may be, two points appear significant. The first is the attitude of the classroom teachers toward such an organization. All members of the board, but especially the reading teacher, work closely with individual teachers. Once a study of a particular child has been made, the reading specialist goes over the case with the teacher or teachers concerned. Joint planning includes not only the actual reading instruction, but other learning situations as well. The classroom teacher, the reading teacher, or both may undertake the remedial instruction

The second factor of note, already implied in the preceding paragraph, is the in-service training aspect of the plan [7]. Teachers are not only concerned in selecting individuals for special work and planning materials to be employed in the light of the information gained through the case study; they are also involved in the remediation. Except in a very few cases where extreme retardation would cause awkward groupings, the classroom teachers handle the special instruction. Thus, in a very practical sense, the teachers learn through working with their own boys and girls.

Composition of Teams. The composition of the professional services board or the cooperative services board depends upon three variables: the reading needs of the boys and girls in the system or systems; existing agencies which may be called on; and professional training in reading instruction of the school faculty involved. These three factors suggest that, before a board is composed, a survey of reading needs, community resources, and teaching resources be made.

SPECIAL CLINICS

Three somewhat different but overlapping clinics are designed to further the handling of special problem cases in reading. These three are the reading clinic, the child-guidance clinic, and a relative newcomer, the learning-disabilities clinic. Before discussing the special functions of each, some general considerations are involved.

Referrals. Almost all clinics depend on outside referrals for their cases. Private physicians, public welfare organizations, youth organizations, schools, and individual parents refer boys and girls to them. Whatever the origin of the referral, the school record is important. For this reason, the majority of clinics seek to work with and through the school office even when the referral is made by the parent or physician. In this way, the school can receive useful help and information, and such procedure also lessens the possibility that a dissatisfied parent will attempt to bypass the school. Usually the parent is informed that part of the clinical routine includes getting the school record. Occasionally, he is asked if he has any objections to such procedure; then, but infrequently, the school is bypassed. This is extremely rare when the school has shown interest in the welfare of individual children and when it makes special provision for reading cases. Such a situation is most apt to occur when the parent feels that the emotional or mental difficulty is such that family pride may be injured. Here a good public relations program, with teachers showing concern for individuals and strong cooperation between school and clinic, usually results in the parents' agreement to help.

Provision of Remediation. Just as there is no reason to embark upon an enlarged testing program unless definite steps are planned to follow up such a program with the necessary adjusted instruction, so there is no point in a school referring a child to a clinic unless the school is prepared to make some positive adjustment of the child's school life.

Many clinics are so overcrowded and have such long waiting lists that, unless the school has the staff and facilities for carrying out the remediation indicated by the diagnosis, the child frequently cannot be taken at all, or at least not for months or even years. Some child-guidance and learning-disabilities clinics, while having reading specialists on their staffs, will frequently not be able to devote the time required for adequate remedial instruction, except for certain cases which may further their research. The school should be able to provide the expert reading instruction called for in the remedial therapy.

Such procedure is also indicated where the only available reading clinic is too far from the school to make daily attendance possible or economical. The minimum time required for testing is usually one day, but many clinics prefer to spread the tests and interviews over a period of from two or three days to a month or more. The school or the reading specialist should follow implicitly any specific recommendations and should make every facility available for the clinic to follow up the case. It is only by this two-way cooperation that the school can obtain the best results from the clinic services; the clinic, in turn, can add to its research function. Schools have not always dealt fairly with clinics in this regard.

Choice of Clinic. A decision may have to be made about the clinic to which a child should be referred. Unfortunately, availability may sometimes be the deciding factor. Where a choice exists, the school's counseling department should know the types of cases handled by each clinic in the vicinity. The following analysis of function should be regarded as a general guide only, for each clinic will have its own particular interest and way of working.

Reading Clinic. Practically every reading clinic has a psychologist, a reading specialist, and a staff member in charge of personal interviews, which frequently include both parents. Such a clinic may or may not have a person qualified to deal with psychiatric problems. For this reason the school should refer to the reading clinic the cases in which the preliminary study indicates that the probable cause of retardation and accompanying emotional frustrations stem from reading difficulties. When this is not possible, the case may be referred to the reading clinic and a psychiatrist will be called in or the case will be referred to a clinic having additional facilities if this is found necessary or desirable.

Child-guidance Clinic. The child-guidance clinic deals primarily with emotional and personality-maladjustment problems which appear to be the cause of difficulty in reading and other school subjects. Frequently the parents are involved in the therapy. Sometimes psychiatric and reading therapy are given concurrently; in extreme cases, little is to be gained from work in reading until the emotional situation, including the home factor, has improved. Before referring a case to a child-guidance clinic, a clear understanding of what may be involved should be determined. This includes reading instruction, by whom it will be given, and the approximate date for beginning such instruction. If the child-guidance clinic is not able to provide suitable reading instruction, a competent specialist who is equipped with all necessary materials should be available as soon as the boy or girl is ready to profit from the remedial instruction.

Learning-disabilities Clinic. The learning-disabilities clinic usually takes more complex cases, including those in which there appears to be the possibility of brain damage. Such a clinic may be operated in conjunction with a medical school or hospital. Like the other clinics already mentioned, it may or may not have the staff to provide remediation in reading, since this is often a lengthy process and not the purpose of the clinic.

Other Clinics. In many communities, there exist certain other special-purpose classes and clinics for individuals with speech defects, the deaf and dumb, spastics, and cerebral palsy cases. Again, the school should be informed of the existence of such organizations and should know what types of difficulty are handled by each of them.

Clinic Sponsors. While a shortage of clinical facilities in education and mental health undoubtedly exists, the shortage may be less than actually appears, since private and civic organizations frequently operate clinics which do not appear in any formal listing. The names of organizations sponsoring such services are mentioned here for two purposes: first, to enable the school to contact such groups to determine whether such facilities exist; and second, to suggest possibilities through which additional services to the community may be sponsored. The organizations are hospitals, the Junior League, Kiwanis, medical schools, Odd Fellows, Rotary, and teachers colleges and universities.

The School's Responsibility. Some reading difficulties are induced by the school, others stem from the home, still others from a combination of the two. Whatever the origin of the reading problem the school has two courses open: to provide special services, including remediation for those found to be in need; or to neglect this portion of the school population which may well amount to 10 or 15 per cent.

Some parents will feel that private remedial work is to be preferred, but the school is more concerned with children of parents who cannot afford private instruction. For them, the local system must and should provide the special services required for successful reading achievement. What form these services take depends upon several factors such as the size of the school, size of the class, training of teachers, availability of special personnel within the system and the community, and, last but not least, the attitude of the entire teaching staff and the administration toward reading.

SUMMARY

The school psychologist can assist a reading program by helping teachers understand the slow learner through a more accurate picture of his intelligence as obtained by means of individual psychometric tests. Projective techniques enable the psychologist to help the maladjusted and the emotionally upset, while performance and other tests permit additional insight into the mental processes of those having blocks to learning.

The case study presents information which has been collected on the subject's physical, mental, and emotional characteristics. The administrator facilitates cooperative teamwork to the end that atypical learners are well served by his school.

The smaller school can obtain psychological assistance by using existing community clinics. Special teachers can be provided through a cooperative services board operating on a local, county, or state basis.

The larger system may well have its own professional services board working within the system but calling on outside assistance in special cases. School principals serve as the line of communication between the professional services board and the classroom teachers.

The reading clinic, the child-guidance clinic, and the learning-disabilities clinic are of assistance in the detection and diagnosis of reading problems. The school should be prepared to work closely with the clinic both in sharing information and in providing remediation when the clinic cannot handle the remedial therapy.

While a shortage of clinical facilities exists, the administrator should be aware of community resources, both actual and potential. The school may provide special services itself or supplement existing agencies.

REFERENCES

1. Barbe, Walter B.: *Reading Clinics Directory,* Junior League Reading Center, University of Chattanooga, Chattanooga, Tenn., 1955.

2. Bogdan, Aniela: "The Work of Reading Consultants," in *Reading for Today's Children,* The National Elementary Principal, vol. 35, no. 1, September, 1955, pp. 202–206.

3. Elsbree, Willard S., and E. Edmund Reutter, Jr.: *Staff Personnel in the Public Schools,* Prentice-Hall, Inc., Englewood Cliffs, N.J., 1954.

4. Hammond, Kenneth R., and Jeremiah M. Allen, Jr.: *Writ-*

ing Clinical Reports, Prentice-Hall, Inc., Englewood Cliffs, N.J., 1953.

* 5. Harris, Albert J.: *How to Increase Reading Ability,* 3d ed., Longmans, Green & Co., Inc., New York, 1956.

* 6. Hayes, Dorothy: "Assistance from Other Agencies," in *Guidance in the Curriculum,* 1955 Yearbook of the Association for Supervision and Curriculum Development, National Education Association, Washington, 1955, pp. 198–214.

7. Marzolf, Stanley S.: *Psychological Diagnosis and Counselling in the Schools,* Henry Holt and Company, Inc., New York, 1956.

8. Robinson, Helen M.: "Clinical Procedures in Diagnosing Seriously Retarded Readers," in William S. Gray and Nancy Larrick (eds.), *Better Readers for Our Times,* International Reading Association Conference Proceedings, vol. 1, Scholastic Magazines, New York, 1956, pp. 152–156.

* 9. Strang, Ruth, Constance M. McCullough, and Arthur E. Traxler: *Problems in the Improvement of Reading,* 2d ed., McGraw-Hill Book Company, Inc., New York, 1955.

* 10. Traenkenschuh, Amelia, and Earl H. Hanson: "Superintendent, Supervisor and Principal as Resource Persons," in *Guidance in the Curriculum,* 1955 Yearbook of the Association for Supervision and Curriculum Development, National Education Association, Washington, 1955, pp. 127–146.

11. Wechsler, David: "Cognitive, Conative, and Non-intellectual Intelligence," *American Psychologist,* vol. 5, no. 3, pp. 78–83, March, 1950.

* 12. Woolf, Maurice D., and Jeanne A. Woolf: *Remedial Reading, Teaching, and Treatment,* McGraw-Hill Book Company, Inc., New York, 1957.

* See Appendix A for annotated list of books for the professional library in schools.

Chapter 10

PARENTS AND PUBLIC RELATIONS

Two differing attitudes toward the reading program of a school are to be found in two recent quotations. The first, as told by Larrick [14], was reported by interviewers making a reading survey. Parents expressed the opinion that "teachers have told us to keep hands off and leave reading to them." The same interviewers also discovered a strong disinclination on the part of parents to go to the school with questions and they "were afraid to help their children with reading."

Freeland [7] refers to a principal who summed up a contrasting parent-school attitude by saying, "We don't have to try to convince parents that we are teaching phonics and word recognition. They are on the 'inside' in this reading program. They know what we are trying to do and furthermore they help us. It's a cooperative undertaking and a beneficial arrangement for all concerned." [1]

The attitude depicted in Larrick's quotations presents a situation which discourages parents from having anything to do with reading. Such an attitude is dangerous to encourage, although at times it may be partially correct. In many instances, once a child becomes emotionally upset, it is true that parents may do more harm than good, for until such time as the situation is improved, tension prevents parents from working with their children to any great advantage. All this, however, is *after* serious difficulty in reading has been encountered. There remains the whole field of preventive relationships in which parents play a most important part. The main purpose of any public relations program in reading is the avoidance

[1] Alma M. Freeland, "Helping Parents Understand," in *Reading for Today's Children*, The National Elementary Principal, vol. 35, no. 1, September, 1955, p. 241. Used by permission.

of complications which may prove detrimental. For this reason the major part of the chapter deals with parent-teacher-school relationships regarding the preventive aspects of reading and leads up to the cooperative atmosphere implied in the latter quotation.

WHY READING ASSUMES IMPORTANCE TO PARENTS

Teachers may well ask themselves why it is that reading assumes a role of such importance in the minds of parents. As Harris [10] indicates, reading is the first of the three R's to be encountered by children starting school. If writing or arithmetic came first, increased attention would be paid to that subject.

Contact with Systematic Instruction. Reading represents the first contact children have with systematic instruction; and parents, through their sons and daughters, are reestablishing a contact after a lapse of many years. Thus, children, parents, and the school system are on trial. In such a situation, it is only natural for parents to feel concerned for their boys and girls.

A Measure of Growing Up. A child starting reading instruction is faced with one of the measures of growing up. If for some reason, knowingly or otherwise, he rebels against this, or if he is inclined to resist authority, his reading often suffers. Thus, children who are maladjusted face their first real test. Up to this time they usually have not had to compete with other children in a series of tests of known difficulty, but now they are faced with tasks which normal children should be able to accomplish.

Basis by Which to Judge the School. Since reading is the first contact with elementary education, it is the first chance parents have to judge their schools. As such, it reveals differences that may exist between the layman's concept of education and that of the teacher and the reading specialist.

According to Larrick [14], parents tend to divide all reading instruction into two categories, the old and the new. The old system—sounding letters and syllables—is contrasted with the new method of learning by sight. Apparently, few parents realize that the two systems are compatible and that much of the new approach involves and incorporates the better parts of the old.

QUESTIONS ASKED BY PARENTS

Parents are naturally vitally interested in the reading program; given the opportunity, they ask many questions both concerning the program itself and what they can do to assist their children. A recent survey [14] indicates that one-fifth of the parents interviewed were interested in the question, "How is reading taught in today's schools?" An equal number were anxious to know what they might do to help their children to read better. More than one-third wanted to know how they could help their children to enjoy reading more, while approximately one-fourth desired information regarding books and magazines that parents could recommend to young readers. This latter group increases in significance when we realize that parental book recommendations are often more acceptable to children than those of either teacher or librarian. At the same time it is alarming to learn of the almost total inability of many parents to make any recommendations at all, let alone adequate ones.

Freeland [7] reports sixteen questions that parents are asking. Of these, seven appear to be of special significance:[2]

1. What can I do to help my child with his reading?
2. What is reading readiness? Why is so much time spent in the readiness period? Why are not children started on books earlier?
3. Why are children grouped for reading activities? Why do not all children in a class use the same book?
4. What is done about remedial reading?
5. What is done to help children read well their geography, history, science, and arithmetic books?
6. What are the "Standards or minimum essentials" for children in each grade? Should they not be expected to meet these standards before they are promoted to the next grade?
7. How can I find out if my child is developing in reading as he should?

Many of these questions, involving the psychology of learning as well as the promotion and reporting policies of our schools, merit the attention of school faculties.

[2] Alma M. Freeland, "Helping Parents Understand," in *Reading for Today's Children*, The National Elementary Principal, vol. 35, no. 1, September, 1955, p. 239. Used by permission.

WHAT BASIC CONCEPTS PARENTS SHOULD UNDERSTAND

From these and other questions asked by parents, it would appear that there are four basic ideas [14] about which the school must educate parents if the reading program is going to be understood and supported by them.

Reading Is Understanding. The first of these basic concepts of reading deals with the comprehension of what is read. In order to comprehend, a child has to do much more than verbalize. He must understand the meanings of words and be able, at least in part, to determine meanings of unknown words from structural clues, context, and such built-in helps as the writer gives him. Further, the reader must have a background of experience in order to have insight into ideas that are being expressed. It is possible to understand every word in a sentence without gaining a clear idea of the author's meaning. The ability to do this becomes increasingly important as the child moves into the middle and upper grades.

Granted one side of the coin of reading is the ability to sound out words. This is the side that parents are most likely to come in contact with when their children read aloud to them. The other side of the coin is comprehension and is not so obvious and not so easily determined. Yet reading without comprehension causes no change in the reader's thoughts. It is this change or reaction to what is being read—called understanding or learning—about which parents need to be aware.

Child Must Want to Read and Find Uses for Reading. A second basic idea which parents should be helped to accept is that children must want to read. The normal child, having seen his parents and other adults gain pleasure from reading, is usually anxious to learn. If his first experiences are successful, he will continue and, because of his desire, will make the extra effort that is sometimes necessary. Parents are in a strategic position to make the most of spontaneous reading situations occurring as a result of watching television, participating in various hobbies, and other everyday happenings. Children's interests should be developed, thus leading into reading rather than the grim alternative—forcing reading upon them.

Reading Is Omnipresent. Third, the parent should learn that reading is not limited to formal school instruction but goes on all the time. The opportunities for reading are countless: advertising signs and labels, street signs, directions, and television commercials. Frequently this out-of-school reading occurs in well-motivated situations with the child having a special reason for his reading.

Children Develop at Different Rates. The fourth, and probably the hardest of these basic concepts for a parent to accept, is that children have different rates of development and that these rates are not constant. This is as true of mental growth as it is of physical accomplishments and is a perfectly normal situation. This concept is basic to the parents' understanding of many of the questions that bother them, such as the need for reading readiness programs and grouping in the classroom. At the same time, a deeper understanding of individual differences in development enables parents to appreciate the problems of promotion and the reporting of progress.

WHEN PARENTS NEED INFORMATION

To cooperate effectively with the school in the furtherance of the reading program, parents need certain specific information which must be available at the right time. If given too late, as when a child has been placed in the not-ready-to-read group in a readiness program, the parent is often placed in an adverse position and is in a poor frame of mind to receive suggestions. Knowing the types of questions asked by parents and the general organization of the reading program, we can foresee when it is desirable and necessary that certain facts be conveyed to parents.

At School Entrance. The preschool survey is more than a census to predict future enrollments if handled by PTA teams [11]. Questionnaires, letters, telephone calls, and individual conferences build up a feeling of mutual interest and confidence. Many schools prepare a bulletin of useful information for the parents of entering kindergarten or first-grade children. Such bulletins present the school's policy on entrance age, health regulations, school hours, absences and tardinesses, school calendar, and many other details. Necessary as such a bulletin is for reference purposes, few schools will wish to stop there.

A worth-while practice is entertaining kindergarten children at a first-grade party. Both parents and children are quick to appreciate what school and reading mean when they see first graders in action

At other times small group and individual conferences are used to spread information. The medical examination and the various screening tests at which the parent is present can be used to reveal physical differences of children, thus paving the way for a better understanding of differences in learning [12].

By these and other means, teachers and children are explaining in different ways the importance of kindergarten activities as a prelude to the instruction in reading that is to follow. If the kindergarten program is explained as it evolves and parents become aware of dissimilarities in children, the purposes of the first-grade reading readiness program will be much more easily understood [5]. Most important of all, parents are being introduced to the school before any tension is built up by formal subjects, with the result that parents develop the feeling that they are partners in the education of their children.

At First-grade Level. As soon as possible after the beginning of the first grade, parents should be informed of the use made of grouping and the system employed by the school in reporting progress. Shortly afterward, any special organization of the primary grades—the possibility that some children will spend four years in those grades while others spend three years or less—should be explained. The promotion policy is then more easily comprehended. This procedure should certainly be considered before there is any question of nonpromotion in an individual case.

Subsequent Years. Assuming that promotion and reporting policies remain the same, the main requirement after first grade is to explain the reading program of that particular year. Reading will become gradually interwoven with subject matter as the child passes from primary to intermediate grades. Special attention will be paid to the importance of work-study reading skills in third and fourth grades and the purposes of remedial reading will be explained in advance.

The practice of waiting until May to inform parents that a child is not going to be passed on to the next grade has little merit. This situation is aggravated when the parent is told that if the child is tutored he may possibly be passed into the following grade. Parents have a right to know how the child is doing and a prior warning should be given when the teacher has any reasonable doubt.

To do otherwise is to undermine the parents' trust in the school, and very often such action accomplishes little more than to make the child feel responsible for upsetting the family. Little can be accomplished in such a setting. The only general exception is when the school operates an adequate summer school program and through it gives the child a chance to complete work satisfactorily and advance with his classmates.

The school will want to make some provision for bringing the parents of transfer students up to date on school policies. One of the most effective ways of doing this is by having the PTA assign a parent to work with the classroom teacher in answering questions informally. The important consideration is to make sure that the new parent understands procedures.

WHY THE READING PROGRAM MUST BE WORTHY OF INVESTIGATION

Turning the white light of publicity on a reading program that is not worthy of interpretation accomplishes little. Parents' questions go to the root of many of the most perplexing issues, not of the reading problem alone, but of our educational system. Unless the reading program is defensible, there is little to be accomplished by inviting the public's inspection.

Faculty Agreement Necessary. A school faculty should be able to reach fundamental agreement on a goodly percentage of the basic issues in reading. A principal [7] recounts how he thought his school had a good reading program until he and the faculty started to examine it. He then found that the members of his staff frequently held divergent views. Subsequent meetings to resolve differences of opinion and institute changes provided a very practical variety of in-service training.

Areas of Concern. Some of the stumbling blocks to faculty agreement are mentioned briefly. The listing is by no means exhaustive, and individual schools may give themselves a clean bill of health on some of these matters, only to find something else that should receive attention.

1. *Curriculum.* Is the curriculum designed with both slow and able learners in mind as well as those in between?

2. *Screening.* Is the screening program for the detection of physical handicaps to learning efficient? Does it receive the support of the medical profession?

3. *Testing.* Is the testing program designed to improve instruction?

4. *Remedial reading.* Is provision made to bring reading-disability cases up to their approximate capacity as quickly and as early in the school program as possible?

5. *Developmental reading.* Do the staff members, both severally and jointly, agree that reading is the job of every teacher? Do classroom techniques and organization substantiate this?

6. *Grouping.* Are groups kept flexible?

7. *Dropout.* Is an effort made to ascertain educational reasons given for dropping out of school? Does this information bring about changes in curriculum and teaching methods?

8. *Promotion.* Is the promotion policy in line with concepts of developmental reading and learning?

9. *Reporting.* Does the method of reporting used actually tell parents what they should know in terms that are understandable?

Complete agreement is not possible on controversial issues such as some of those just mentioned; but, having thought through these and other issues, the staff will know where it stands. Of course, some disagreement is a healthy condition. However, the general public will misunderstand and mistrust a faculty that disagrees about fundamental policies. Discriminating teachers should be able to profit from the discussion of these and other questions.

Parental Survey. Most schools will be inclined to think that they know what questions parents wish to have answered, yet the staff may want to determine fairly early in its self-examination what problems are uppermost in the minds of parents. This step should not be taken, through formal or informal methods, until enough agreement has been reached to make answering such questions possible, for once this step has been taken there can be no drawing back.

WHERE PARENTS CONTRIBUTE TO READING

Reading is an all-school program, but it is not necessarily an all-in-school program. Parents are correct in frequently reiterating the question "What can we do to help in reading?" for children can and do profit from parental assistance of the right kind. Rather than adopting a hands-off attitude, the school should help parents understand the reading program and show them what may be done to help their children in reading [3]. To this end a number of books have been written by such authors as Aho [1], Artley [2], Duker and Nally [4], Frank [6], Monroe [17], Robinson [18, 19], and Witty [22]. While many of these are such that individual parents may profit from reading them, more effective results are usually obtained when a discussion group studies them.

By Providing Experiences. Parents need to be alerted to the contribution of out-of-school and preschool experiences. A car ride, a visit to a farm or a zoo, and a trip to the beach provide new interests, new words for growing vocabularies, and a new background of information. Playing games that increase observation while passing away the time spent on a journey and answering a child's questions about things he sees stimulate interest and satisfy curiosity. Conversation with adults—as when a father shares his hobby with his son or takes him on a hike—adds new meaning to words. A child with few experiences brings little to his reading, but a child who shares a full family life usually possesses good listening and speaking vocabularies, a wide variety of interests, a useful fund of information, and a habit of observation and curiosity.

Many of the popular children's television programs are excellent for supplying vicariously this background experience necessary for reading. Parents and older brothers and sisters can answer questions and show the young reader how reference books and library books supply additional knowledge.

By Environment. The parent who wishes to help his child in reading should be made aware of the importance of home environment. The reading done by parents sets an example for the child to follow. If he grows up in a home where reading is a part of everyday living and books are familiar companions, he, too, will accept reading and will grow up to love books. When a difference of opinion results in the use of atlas, dictionary, or encyclopedia to settle questions among the various members of the family, children will soon seek these same sources of information to corroborate their statements.

A second factor contributing to the reading situation is the attitude of the parents toward the school and the progress the child is making in it [9]. When parents feel that they are a part of the school, working with its teachers rather than being excluded, their attitude toward the school will be one of acceptance and partnership [4]. They have faith in the school because they know what is going on and, having assisted in the program's implementation, wish to cooperate.

By Helping with Reading. Providing experiences and setting a pattern designed to show the child that pleasure may be derived from books is actually helping with reading instruction. The parents should be aware that this attitude is most important even before the child starts kindergarten; as the child begins school, there are many things directly concerned with reading that may be done, provided the other has come first.

The child enjoys being read to provided the books selected are interesting to him and touch on his experience. As the child starts reading, the parent will take time to listen to him read from supplementary books he is familiar with at school. From the teacher, the parent will have learned how to deal with words that the child does not readily recognize. As reading improves, the mother will contrive situations, such as reading directions and recipes, that will give practice while illustrating some of the purposes for reading.

The beginning reader should be encouraged to take books home because the child needs to do large amounts of easy reading in order to develop his recognition vocabulary. Supplementary readers and library books chosen under guidance provide this practice material. Most school systems refuse to permit a child to take home the basal readers. Parents often misunderstand the reason for this ruling and believe it is an attempt to prevent their assisting in reading instruction. Nothing could be further from the truth. The reason basal readers are not brought home is that many children can memorize whole stories by hearing them read a few times. Memorization is not reading and to permit it complicates teaching, and voids available material. If the parent can realize that introducing new material, new techniques, and new reading skills can best be done by the teacher while he supplies the leisure reading, much will have been accomplished. Provided parents exercise patience in reading situations, there should be no objection to this arrangement.

By Guidance in Book Selection. The parent who undertakes to provide a guided reading period at home profits from some help in selecting appropriate books [15]. Many parents can do little better than to recommend books they liked as children. The cascade of books now being published is enough to bewilder the parent who knows little or nothing about reading difficulty and who may be unaware of his own children's rapidly changing interests. Two types of books should be considered: those for children to read themselves, and more difficult ones for the parents to read aloud. The school should take the initiative in helping parents learn the reading interests of their children and to choose suitable reading materials.

The classroom teacher is the logical person to supply much of the guidance in book selection, particularly regarding difficulty and interest. Through everyday instruction, the teacher has information regarding reading levels and the changing interests of boys and girls at her finger tips. Some teachers send home timely hints for Christmas and birthdays and supply suggestions for summer reading. A more ambitious plan incorporates each child's favorites into a master list for the grade. This is duplicated and taken home by each child. Such lists are usually keyed to indicate general levels of difficulty and may be organized under various interest headings. Book suggestions are commonly a part of almost every individual conference between parent and teacher.

Book shows and exhibits afford another means of conveying information to parents. Book fairs may be sponsored by the individual school with the librarian and the teachers cooperating, by the local public library, PTA, or by the publishers themselves. The efficacy of such displays has been improved by permitting children and their teachers to attend before the general public is admitted. In this way, children can locate books that interest them personally and can point them out when they attend later on with their parents.

By far the most ambitious undertaking to improve parents' knowledge of children's books is the library-sponsored discussion group or class. One outcome of such a study may be reading aloud books selected by each member of the family. The Illinois Congress of

Parents and Teachers and the Chicago Public Library have been jointly sponsoring such a guidance program in book selection since 1936 [20].

By Establishing Good Reading and Study Habits. At times parents have questioned the advisability of the school assigning work to be done at home. Some parents, taking the presumably easy way out, are forced to do their children's homework and resent the lack of carryover of reading and study skills. With a well-planned cooperative program at the beginning of reading instruction, children should be well on their way to independence in reading and able to handle their homework assignments long before they reach junior high school. The home environment and the parents' attitude toward their school will be a positive one for having had a share in the planning and the instruction.

PUBLIC RELATIONS

The *who, what, when, where,* and *why* of the parent and public relations program are important, but equally essential is the *how.* Under the coordination of the reading specialist and assisted by classroom teachers and students, schools are turning to television to acquaint the public with effective modern methods of reading instruction. Newspaper and magazine articles are read by millions; report cards, pamphlets, bulletins, and books reach many more. These media are often effective and should therefore be continued. But in order to reach everyone, the oldest medium of all, word-of-mouth advertising, should not be neglected. Parents should and can be the most convincing salesmen for our schools and our reading programs. Parents need to be involved in the learning process. They need to see for themselves. Once they are convinced—a satisfied customer is the best advertising.

How, then, can the schools involve parents? What are the ways by which a school can spread understanding of that which they are seeking to accomplish?

Grade Conference. One of the more commonly used methods is the grade-mother conference. This reaches larger numbers than does the individual conference. It is particularly effective when general information on some aspect of reading, such as the purpose of the reading readiness program, must be imparted. The group meeting continues to flourish; of late, successful attempts have been made to expand its usefulness and enlarge its scope by including fathers as well as mothers.

Parents' Club. One outgrowth of the grade conference is the parents' club [21]. As reported, it was employed in a fourth-grade situation to acquaint parents with the unit method of reading instruction as applied to subject-matter reading. Parents were invited by the class to sit in at the culmination of each unit throughout the school year. The first half-hour was devoted to various class activities which demonstrated the work accomplished during the unit. The second half-hour gave the parents a chance to discuss the learnings achieved, including the reading, writing, and spelling that had been done.

Various activities were employed in the parents' part of the meeting to show many of the difficulties inherent in reading. McKee's symbol alphabet [16] was used to show the problems of ready recognition as opposed to word-by-word reading, and legal documents were brought in to show the necessity of having background concepts in order to understand meaning. At the end of the year, during which attendance at the meetings increased by leaps and bounds, parents felt that [21]—

1. The close relationships between the parents and the teacher had freed them to comment and to suggest without fear or embarrassment.

2. A parent and his child could now discuss the school program on a level of understanding not possible before as a result of which a new feeling of companionship arose.

3. A friendly, relaxed relationship with the teacher made parents look forward to conferences about their children and forestalled . . . home-school misunderstandings.[3]

Parents appear to be eager to learn about their schools once they feel they are wanted. Impersonal programs and articles appearing in the public press cannot reach individuals with the same impact as can continued observation, discussion, and evaluation of the

[3] Clare C. Walker, "A Parents' Club for Interpreting the Reading Program," in *Reading for Today's Children,* The National Elementary Principal, vol. 35, no. 1, September, 1955, pp. 256–257. Used by permission.

progress made by their own children. Parents become partners in the learning process. What they know, they understand; when they understand, they believe.

Some Problems. One of the complaints of teachers is that the very parents they want to attend meetings often are the ones who fail to appear. By giving the children of such parents parts in the program, this difficulty is usually overcome. A second problem faced by teachers is that parents of older boys and girls tend to visit school less frequently. Part of this is caused by a natural inclination on the part of growing adolescents to be on their own. Little harm results in schools where an early start has been made in building up parent-school relationships, since the parents are strong supporters of school policy. But parents who have not participated in earlier years may continue to be adverse or negative in their attitude. The answer appears to be to build up an attractive primary and intermediate grade program, while doing all that is possible by means of individual conferences, meetings for new parents, and back-to-school nights.

Back-to-School Nights. At the junior high level, many mothers and fathers are attracted by a back-to-school evening program. Name tags and their son's or daughter's class schedule are handed them as they enter the school building. The evening is spent "attending" classes except for a brief talk by the principal or guidance director. The teachers find this type of program an excellent way of meeting parents and talking briefly about their subjects. In the opinion of many teachers this is far superior to older parents' nights when long lines of parents filled the corridors outside each classroom and besieged each teacher with the question, "How is my son doing?" Group meetings can never be the effective situation in which to answer individual and personal questions. These should be reserved for individual conferences.

Another form of back-to-school evening appealing to the parents of elementary school children is the Then-and-Now program in which grandparents and their grandchildren demonstrate the difference in methods of learning to read [7]. One grandmother was heard to say to her grandson as they were leaving the stage, "What a lucky boy you are. Imagine having all those wonderful books. McGuffey indeed!"

PTA Meetings. Some schools have frankly copied business methods in using charts for the portrayal of statistics on reading improvement. The impersonal nature of graphs makes it possible to depict differences in mental endowment and reading ability without the risk of hurting the feelings of individual parents. Parents are more receptive to reading readiness, classroom grouping, and the promotion policy of the school once they become accustomed to the idea of differences in abilities.

Usually a major part of at least one meeting per year may be devoted to a report on reading progress. Frequently the interest aroused by such a meeting serves as the impetus for other reading-centered PTA activities. One of the outcomes of the reading-progress report is likely to be a revision of the report card to include a place for recording the child's reading level. Individual parent-teacher conferences invariably include a consideration of the child's reading ability.

A somewhat different approach to public relations is explained in detail by one school principal [13]. As PTA interest in reading is increased by having supervisors, classroom teachers, children, and administrators explain the various phases of reading instruction, a more ambitious scheme becomes possible. As in previous suggestions, the key to success lies in involving the parents [8]. In this case, the PTA members report to the group what they as parents have found out about the reading program [13].

Teachers were asked to suggest the names of mothers and fathers who were interested in school affairs and who would be able to speak convincingly before a large group. From these names the PTA chairman, under whose personal direction the committee worked, chose six—one for each grade. By talking with classroom teachers, by observing actual instruction, and by studying materials, the six parents gradually corrected their own misunderstandings and answered many of their own questions. Monthly meetings enabled them to share ideas and served to give coherence to the study. The method selected for presenting their findings to the public was that of a panel discussion with the principal acting as moderator. Several other possibilities exist by which parents may be involved in the work of the school.

Many particular values can be obtained from such a procedure. It is more convincing to have parents—rather than teachers—commend the school program. At the same time, the principal is able to comment on areas that need improvement and indicate future plans. Since the interpretation of the reading program is made by lay people who may originally have had misgivings and questions similar to those entertained by the audience, the discussion can be both understandable and informative.

SUMMARY

The school is concerned, among other things, with the preventive aspects of parent-teacher-school relationships. Since reading affords the child his first contact with systematized instruction, both child and school are on trial in the eyes of the parents. Parents are naturally curious regarding modern methods of teaching reading and are frequently misinformed.

Parents need help in understanding that reading is comprehension, that children must want to read and must have uses for reading, that reading goes on all the time in and outside of school, and that, like physical achievements, reading develops at different rates. Furthermore, parents need particular kinds of information concerning the school at specific times.

Before a school can inform parents of the reading program, it must ascertain that it has a program worthy of the name. This self-examination should include faculty agreement on fundamental issues. Parents can contribute to reading instruction by providing out-of-school and preschool experiences, by setting an example of love of reading in their homes, by providing time for leisure reading, and by recommending books.

An active public relations program involves parents. Grade conferences, parents' clubs, back-to-school nights, and PTA meetings in which parents become actively engaged in the reading program are all methods of disseminating information.

REFERENCES

1. Aho, Ebba: *Your Child Learns to Read,* Board of Education, Minneapolis, Minn., 1949.

2. Artley, A. Sterling: *Your Child Learns to Read,* Scott, Foresman and Company, Chicago, 1953.

3. Dolch, Edward William: "If Parents Help with Reading," *Elementary English,* vol. 31, pp. 143–146, March, 1955.

4. Duker, Sam, and Thomas P. Nally: *The Truth about Your Child's Reading,* Crown Publishers, Inc., New York, 1956.

5. Elinsky, Dolores, Mary E. Farrell, and Dorothy M. Penn: "Parents Learn about First-grade Reading," *The Reading Teacher,* vol. 8, pp. 227–233, April, 1955.

6. Frank, Mary, and Lawrence Frank: *How to Help Your Child in School,* The Viking Press, Inc., New York, 1950.

7. Freeland, Alma M.: "Helping Parents Understand," in *Reading for Today's Children,* The National Elementary Principal, vol. 35, no. 1, September, 1955, pp. 236–244.

8. Gansberg, Martin: "Let's Put the P.T.A. to Work," *Clearing House,* vol. 30, pp. 375–376, February, 1956.

9. Grayum, Helen S.: "How Parents' Attitudes Affect Children's Reading," *The Reading Teacher,* vol. 7, pp. 195–199, April, 1954.

* 10. Harris, Albert J.: *How to Increase Reading Ability,* 3d ed., Longmans, Green & Co., Inc., New York, 1956.

11. Jones, Daisy M., Glenn Cross, and H. G. Walters: "The Principal Helps with Reading," in *Reading for Today's Children,* The National Elementary Principal, vol. 35, no. 1, September, 1955, pp. 192–196.

* 12. Kawin, Ethel: "Guidance Specialists as Resource Persons," in *Guidance in the Curriculum,* 1955 Yearbook of the Association for Supervision and Curriculum Development, National Education Association, Washington, 1955, pp. 101–113.

13. Lacosse, Robert H.: "Parents Report on Reading," in *Reading for Today's Children,* The National Elementary Principal, vol. 35, no. 1, September, 1955, pp. 248–251.

14. Larrick, Nancy: "How Can We Secure Parent Co-operation?" in William S. Gray and Nancy Larrick (eds.), *Better Readers for Our Times,* International Reading Association Conference Proceedings, vol. 1, Scholastic Magazines, New York, 1956, pp. 101–105.

15. Larrick, Nancy: *A Parent's Guide to Children's Reading,* Doubleday & Company, Inc., New York, 1958. (Also published by Pocket Books, Inc., New York, 1958.)

* 16. McKee, Paul G.: *The Teaching of Reading in the Elementary School,* Houghton Mifflin Company, Boston, 1948.

17. Monroe, Marion: *Growing into Reading,* Scott, Foresman and Company, Chicago, 1951.

18. Robinson, Eleanor G.: *Helping Parents Understand the Reading Program,* Ginn Contributions to Reading, Ginn & Company, Boston, 1951.

19. Robinson, Eleanor G.: *A Letter to Parents,* Ginn & Company, Boston, 1951.

20. Rollins, Charlemae: "Discussion: How Can We Secure Parent Co-operation?" in William S. Gray and Nancy Larrick (eds.), *Better Readers for Our Times,* International Reading Association Conference Proceedings, vol. 1, Scholastic Magazines, New York, 1956, pp. 105–106.

21. Walker, Clare C.: "A Parents' Club for Interpreting the Reading Program," in *Reading for Today's Children,* The National Elementary Principal, vol. 35, no. 1, September, 1955, pp. 252–258.

22. Witty, Paul A.: "Answers to Questions about Reading," *National Parent-Teacher: The PTA Magazine,* September, 1955. (Reprint.)

* See Appendix A for annotated list of books for the professional library in schools.

Chapter 11

THE ADMINISTRATOR'S ROLE IN READING

Of the four language arts—speaking, listening, writing, and reading—the most important in some respects is reading. While listening and speaking come first in point of time and contribute to vocabulary development, reading is, as we have seen, the first contact a child has with systematized instruction. As a result, parents tend to evaluate a school through their child's success in reading. Fortunately, a great deal of attention has been paid to the improvement of beginning reading by teachers and book publishers. Every effort should be made to improve and strengthen the primary grade reading program through experimentation. However, the further development of reading skills beyond this level and the necessity of remediation for some students create problems. Administrators who are vitally concerned with the continued improvement of public education are rightly alarmed when there are indications that the school has but scratched the surface of the child's reading potentialities.

WHOLE-SCHOOL ATTACK ON READING

Reading cannot be regarded as the function of one area of the school system, such as the primary grades, nor should it be left entirely to one subject-matter department, such as the English department in the secondary school. Reading instruction involves all teachers and all subjects at all grade levels from kindergarten to college [5]. Some over-all agency—a part of the school, yet sufficiently removed from individual classrooms for an entire view—is needed to coordinate the program.

Reading Basic to Learning. No other branch of instruction affects learning so profoundly as does reading. Teachers are finding that the lecture method, while successful in imparting information, does not equip the student with the reading and study skills necessary for successful learning in college. Thus the student is able to get into college, but he is not always equipped to stay there [13]. The single-textbook approach to reading fails to provide for the vast differences in ability now met in the upper grades of elementary school and in secondary schools, and such an approach does little to build up the love of reading so desirable in adults [4].

Coordinating the Reading Program. Until recently, the chief offenders have been the junior and senior high schools, which have tended to ignore reading instruction [1] both as a separate subject and as a concomitant to subject-matter teaching. Much is now being done in some schools in these areas [5]. However, cooperative planning by the entire faculty under the leadership of the main administrator is required to carry forward the work started in the primary grades and to ensure a successful application of skills and techniques at the secondary level.

LEADERSHIP RESPONSIBILITIES OF THE ADMINISTRATOR

Once the fundamental importance of reading has been recognized, three main areas present leadership possibilities. These fields are (1) the professional growth of teachers, (2) coordination of staff effort, and (3) public relations. They are not mutually exclusive, since progress in one permits and demands advancement in the two remaining areas.

Professional Growth of Teachers. Every improvement should be made by teacher training colleges and schools of education in the professional training of teachers. But unifying a teaching staff composed of individuals of varying backgrounds, education, and philosophy calls for a well-planned, concerted effort toward the in-service growth of teachers. By workshops and reading conferences, courses and seminars, case studies and parent-teacher meetings, the attitude of teachers toward developmental learning can be strengthened. Such programs foster an atmosphere conducive to action research based on a sound philosophy of reading, yet permitting the individual freedom for experimentation.

As teachers seek to discover for themselves what others have done and are doing about the solution of reading problems, professional libraries will be increasingly demanded. The interested administrator will find that the books listed in Appendix A form a nucleus for a professional library to which other books should be added as the demand increases.

Coordination of Staff Effort. As teachers grow professionally and recognize their varying contributions to the reading program, the importance of coordinating their efforts grows also. This coordination of staff effort must be both horizontal and vertical.

The teachers of any one grade require assistance to ensure that the necessary reading experiences are provided so that boys and girls may continue to develop. In order that this development may be forwarded, special services—afforded by the school nurse, school psychologist, guidance department, and the reading teacher—should be readily available to the classroom teacher. This situation exists in the elementary school where one teacher may have the primary responsibility for a group of children. It is of even greater importance in the secondary school where such responsibility may be shared by several teachers in different departments.

At the same time the vertical coordination of the reading program fosters continuous development by taking each child where he is in reading. Provision should be made for continuing reading instruction both in the intermediate grades and in junior high school.

Central or consolidated schools have an advantage over separate elementary, junior high, and senior high schools in this respect. But whether a single administrative officer is responsible, or whether two or even three are involved, the need for coordinating what teachers at other levels are doing still exists. For learning to be effective, each member of the teaching staff must know where and to what extent his efforts fit into the picture. To do this most efficiently, avoiding duplication of effort yet affording the necessary practice and review, each teacher must know what provision for reading instruction has come before and what will follow. In the last analysis, the coordination of the instructional program—in reading or any other field—is the primary responsibility of the school principal, working in conjunction with the other principals in the system.

Public Relations. The third area in which the school looks to the administration for dynamic leadership is public relations. If the taxpayer is to continue to give increased support to our schools, he must be educated in the meaning of developmental learning and must become acquainted with its implications both to the school and to society. An informed public is generally a cooperative one.

Yet another group in the community should be enlisted in active support of the reading program. This group consists of members of the medical and allied professions who may be called upon from time to time to assist directly or indirectly. Among this group are psychologists, psychiatrists, pediatricians, ophthalmologists, optometrists, and general practitioners. Without their professional assistance, we cannot be sure that boys and girls are physically and emotionally able to profit from instruction.

Finally, to build an effective reading program, parents must participate. Some of the criticisms of reading instruction come from parents of boys and girls who are failing to make suitable progress. Other criticisms come from fathers and mothers who feel there is something wrong with an educational system that passes children through the grades, only to have them denied admission to college [12]. In each case the administrator is faced with a twofold problem. Is the reading program doing the best it possibly can for individuals of widely differing abilities? Are the reporting practices of the school presenting a realistic and understandable picture of a young person's chances of success? First, attention must be devoted to putting the school's house in order; second, parents must be on the inside so that they, as well as the school, may be aware of what is realistically possible for their sons and daughters.

Public criticism of our schools can frequently lead to improvement of existing educational programs, but only under the intelligent leadership and coordination of the administrator. Teachers themselves are frequently too close to the instructional program to see what needs to be done; when they are aware of the situation, they need the backing of the administration and the cooperation of the entire staff.

Lay people are the foundation of the public school system in a democracy, but they are sometimes apt to judge on the basis of insufficient evidence and to suggest impractical solutions. Careful leadership can frequently salvage what would otherwise prove to be a critical situation. One such case, involving a member of the board of education, resulted in the superintendent countering a proposed change in primary reading instruction by suggesting a complete evaluation of the total reading program [9]. The school system found that in general boys and girls were reading well above the national norms but that about 10 per cent were not reading up to their ability. Provision for more emphasis on reading for this group resulted in a better reading program for the school.

To assist members of a teaching staff in realizing their many overlapping but different functions in reading, to coordinate the efforts of teachers so that every young person may make maximum growth, and to interpret such a program to the general public is not an easy task.

LEADERSHIP AT VARIOUS LEVELS

Developmental reading is a grass-roots movement, depending on the classroom teacher for its day-to-day progress and upon the local principal for its coordination. But leadership should be forthcoming at the county and district level, the state level, and the national level for reading instruction to receive its rightful emphasis in education.

National Level. The U.S. Office of Education, while primarily a fact-finding and reporting body, can do much to foster reading instruction. The present national emphasis upon the teaching of science and mathematics should eventually expand to also embrace the teaching of reading, which is basic to the two other subjects. Many of our most capable students are content with average performance or with indifferent achievement. That each and every student should achieve according to his capacity is the only sane approach to learning.

In addition to determining states that are backward in their provisions for reading and those that are outstanding, the U.S. Office of Education, through groups similar to the White House Conference on Education, can provide intelligent leadership. If and when Federal aid to education becomes a reality, states administering Federal funds should consider not only the lack of reading materials in backward areas, but also the lack of good reading habits and reading material in the homes. In other words, improvement of the education of boys and girls necessitates vigorous attempts to improve the home environments from which they come.

More specifically devoted to reading is the recently formed International Reading Association. The merging of the International Council for Reading Instruction and the National Association for Remedial Teaching has resulted in one professional organization at the national level. The reports of yearly conferences, local councils, and the organization magazine *The Reading Teacher* spread information regarding reading throughout the country.

The National Congress of Parents and Teachers is another national organization which has shown itself willing to cooperate and which recognizes the vital necessity of keeping parents informed.

Finally, the National Education Association, with its many affiliated groups—the Department of Classroom Teachers, the Association for Supervision and Curriculum Development, and the Departments of Elementary and Secondary Principals, to name but a few—has shown itself to be aware of the fundamental importance of reading instruction. Illustrative of this awareness is the series What Research Says to the Teacher, especially the issue entitled "Reading in the High School" [6].

There are, of course, many other national organizations and magazines which might be mentioned. The important consideration is that the channels for disseminating information exist. However, it remains for the chief school administrator to establish a school climate conducive to experimentation and reporting successful methods and techniques.

State Level. Much of what has been said concerning national organizations applies equally well at the state level, since the latter organizations tend to parallel those on the national level. In addition, the various state education departments afford facilities in at least three areas—research, publications, and resource specialists.

In some states, research includes the preparation of reading tests, norms, examination of textbooks for state adoption, and making state-wide reading surveys. Additional research is always a possibility, but state research departments can be of practical assistance only as state organizations of classroom teachers, working with and through local principals, make their needs known.

Research organizations are faced with the necessity of translating pure research into practical forms which are usable in the classroom. In the past, they have reported their findings. They have not always proceeded to the next step, illustrating new methods and techniques which apply the research findings to actual teaching situations. Failure to do this may have been caused, at least in part, by a desire to avoid "recipe dispensing." Still, it is much easier for a small group to indicate how classroom instruction can be modified than for the much larger group of teachers to work out their individual applications.

By the publication of forward-looking curricula, syllabuses, and specific bulletins on various aspects of reading instruction, state departments of education, working closely with state organizations of teachers, may constructively affect reading instruction. Individual classroom teachers and principals of local school systems should be encouraged to work with state personnel on specific reading problems. One of these is the preparation of suitable materials for states requiring the teaching of the state's history. Although the publication of state history books is not unprofitable, existing texts tend to be poorly written, not carefully regulated as to difficulty, and are not always up to date.

Another area in which better-than-average classroom teachers can cooperate with state departments of education is the preparation of unitary teaching materials. The criticism against this practice has been that such preparation would tend to stifle individual initiative. In the light of the present acute teacher shortage and the resulting employment of many partially trained teachers on an interim basis, such claims are ridiculous. To force all such teachers to work out every teaching unit is a palpable waste of time. Granted, they should know how to do this. Those who become master teachers will continually be improving such units. But to ask every teacher to go through the laborious process for every unit taught is to admit that teachers have no capacity to learn from example. Regimentation can be avoided by providing several illustrative units on each grade level rather than the entire course. Possible activities and suitable reading materials at many different grade levels, together with usable visual aids, would provide the desirable flexibility.

Some states combine publications with the third function of the state education department—that of aiding teachers by the allocation of resource personnel. One of the bulletins growing out of such a program is *The Road to Better Reading*, issued by the New York State Education Department [11]. Several regional conferences, at which nationally known reading consultants spoke, were followed by a series of local study-skills conferences covering the elementary and secondary reading levels. The bulletin presents the best thinking of many of these meetings.

The Bureau of Elementary Education of the California State Department of Education offers an example of what can be done in providing consultant services for county and district groups [10]. Elementary teachers of Stanislaus County decided by a margin of over 70 per cent that the subject with which they needed help was reading. After preliminary planning meetings attended by principals, district superintendents, county staff, and members of the Bureau of Elementary Education, an all-day institute for classroom teachers was held. This was followed by a number of grade-level meetings at which teachers and consultants exchanged views. As one principal expressed it, "My teachers used to be worried about reading, now they are excited about it" [10].

Many other instances of the close cooperation between state and local groups could be given. Two points appear to be significant enough to be worth mentioning. The usual organization of state departments of education tends to parallel that of the local school system. With elementary and secondary sections, they are faced with a problem of vertical organization similar to that faced by our schools. Unless a deliberate attempt is made, both teachers and secondary divisions of state education departments are likely to look upon reading as a concern solely of the elementary schools. Specific plans should be worked out by state education officials to ensure on the secondary level subject supervisors recognizing the reading problems implicit in the subjects they supervise. As the demand for coordinated reading instruction above the elementary grades increases, state departments may need to provide reading coordinators and consultants to continue the work of primary and intermediate reading supervisors. Certainly some method of avoiding any breakdown between elementary and secondary levels is as imperative in state education departments as it is in the individual school system.

The second point grows out of the first. As state departments recognize the nature of reading growth, they will be more and more concerned with the developmental, corrective, and remedial aspects of reading instruction in the secondary school. Definite steps should be taken to establish the professional status of the reading specialist [8] in somewhat the same way as many states have done in the matter of guidance personnel and school psychologists.

County and District Levels. The various school administrators at the county and district levels share the problems of the local school administrator. They must be alert to the varying needs of the schools in their area, realizing that no two communities are quite alike. By planning with local principals, the services of state departments of education may be focused on in-service training courses, conferences, and institutes. The county administrator thus provides two-way communication between the local school unit and the state. Needless to say, to be of utmost service, these channels of communication must be kept open at all times.

A second contribution at the county or district level includes supplying additional services which individual school districts cannot afford. These services vary widely with the location, size, and economic status of the community. They may include some or all of the following: guidance personnel, medical personnel, and special teachers, such as reading specialists and supervisors. Some pieces of equipment, notably screening devices for vision and hearing testing, may also be handled on a group basis. Where this is done, a single individual should be held responsible for such equipment. Careful scheduling of shared screening devices tends to ensure maximum use.

Local Level. Last, but by no means least, in this consideration of the leadership potential at various levels is the local school system. Just as the classroom teacher is the backbone of reading instruction, so is the local administrator a key figure. The school principal, elementary or secondary, has the responsibility for initiating, developing, supporting, and interpreting the reading program in the community.

ESTABLISHING THE READING CLIMATE OF A SCHOOL

The ways in which a school may become aroused about the importance of reading are many. In some cases public criticism results in an increased awareness of the situation; in others, individuals and groups of teachers realize that the needs of the slow learner and the gifted are not being met. However criticism develops, the administrator is alert to detect it and to move toward solving the problem. Frequently the point of departure is the establishment of a reading survey.

Reading Survey. As has already been indicated, two alternatives present themselves: the reading survey may be made by an outside agency, or it may be carried out by the school staff. The second of these two alternatives, while time consuming, is by far the better procedure [7] to adopt if the administrator wishes to further faculty thinking in matters of curriculum, promotion, and reporting.

The administrator's part in such a reading survey is not easy for there will almost inevitably be much groping and pursuit of many false trails. He will at times feel thwarted, tempted to short-circuit discussion as teachers move hesitatingly toward the solution of difficulties [3]. As teachers resolve problems, the time may come for extra assistance in the form of the addition of a reading specialist or a curriculum consultant to the staff. At other times, an outside consultant may be called in to add an objective viewpoint to aid in the solution of troublesome questions; usually, this will not occur before the staff has had adequate time to examine the matter for itself. The magnitude of the task before the administrator is the measure of his opportunity.

While the teachers under the leadership of the Reading Improvement Committee are conducting the survey, there are several ways by which the administrator may give concrete evidence of his support.

Selection of Teachers. One of the more effective ways by which a principal can influence the reading climate of a school is by his selection of new teachers. Most hiring officials have their own methods of evaluating the probable contributions of the teachers they interview. The administrator who is interested in developing a faculty which will cooperate effectively in providing for widely differing reading abilities will wish to inquire into such things as what experience the prospective teacher has had in working with groups of boys and girls within the larger class group. The basic assumption upon which the philosophy of developmental reading rests is that children learn at different rates, and one of the principal ways of providing for differences in reading ability is small-group instruction within the classroom. While this is particularly true of the primary and elementary grades, we now recognize that differentiated reading instruction should be carried on both in junior and senior high school, to be fully effective.

The administrator will seek answers to other questions. Has the prospective teacher recognized the basic importance of reading in his grade or subject? Is his educational philosophy compatible with the school's concept of child growth and development? Is he sympathetic to the idea that not all children learn at the same rate and does he make provision for differences by incorporating reading materials of different levels of difficulty wherever and whenever possible?

One of the better-than-average secondary schools in the East has been asking its prospective teachers if they were challenged by the opportunity afforded for working with slow learners. The rejection of slower sections by established staff members had become so habitual that the administration felt it necessary to select some new teachers interested in working in this area. A determined effort to obtain teachers qualified by temperament and training to instruct the less gifted strengthens the staff.

Assignment of Teachers. While an administrative official can mold a faculty over a period of years by judicious selection of new teachers, he is still faced with the problem of members already on the staff. Fortunately for him, most experienced teachers are quite receptive to new ideas. Once they have convinced themselves that provision for differences in learning and reading abilities does improve instruction, they tend to be more influential than newer members of the staff. Yet there are likely to be some on every teaching faculty who believe in rigorous and ruthless elimination of students who are not up to grade level.

Teachers, being human beings, have strengths and weaknesses. The successful administrator knows these strengths and weaknesses and places his teachers so that their strengths are emphasized and their weaknesses minimized.

Suppose a school has two elementary teachers on its staff who make no secret of the fact that they feel they are hired to teach their particular grades, using the books prescribed for those grades, regardless of the fact that some will not be able to read them and thus will learn little or nothing from the printed page. The administrator of such a school will probably assign these teachers so that boys and girls will not be taught by them for two consecutive years. Usually such teachers will do a superior job with the better-than-average pupils. The size of slower sections might well be kept smaller and every effort should be made to secure abundant supplies of reading materials at the appropriate levels of interest and difficulty. Far too often, the able teacher is overloaded with retarded readers, many of whom are difficult to teach, and at the same time deprived of necessary supplies. As every administrator knows, the result is the loss of the teacher to the teaching profession.

The tendency toward uniform salaries, based on training and experience, has reduced to some extent the feeling that moving from the elementary grades to junior high or from junior high to senior high is a promotion. We need good teachers at every level, but particularly we need them in the primary grades. Nevertheless, the administrator who wishes to ensure the learning of children at all levels of ability will sometimes find it advantageous to assign a teacher to an upper grade with the idea that he may be better fitted to work with a slower group. Ideally, the administrator of an average-sized school would like to have at least one such teacher in each grade above the primary and, wherever possible, one in each subject in the secondary school.

What has been said about providing properly trained and temperamentally qualified teachers for those of limited mental ability also applies to the selection of teachers for those of above-average mental ability. Here, too, reading is important, but with able learners the problem is to enable them to realize their potential in both reading and subject matter.

Scheduling. The scheduling of boys and girls is largely the duty of the guidance department, but the administrator should be ready to assist in improving schedules. Wherever possible, students should be placed in sections that will challenge them. For many boys and girls this will mean individually prepared programs, since they will not necessarily be placed in the same homogeneous section for all subjects. The administrator can be of great help in supporting the guidance department in conferring with parents as well as students in this matter, as indicated in Chapter 7.

If a system is forced to go on a two-shift school day, because of overcrowded buildings, the administrator should examine the possibility of alternating morning and afternoon sessions so that all children have equal learning opportunities. The necessity for working mothers to arrange for child care precludes too frequent alternation. Possibly a change every half year or every year is all that should be attempted, and this only with adequate notice of the proposed change. Part-time work of students at the secondary level may make this procedure impractical.

The split-session school day also presents the administrator with a temporary advantage in scheduling teachers. Special reading instruction may be provided for some boys and girls while other teachers are engaged in in-service training programs such as the preparation of unitary materials or curriculum revision.

Budgetary Provisions for Reading. The local administrator can affect his school's attitude toward reading by budget provisions for reading supplies. For the elementary program these should include adequate reading readiness materials and tests; replacement orders of basal, cobasal, and supplementary readers and workbooks; special-purpose materials, such as games and devices for providing drill; and books at several levels of difficulty for each classroom library, including books for reluctant readers [4] and for boys and girls who may be reading below grade level in the upper grades.

For subject-matter teachers at the secondary level, supplies should include classroom libraries composed of trade and supplementary books, bulletins, magazines, reprints, and multiple copies of easy and difficult textbooks. Where work is contemplated in corrective and/or remedial instruction, provision should be made for additional oral- and silent-reading tests; charts and graphs to record progress; workbooks devoted to phonics, study-type reading skills, and speed-of-comprehension exercises; games and practice materials; and other special-purpose supplies for reading-disability cases.

Obviously special materials are required when specific work is undertaken with reading-disability cases, slow learners, and superior students. Many schools set up a reading program and secure the services of an adequately trained teacher, but fail to provide sufficient money to furnish essential reading supplies. In subsequent paragraphs, suggestions will be made regarding some of the above budgetary provisions.

Policy on Workbooks. Some schools refuse to permit the use of workbooks; others refuse to let children write in them. Such prohibition is usually caused by the past misuse of workbooks as busywork. The policy of making workbooks nonconsumable originates from a false concept of economy. To deny the use of professionally prepared materials for such a reason is shortsighted indeed. Either children do not receive the necessary drill, or teachers are forced to prepare material which they are often not qualified to write and to devote time to duplicating or mimeographing which could be more profitably used in improving instruction.

Reading Materials. Many schools suffer from an insufficient quantity of reading material. At the elementary level, a single basal series with no supplementary books provides a threadbare, poverty-stricken reading program. From the first grade on, children need wide reading so that they will meet familiar words in new contexts, thus gaining practice in word recognition and shifts in meaning of common words. At the secondary level, a single text, no matter how excellent it may be, does not provide for differences in reading ability within a class. This is especially true of English anthologies. Not only do they fail to provide materials of different levels of difficulty, but they do not contain enough materials for a year's reading. The practice of incorporating a novel in the anthology further tends to reduce flexibility.

The policy of using several texts of differing degrees of difficulty deserves consideration. Not all teachers are ready for this type of teaching. Certainly there is little to be gained from forcing teachers to employ methods for which they are not professionally equipped. Conversely, an administrator should welcome requests for the purchase of several texts wherever financially practical and should seek to further in-service training in their use.

Machines. In discussing budgetary provisions for the reading program, the administrator should possibly be cautioned against the too early inclusion of appropriations for machines to teach reading. They do have their place, but, in the final analysis, the first items to improve a reading program are *suitably trained teachers* with *adequate supplies* of properly prepared and selected reading material. To spend hundreds of dollars for a piece of equipment that is used sporadically or gathers dust is poor economy [2]. Yet it is very difficult to convince parent-teacher associations and alumni that something more fundamental than mechanical equipment is needed. All this points up the need for a dynamic and ongoing public relations program. True, there are times when machines are valuable. However, the first move should always be to free teachers whose philosophy and training particularly suit them to reading instruction and to aid them with professionally prepared reading materials. As they influence others, the time comes for a reading specialist and some of the more useful equipment.

However, there should be no delay in the purchase of mechanical equipment for screening for visual abnormalities. Provided a good working relationship has been established with eye specialists, a suitable device should be obtained early and used yearly. Hearing loss does not appear to be as significant a factor in reading retardation, and, at least at the beginning of a reading program, simpler methods may be used to screen for hearing loss.

Book Selection. If the school is a small one, many of the decisions regarding book selection and adoption will necessarily devolve upon the principal. In larger schools, such selection will involve one or more of the following people: the supervisor, curriculum coordinator, or department head. Each school works out its own procedures within budgetary and structural limitations.

Two points regarding book selection are of vital importance. First, the selection of books should be a continuous process. One person in each area, subject, or grade should be designated to familiarize himself with new books as they are published. Sample copies should be ordered and tried out with selected boys and girls. Thus a nucleus for multiple texts is available, and the staff is always ready to suggest suitable books when money is obtainable for their purchase. Second, teachers and administrators should be encouraged to write to publishing companies stating their requirements, pointing out the strong and weak points of existing books, and indicating areas lacking suitable coverage, as when changes in state or local syllabuses are made.

At a meeting of the New England Reading Association, Durrell asked a group of publishers' representatives why more texts on several levels of difficulty were not obtainable. The answer was that there appeared to be little or no demand for them by classroom teachers.

In-service Training Programs. Another way in which the administrator can affect the school's reading climate is through the in-service training program. Frequently a faculty meeting, or a series of meetings, may be devoted to reading and allied subjects. Those who face teachers at the close of a busy school day tend to favor released time for such meetings if attendance is compulsory. If attendance is voluntary, the meeting may be held at the close of school, provided a coffee break is included. The administrator should be alert to recognize signs indicating that some of his faculty, such as junior high teachers, do not feel involved in the subject of reading.

A combination of required and voluntary meetings works out well. For example, a meeting on released time for everyone may be followed by one or more voluntary meetings.

From a meeting to an in-service training program is often a logical step. Whether such a program is formalized by credit from a college and/or local board of education depends upon location, the numbers involved, and, of course, other commitments of the faculty. The administrator will often find a teachers' club willing to sponsor such courses. Some boards of education foot the bill, although difficulties are apt to ensue when college credit is involved and when neighboring communities cooperate. Such meetings are usually scheduled in the late afternoon or evening.

Other in-service training programs consist of one-day workshops at intervals throughout the year and two- or three-day institutes at the beginning of the school year. It seems probable that in the not too far distant future some boards of education will employ teachers on a twelve-month basis with a one-month vacation. During the summer, teachers will be engaged in one or more of the following areas: teaching the summer term of regular classes, supervising summer camp or playground, pursuing formal study, or improving curricula and preparing materials in local workshops. When and if this day comes, an almost ideal workshop atmosphere should be forthcoming, with teachers employing school library facilities with additional resource materials and possibly some outside direction.

Rate of Progress. Finally, the administrator seeking to establish the reading climate of the school must be an accurate judge of how fast the school, the staff, and the community are prepared to move. To attempt to proceed too quickly undoes much that has already been accomplished by small groups of teachers. At the other extreme is the principal who, having welcomed each class back to school, whispered to the teacher as he was leaving each classroom, "This year we are emphasizing reading." No meetings, no committees, no speakers followed. Small wonder little or nothing was accomplished that year.

The administrator is concerned with the educational philosophy of two groups, one within the school and the other outside it. The first group consists of teachers who need leadership to see that provision for differences in learning is a logical extension of earlier work in reading. The second group is composed of lay people who, through an intelligent public relations program, must be won away from the belief that uniform textbook requirements, common school or state examinations, and vigorously applied grade standards result in better educational opportunities. We have just about reached the conclusion that creativity cannot be mass-produced.

What both groups forget is that practices which worked with the school population of thirty or forty years ago are not effective today. While in some ways it might be easier to return to a system which tended to turn out a more uniform product, that way does not provide the utmost opportunity for all students. In order that each may become all that he is capable of being, teachers and lay people alike must be brought to the realization that the school's responsibility is not confined to one portion of the school population. Slow learners and students of average ability, no less than able learners, must be helped to develop their full capabilities. Awareness of the needs of each group results in raising the levels of performance.

SUMMARY

Reading presents the first contact child and parents have with systematized instruction, and reading is basic to many branches of learning. Since all teachers at all grade levels are involved, coordination of the reading program becomes the responsibility of the chief school administrator. His leadership responsibilities include (1) the professional growth of teachers, (2) coordination of staff effort, and (3) public relations.

Leadership is necessary at the national, state, county, and district level as well as in the local school system.

The reading climate of a school may be influenced by a reading survey, by selection and assignment of teachers, by scheduling, and by budgetary provisions for reading. In this last category, the policy on workbooks and materials of instruction, the place of mechanical equipment, and the selection of books are important.

The attitude of a school toward reading may be improved by in-service training programs. In this, as in everything else, the administrator must be an accurate judge of how fast to proceed.

REFERENCES

* 1. Bond, Guy L., and Eva Bond: *Developmental Reading in High School*, The Macmillan Company, New York, 1941.

2. Davis, L. R., and Jacqueline Davis: "What Principals Should Know about Remedial Reading," *Clearing House*, vol. 29, pp. 298–300, January, 1955.

3. Donelson, Raymond: "Tackling Reading Problems Together," in *Reading for Today's Children*, The National Elementary Principal, vol. 35, no. 1, September, 1955, pp. 219–222.

* 4. Dunn, Anita, Mabel Jackman, and Bernice Bush: *Fare for the Reluctant Reader*, CASDA, New York State College for Teachers, Albany, N.Y., 1953.

5. Early, Margaret J.: "About Successful Reading Programs," *English Journal*, vol. 46, no. 7, pp. 393–405, October, 1957.

6. Fay, Leo C.: "Reading in the High School," *What Research Says to the Teacher*, Department of Classroom Teachers, American Educational Research Association Series, no. 11, National Education Association, Washington, 1956.

7. Hicks, Vernon: "A School Staff Surveys Its Reading Problems," in *Reading for Today's Children*, The National Elementary Principal, vol. 35, no. 1, September, 1955, pp. 208–212.

8. Leavell, Ullin: "Discussion: Clinical Procedures in Diagnosing Seriously Retarded Readers," in William S. Gray and Nancy Larrick (eds.), *Better Readers for Our Times*, International Reading Association Conference Proceedings, vol. 1, Scholastic Magazines, New York, 1956, pp. 157–158.

9. Misner, Paul J.: "Administrative Steps in Providing for Retarded Readers," in William S. Gray and Nancy Larrick (eds.), *Better Readers for Our Times*, International Reading Association Conference Proceedings, vol. 1, Scholastic Magazines, New York, 1956, pp. 165–167.

10. Pratt, Miriam L.: "Working Together to Improve the Reading Program," in *Reading for Today's Children*, The National Elementary Principal, vol. 35, no. 1, September, 1955, pp. 213–218.

11. *The Road to Better Reading*, Bureau of Secondary Curriculum Development, The State Education Department, Albany, N.Y., 1953.

* 12. Strang, Ruth, Constance M. McCullough, and Arthur E. Traxler: *Problems in the Improvement of Reading*, 2d ed., McGraw-Hill Book Company, Inc., New York, 1955.

* 13. Townsend, Agatha (ed.): *College Freshmen Speak Out*, Committee on School and College Relations of the Educational Records Bureau, Harper & Brothers, New York, 1956.

* See Appendix A for annotated list of books for the professional library in schools.

Chapter 12

ORGANIZING SCHOOL READING PROGRAMS

The Reading Improvement Committee, aware that the changed school population has resulted in wide differences in reading ability and that reading instruction is fundamental to successful learning in all curriculum areas, seeks to identify and eliminate as many causes of poor reading as possible. Teachers at all levels, both elementary and secondary, are alerted to the continuing nature of developmental reading. By means of a school survey, the reading climate of the school is ascertained and necessary changes are made in the testing program. Staff members in all departments and levels of the school are aware of their unique contributions to various phases of reading instruction; they are also aware of the help forthcoming from the reading specialist and related services. Furthermore, in their consideration of the reading program, they have been careful to enlist the support of the community, parents, and the boys and girls whom they teach. The administration has provided leadership and has actively supported the teachers in their efforts. All this has taken considerable time and much hard work. Certain revisions in school organization which will further the reading program and improve the learning situation have yet to be made.

CHANGES IN BASIC SCHOOL ORGANIZATION

The Reading Improvement Committee and the administrator are concerned with both the immediate and the long-term improvement of reading [21]. The former includes what can be accomplished in a comparatively short period of time within the existing framework. The latter concerns changes in basic school organization which, over a period of years, will strengthen reading instruction and thus provide a better education for boys and girls. Since schools vary a great deal in organizational patterns, what would be a major change for one school might be a relatively simple readjustment for another in a different stage of development.

Typical Organizational Patterns. What started out as an 8–4 organization of elementary and secondary school in many parts of the country has now become a 6–3–3 arrangement or even a 3–3, 3–3 plan—a division into primary and intermediate grades in one building and junior and senior high in another. Many local variations exist, some of them brought about by expansion due to overcrowding of existing school buildings. To most of these plans a pre-first-grade year of kindergarten has been added. Such systems are geared to the average child and work well with him, but they lose much of their effectiveness where the slow to mature and the early to mature are concerned. Both of these groups are present in our schools in about equal numbers.

Kindergarten. The indications are that kindergarten, despite some objection to its name, is here to stay. The more we learn about the reading process and the background experiences that further it, the more important kindergarten becomes. Yet many a school system, faced with the necessity of economizing, has contemplated abandoning this important phase of schooling. It is worth noting that at least one of the reorganization plans considered here would make the kindergarten an integral part of the beginning grades [25].

Reorganization of Primary Grades. The principal reorganizational plans affect the early grades of school. The attempt is being made to fit the program to the child rather than forcing the child—by retention, chronological promotion, or acceleration—to fit established grades.

One such plan is that recently adopted by New York City schools in which children who have not demonstrated achievement in line with their ability are retained a second year in the third grade [10]. While it is still too early to pass on the merits of such a plan, it would appear that this modification may be made with the least disturbance of the *status quo.* At the same time it does little to improve the initial teaching situation facing teachers in grades K to 3. From the viewpoint of the child who is retained an additional year in the third grade and his parents, there remains the stigma attached to nonpromotion. While such a plan may be suitable for some school systems, there are other arrangements which deserve consideration.

If an elastic time limit for accomplishing the work of the first three grades is provided and if the usual grade designations are removed, pupils may proceed through the work usually taught in the first three years of school at the pace best suited to their learning abilities. Thompson [21] points out that the customary assignment to grades in May or June is eliminated and progress is continuous throughout the primary grades. The above-average child completes the work in two years, while the slow learner takes four. Although such an ungraded procedure might logically be applied to the intermediate grades, it has so far been largely confined to the primary school. There are indications that the scope of the program should be enlarged to include subjects other than reading. Under such a system a teacher may move along with the children or not, as local conditions warrant. The ungraded plan works well when combined with a reading-levels approach to instruction.

A somewhat more radical change is suggested by Woodring [25]. Consisting of a primary, middle, and high school, the Woodring plan combines kindergarten and the first two grades in an elastic block which will take from two to five years to complete. Essentially, the plan is designed to speed up college entrance for the able learner while permitting the slow learner to leave school at sixteen or less in some circumstances.

Philosophy Leading to Change. Our commonly accepted grade designations are a relic of outmoded thinking. They fitted a concept of education that called for separate hurdles, each to be achieved before going on to the next. The practice of applying grade standards has necessarily given way in the face of our attempts at universal education and a deeper understanding of variations in ability to learn [21]. Chronological promotion, employed in a vast majority of cases, has further weakened the orderly division of subject matter. Yet the designations of the older system are retained, causing confusion to parents and perplexity to many secondary school teachers.

When a child is promoted in spite of not learning to read, all subsequent teachers need to meet the demands created by this situation, or such an individual will be passed on from grade to grade without receiving instruction geared to his level of ability. At the other end of the scale, the above-average student who may be ready to read in kindergarten or before is usually forced to lock-step his way through the grades. Yet a third individual handicapped by existing methods is the child of above-average ability who, for any one of a combination of reasons, is not ready to read in first grade. At least one reading authority [11] suggests that such a child is poorly served by the present system of chronological promotion.

Preparation for Change. Whatever the reorganization decided upon, community, parents, and teachers must be prepared for such change. Almost all are accustomed to thinking in terms of grade designations and any attempt to change existing patterns is doomed to failure unless all concerned are brought along in their thinking [12]. This means acquainting everyone on the staff and in the community with the reasons why such proposed changes are advisable and necessary, the advantages to be gained from such plans, and a realistic recognition of possible disadvantages.

As indicated earlier, one of the better ways of bringing about a new philosophy is to involve those concerned in the planning. The teachers should probably come first, but lay people should be included as soon as possible. This may be a lengthy process, but any school which has experienced difficulty in other areas, such as a change in reporting practices, will recognize the wisdom of going slowly in the initial stages.

When the plans are finalized and a change is to be made, as for example the introduction of the ungraded plan in the primary school, a good procedure is to initiate such a change a year at a time, beginning with kindergarten or first grade. This procedure is termed the *step plan.*

CHANGES POSSIBLE WITHIN PRESENT FRAMEWORK

Primary Grades

The Reading Improvement Committee and the principal may feel that the community, the parents, the board of education, or even members of the teaching staff are not yet ready for changes involving the organization of the school. There remains much that can be accomplished within the existing framework. However, teachers should be brought to the realization that changes involving the earlier years of a child's education have a profound bearing upon what ought to be done in later years. This fundamental point escapes some secondary school teachers and many critics of our educational system.

Reading Readiness—Kindergarten and First Grade. The reading readiness period assumes a position of strategic importance in the organization or reorganization of the school reading program. The readiness program, as we have seen, enables children of varying backgrounds and stages of physical, social, emotional, and mental development to get off to a good start in reading, thus avoiding one of the principal causes of failure attributable to the school.

The first essential is to determine if there actually is a readiness program. Children who are not yet ready to read should be made to feel that they are gainfully employed and not engaged in busy-work or waiting until the time when they are ready to read. Durrell's listing [6], "Check List of Instructional Needs in Reading Readiness," will help the administrator and the teacher assess the program.

Principals and elementary supervisors are likely to face two problems in school systems which actually have reading readiness programs in operation. The first is to restrain the enthusiasm of teachers; the second is to allay the anxiety of parents.

Teachers, especially inexperienced ones, need help and support in resisting a very normal impulse to rush into formal reading instruction before children are ready. Much help may be gained from the wise counsel of an experienced teacher, who is placed in charge of the reading readiness program in each building. Teachers profit from help in selecting, preparing, and organizing materials, which they should be encouraged to share with other teachers. Appropriate games, stories, and poems should be selected, not only for their interest to boys and girls, but also for the contribution they make to a sequential readiness program. Very often a teacher feels forced into reading instruction against her better judgment because of the lack of suitable material for the readiness program. Administrators who have issued prohibitions against the use of workbooks or who fail to provide adequate tests, materials, and supplies are thus doing the reading program a serious disservice.

If parents are expected to cooperate in the reading readiness program, they must be completely informed about the purposes and principles of such a program. To do anything less is to run the risk of overanxious parents spoiling the effectiveness of the readiness program while giving the school a bad name at the same time. Axiomatic in this public relations program are the facts that (1) parents must be informed *before* their children enter the first grade, and (2) no amount of publicity will make a good program out of a bad one.

Primary Reading. In order to provide greater elasticity in meeting the instructional needs of children of varying learning abilities, many schools are adopting a system of reading levels rather than the older grade designations.

Such provisions are by no means new. One of the first programs incorporating reading levels was developed in Cleveland and was reported by Margaret White in 1938 [24]. The elementary school was organized so that a pupil could pass from one level to the next as soon as he was deemed ready. Since that time, various plans designed to promote continuous progress have been developed. Fresno, California, divides the work of the first six grades into twenty-one reading levels, four for each of the primary grades and three for each of the intermediate grades [10]. Basal readers and supplementary texts are organized according to these reading levels, with the result that an abundance of material is available at each level. A child normally would take three years to complete the twelve levels of the primary division but, regardless of the room he may be in, he progresses from one reading level to the next.

Pygman [15] reports a variation of the above plan in which the work of the ungraded primary school is divided into eight levels, four in the first year, two in the second year, and two in the third year. Advantages claimed for this procedure include thorough teaching of basic skills, avoidance of any feeling of failure, and an increased interest in work that is constantly new and challenging to young readers.

The reading-levels approach to primary reading instruction may be used with existing grade designations. In fact, it is really an extension of the basal, cobasal, and supplementary readers plan. If a child is not deemed ready for the next level, he reads another book on the same level. Many successful teachers provide continuous and continuing reading instruction despite the existence of grade designations. However, the existence of such grade labels is likely to promote the possibility of some primary or intermediate teachers continuing or reverting to the grade-standard concept. Reporting practices are also complicated, sometimes misleading parents and aggravating possible misunderstanding of the purposes of contemporary education on the part of the general public.

Finally, the establishment of reading levels may serve as a steppingstone toward the subsequent abolition of the conventional grade designations. As teachers and parents become accustomed to thinking in terms of levels of reading instruction, they will become more ready to accept the elimination of outdated grade names.

Intermediate Grades

The reading instruction program of the intermediate grades varies considerably from one school system to another. Some schools follow a conservative basal-reader approach; others employ both co-basal and supplementary readers. The continuation of the reading-levels provision for instruction, either with or without formal grade designations, is gaining adherents. Variations may also exist within a single school system.

Provisions for Differences in Reading Ability. Some schools, by scheduling reading instruction at the same time in all classrooms, are able to move groups of children to a teacher working at a particular level. Where there are several sections of the same grade, this provision has some advantages from the individual teacher's point of view, although the advantages tend to be overshadowed by accompanying difficulties. The paramount difficulty is that of coordinating reading-class reading with that done in subject-matter areas. A second objection is that groups so formed tend to have a homogeneity which may tempt the teacher to treat the whole group alike. The end result is more pupils for the teacher to know and less and less provision for individual differences. Perhaps this pattern of organization is better adapted to subjects such as arithmetic than it is to reading instruction. However, many school systems believe that the self-contained classroom has more to offer.

The method occasionally followed in conjunction with the above scheduling of reading classes—shipping boys and girls up or down to the grade room at which level they are reading—has little advantage. Such a practice is an admission of the meaningless nature of grade designations, even more difficult to coordinate, and likely to result in children of widely different ages and interests being forced to work together. The effect may be beneficial to children sent into a grade room higher than their own, but the impact upon those who "entertain" the younger readers is, to say the least, questionable. The less said about the effect upon those who are asked to report to rooms of a grade level lower than their own, the better.

Implicit in both accommodations outlined above, there is tacit recognition of the necessity for homogeneous grouping without frank admission of it. The total effect on boys and girls is probably much worse than homogeneous grouping would be, for they are faced daily with the fact that they are not achieving as their age group and associates are. A simpler solution to the entire problem would be recognizing that individuals differ in ability. Provision for differences is one of the major responsibilities of the classroom teacher, aided by the specialists and the administrator wherever possible [17].

Homogeneous Grouping. A better instructional program frequently results from continuing the reading-levels approach into the intermediate grades. This really amounts to a form of homogeneous grouping. Admittedly, such procedure does not ensure the same level of ability in work-study reading skills. While provisions still must be made for individual needs in the various skills—which together form the complex pattern of abilities known as reading—there is much to be said in favor of continuing the levels approach to reading.

Sometimes attempts are made to avoid the criticism that homogeneous grouping is not democratic by giving each teacher a combination of groups. Under such a system a teacher might have a fast and an average group, or an average group and a slow group, but probably not a fast and a slow group. This, like the names given to reading groups in the primary grades, succeeds in fooling no one—certainly not the boys and girls involved.

Unfortunately, the continuation of planned reading instruction in the intermediate grades, whether on a levels system or the more conventional basal-reader approach, often fails to provide an optimum reading program. At least two additional provisions are necessary.

Study-type Reading Skills. First, instruction in work-study reading skills should be given as reading is introduced in the content areas of social studies, health, and science. In these subject-matter areas the instruction anticipates junior high school, where each teacher assumes the responsibility for teaching the reading skills required for the successful comprehension of his subject. However, the intermediate grade teacher has a decided advantage over the departmentalized junior high teacher; he knows his boys and girls much better and so can more readily help them to master the study skills required to read content subjects with comprehension.

Remedial Instruction. Second, adequate provision should be made to assist boys and girls who are not reading up to their indicated capacity. Theoretically, continuation of the reading-levels approach or the basal-reader approach might be supposed to take care of such problem cases, but this is not entirely true. The main reason for this is that these forms of instruction are mainly concerned with narrative reading. Thus, a child who is not reading at the equivalent of the fourth-year level in narrative material may not have mastered the principles which enable him to engage in work-type reading and he may not be ready for them. Partly for this reason, schools having reading teachers usually start remedial programs at what would correspond to the third or fourth grade [6].

When individual classes are kept relatively small (i.e., under twenty-five), the classroom teachers may provide the remedial instruction, assisted in some phases of testing, diagnosis, and selection of materials by the reading teacher. However, where classes are larger, the reading teacher frequently works directly with small groups of children. The suggestion made by Durrell [6], stressing the necessity of careful coordination of remedial teaching and regular classroom instruction, is well taken.

Once more, there can be no one best answer to the question of which organizational pattern a given school should adopt in the intermediate grades. In the final analysis, such a decision depends

234 READING IN YOUR SCHOOL

on the training of the teachers, the number of sections at each level, and the extent to which the community and staff have been helped to rethink their philosophy of the teaching of reading.

Junior High

Continuation of reading instruction in the earlier years of the secondary school is a logical extension of the elementary program. The need for such instruction is brought about by our changed school population, since not everyone in the same grade has the same reading ability and a recognition that reading skills, initially taught in the primary grades and developed in the intermediate grades, are capable of further refinement in secondary reading situations.

As a matter of fact, the expansion of the teaching of reading to the seventh and eighth grades is nothing new. Under the older 8–4 school organization, reading instruction was quite regularly part of the program. Furthermore, such instruction was given by a teacher who had students for all subjects and thus knew their strengths and difficulties in subject-matter reading. The continuation of reading in the first two years of early secondary education is the restitution of a vital part of children's education that was lost when school organization shifted to a 6–3–3 form.

The principal difference in instruction between sixth grade and junior high school is the introduction of departmentalization, resulting in a problem on the part of boys and girls of adjusting to more than one teacher. Such departmentalization tends also to emphasize subject matter and sometimes results in less flexibility. A report of the Association for Supervision and Curriculum Development points out that the teacher's training as a subject specialist [9]—

. . . makes it especially difficult for him to feel comfortable about varying his expectations to insure a better "fit" with the capacities, interests, and needs of individual students. Despite the fact that the providing of this "fit" is a requisite for effective subject matter achievement, the making of such accommodations is often perceived as the "lowering of standards" and hence is rejected.[1]

[1] Harold G. Hand, "Relationship of Guidance to Instruction," in *Guidance in the Curriculum*, 1955 Yearbook, Association for Supervision and Curriculum

The question is not one of subject matter versus methodology, since the two are of equal importance. Schools must emphasize content and courses need to be strengthened; but, by the same token, schools must recognize differences in boys and girls by actually providing for these differences.

For years, phrases like the familiar "provision for individual differences" have been bandied about by educators. Yet the average secondary school teacher, hampered by inadequate materials, confronted with set courses of study which must be covered, and plagued by examinations—by the results of which he is sometimes judged—often makes very little, if any, adjustment to individuals.

A well-conceived reading program provides for the continuing development of reading skills, helps seventh graders adjust to the reading demands of various subjects, and ensures provision for differences in reading ability [8].

A junior high reading program should be concerned with three kinds of instruction. They are (1) the *developmental*, which continues the upward expansion of reading abilities in all subjects; (2) the *corrective*, which is designed to provide specific work in reading areas in which individuals and groups are found to be weak; and (3) the *remedial*, which seeks to salvage boys and girls who have the capacity but are so retarded that they can profit little from either the developmental or the corrective program.

Developmental Reading Instruction. The best approach to reading instruction undoubtedly is for every teacher to handle the reading techniques demanded by his subject. Among other things, this includes the use of several texts in a two-track or three-track program, or the multilevel unit. There are indications that teachers are concerned with such methods [14]. The employment of the core or block program, which permits teachers to work with fewer different individuals in the course of a day, also has implications for the teaching of reading [17, 22].

The very fact that developmental reading depends on every teacher in the entire school system—to challenge reading interest, supply reading materials within each individual's capacity, and re-emphasize reading skills which need amplification—is at the same

Development, National Education Association, Washington, 1955, p. 10. Used by permission.

time its strength and its weakness. Reading is involved in the study of every subject; reading remains one of the best approaches to learning. But, at the same time, the evaluation of the effectiveness of such a program is extremely difficult. This does not mean that a developmental program should not be undertaken, but it does mean that the Reading Improvement Committee and the administration must be prepared to discover, when problems of evaluation have been solved, that wide differences exist between teacher and teacher. This is natural since teachers, as human beings, are fallible.

Because of these inequalities in the effectiveness of the developmental reading program, an existing program usually profits from supplementation. Emphasis should be placed on the fact that the developmental program should come first. The supplementation of it by a corrective program does not remove the obligation of the classroom teacher, since it aids and abets him in his efforts.

Corrective Reading Instruction. A developmental reading approach may not be equally effective with all students, yet the school is concerned with the preventive side of reading. For these and other reasons, many schools are examining possible ways of continuing definite reading instruction in the junior high school. Several provisions for this type of program exist; some plans fit individual requirements better than others.

1. *The reading home room.* The first provision for preventive reading instruction utilizes the existing home-room periods. Two changes may be necessary. The period may need to be lengthened, since less than thirty minutes of instruction is usually ineffective. The customary heterogeneous assignment to home rooms may need to be modified in order to cut down the range of abilities within any one room. Because the home room is the basic unit of organization of the school, some critics feel that to modify this structure would be undemocratic, even in schools employing homogeneous grouping for subject-matter instruction.

A more serious objection would appear to be that not all home-room teachers are interested in teaching such classes. Some are not qualified to teach reading to the group to which they have been assigned for administrative home-room purposes. However, where guidance personnel are reading-conscious [18] and can provide help in planning materials and methods of instruction, the reading home room can be very effective. The home-room reading program requires very careful supervision, since there is always the temptation to turn the reading class into a study period.

A method of organization which removes some of the above objections is to assign students requiring instruction to the home rooms of teachers qualified in reading and to assign the others to the more usual activities of the home room. This is a possibility where other methods of organization are not feasible, but many of the preventive aspects are likely to be lost, since not every boy and girl would receive instruction under this substitute plan.

2. *Special English section.* A second method of providing reading instruction is to set aside a special section or sections of English for those having reading difficulties. Practically the only advantage obtained by this system is that no additional staff is required [7]. Such sections are difficult to schedule, reach only a part of the total grade population, and frequently result in a poverty-stricken offering which is unsuccessful both in English and in reading. Children, including slow learners, profit from regular English-class instruction geared to their abilities. To ask English teachers to supply the necessary work in English plus instruction in reading skills within the five-period week is to ask the impossible. Work-type reading of the kinds found in the content subjects is not common to the English curriculum. Yet this study-type reading is frequently exactly what those who are having reading difficulty would profit from the most.

The assumption that the English department of a school should be responsible for the entire reading program is about as sensible as assigning one department to revise the whole school curriculum. Every department has equal responsibility, and English teachers are not usually trained in teaching reading in subjects other than their own. The danger in selecting the English department is that other teachers will tend to feel that reading instruction is the affair of the English department.

A school might better provide a specially trained teacher to head up the work in reading, assisted by teachers from all departments. Other elements of the language arts program merit consideration. For example, the class load of the English teacher could be reduced [4], since it is not the number of preparations that affect the writing part of the language arts program but the number of corrections.

Of course, a better way to implement a strong developmental learning program is to have each teacher assume responsibility for the language arts in his subject. This would include listening (note taking), speaking (various forms of oral reports), writing (spelling, paragraph organization, grammar, and sentence structure), and the work done in reading. Such a developmental language arts program in all subjects is a logical extension of a developmental reading program.

3. *Double English period.* An alternative provision for reading under the auspices of the English department is to increase the number of English periods by three to five per week. Such scheduling removes the criticism of attempting too much in the regular five-period week, but it does not eliminate many of the other objections to the special English section. The double-period English class is fairly common. Blair [2], reporting a study made by Hills, found the special English section to be second in popularity to the special reading class. If qualified teachers are available and recognize that study-type reading techniques must be included, an effective program may result.

4. *Special reading class.* One of the more recent provisions for reading instruction is the special reading class scheduled from two to five periods per week for all students of a particular grade. Usually sections are homogeneously grouped to facilitate the handling of materials and instruction. Since much of the teaching is small-group work, the size of such classes is better kept to twenty-five or less.

The special reading class may be found masquerading under many names in school systems where it has been established for some time. Some school systems call it Spelling; others call it Vocabulary or Research. Frequently, upon close examination, the course will be found to be essentially a reading course which may or may not be in need of revision. Some schools call such a course Remedial Reading. This name is unfortunate indeed and sometimes gives rise to emotional problems on the part of the boys and girls concerned and needless anxiety on the part of their parents. Seventh-grade Reading is a simple enough name and it is without the stigma often attached to the words "remedial" and "clinic."

Occasionally the only possible way to provide for reading instruction at the junior high level is to schedule groups out of existing study halls or library periods. This is usually a relatively poor way of organizing a corrective reading class because it does not reach everyone in a given grade. Even when it does reach everyone, a class composed of different individuals each day presents almost insurmountable problems of organization, unnecessary paper work, and the constant shuffling of folders and materials. The effectiveness of the teacher is reduced and much class time is devoted to handing out and collecting papers and books. Both study hall and library periods can be used to advantage, however, where smaller groups receive remedial instruction.

Who Should Take Corrective Reading? The question can be answered by saying that probably all seventh graders can profit from such a course at the beginning of junior high school. Of course, such an answer must be modified according to the degree to which intermediate reading and seventh-grade developmental programs function effectively. In schools where both programs are relatively good, the amount of time devoted to corrective reading may be reduced to two or three periods per week. Many schools schedule reading classes on days when the seventh grade is not taking home economics, manual arts, or music.

Who Should Teach Corrective Reading? A simple answer would be to say those teachers who are properly qualified and who have evinced an interest in this type of work. Unfortunately, the mere fact that the teacher can read does not imply qualification to teach the course. Schools are often forced to draft teachers with no training or interest to fill out their program. Occasionally the teaching of a single reading class is divided up between two or more teachers. Reading programs employing these practices stand little chance of being effective.

School systems having a reading specialist frequently assign him to teach one or more sections while supervising the work of other teachers also teaching the course. In this way a certain amount of on-the-job training is possible and the shortage of qualified teachers is minimized.

A question concerning the organization of corrective reading classes remains. Should credit be given students for such work?

The answer depends in part on the type of provision for reading instruction that the school decides to use. If reading is taught as part of the work in English, credit is allowed [2]. However, where the reading or guidance department assumes responsibility for the work in reading, usually no credit is given.

Many factors will have to be weighed by a school setting up a corrective reading program before a decision can be reached regarding departmental organization. Among these factors are (1) the probable effect upon teachers of subjects other than English and reading, (2) the availability of teachers and of time in the schedule, and (3) the status of the developmental and remedial programs. The writer happens to lean toward a separate reading department for junior high school, but he is inconsistent in that he feels certain senior high programs are better administered through the English department. The Reading Improvement Committee and the administration will find that Blair [2] and Early [7] are informative in their descriptions of reading programs. The solution is for each school to determine the matter for itself on the basis of the known facts, not forgetting that whatever plan offers promise of the best instruction for boys and girls is best for that particular school.

What Is Taught in Corrective Reading? The content depends upon the reading needs of the group, as determined by appropriate tests. Care should be exercised to see that the class does not become another single-textbook course, for levels of reading ability should be carefully observed. Many books on reading give helpful lists of materials. Of those listed in Appendix A, teachers will find Blair [2], Harris [11], and Strang [20] among the more useful.

Work usually centers around several of the following: vocabulary; word analysis, including phonics; spelling; critical reading; locational skills; dictionary usage; newspaper and magazine reading; learning to read content subjects; study-type and speed-of-comprehension materials at different levels of difficulty; and guided free reading. Mechanical equipment is used sparingly, since comprehension is more important than speed. With good readers, however, judicious use of machines will improve reading.

Remedial Reading. This type of course is perhaps better called Personal Reading Improvement rather than the commoner names Remedial or Clinic, for reasons previously stated.

One of the more popular ways of setting up a remedial class is to establish one room as a reading laboratory to serve as headquarters for reading instruction, with an office for the reading teacher, and as a central point where teachers may become acquainted with newer materials. Students may be referred to the laboratory by the guidance department, other teachers, the reading teachers, or by student or parental request. Personal reading students are scheduled through the guidance department. Such a system permits a maximum amount of flexibility, since the reading teacher can take individuals from other reading classes and from study hall and library periods.

Here, at the risk of being repetitive, the point should be stressed that little is to be gained from forcing slow learners unduly. If their mental capacity is limited, as determined by appropriate intelligence tests (i.e., those yielding a verbal and a nonverbal score) supplemented by individual intelligence tests where indicated, these students belong in the regular classroom in both homogeneously and heterogeneously organized classes with teachers using properly adjusted materials. It is wasteful of a reading specialist's time to load his program with students of limited ability. However, the reading teacher may be very useful in helping regular classroom teachers with materials and techniques.

Reading Program—Grades Eight and Nine. If one of the better methods for providing instruction in corrective reading has been used in the seventh grade, and if it was designed to take every seventh grader at his own reading level, it is common administrative practice to continue instruction in eighth and ninth grades for reading-disability cases who have not yet reached their indicated capacity. The developmental reading program should provide for reading growth in all subjects for other students. A careful watch is maintained—via periodic tests and teacher reports in all subject areas—to apprehend any who may begin to falter. In this way, the time of students who are making satisfactory progress in reading is not spent in the corrective reading class with its specific instruction, but rather in wide reading in all subjects.

Local conditions, particularly the numbers involved, may make it administratively necessary to continue special reading-class instruction for eighth and sometimes ninth graders. Such programs are a cross between corrective reading classes and remedial instruction. Such classes should be kept as small as possible—not over ten or twelve students—so that each may make the greatest possible gain in order to profit from regular classroom situations. Reading gains made in group remedial classes of this size are almost never as great as those achieved by individual instruction.

Summer Programs. In the last few years another provision for reading, a summer reading program, has become increasingly popular. All varieties of offerings may be found.

The better courses appear to have the following characteristics. They are limited in enrollment, often admitting students on the recommendation of previous teachers. When the numbers are kept small and the instruction is provided by competent reading teachers having access to school records, much can be accomplished. Sometimes boys and girls report only at stated hours and are dismissed when the instruction period is over. This organization of the summer reading program resembles the clinic or reading laboratory for work in reading.

At other times summer reading instruction is an addition to an already established subject program. Children attend morning or afternoon sessions or both. Classes tend to be larger and the work is preventive rather than remedial. In many ways this type of provision for reading approximates a seventh-grade reading class.

The third, or developmental, part of the summer reading program is present when regular subject-matter instruction forms the entire summer offering. When this is not the case—even to supplement it where it does exist—there are many excellent summer reading programs sponsored by local public libraries. Schools, as well as individual parents, should advertise and support these useful adjuncts to the developmental reading program.

In addition to the three types of public school programs mentioned previously, private schools often offer work in reading. Here again, if numbers are kept limited to permit individual and small-group instruction, these offerings can be very effective. However, at least in some cases, undue emphasis may be placed upon the use of mechanical equipment with individual rates charged for what amounts to group instruction.

Yet another provision for boys and girls who could profit from additional reading instruction is to be found in summer reading camps. These are usually sponsored by private individuals or by universities. They often afford a happy combination of reading, tutoring in certain subjects, and camping experience. If a young person is reluctant to spend a summer at home studying, this type of instruction can be a desirable compromise.

Finally, many colleges and universities provide free clinic facilities in conjunction with the remedial reading courses scheduled for teachers as part of the summer session program. While the amount of instructional time is likely to be somewhat limited, such work is generally carefully supervised.

There is as much divergence in the types of summer reading programs as there is in methods of organizing reading programs during the regular school year. For this reason, the guidance department or the reading specialist should have available an up-to-date listing of various public and private agencies supplying reading instruction during the summer months. The ethics of the situation demand that the school furnish adequate information to reputable organizations. In turn, school authorities have a right to expect detailed reports of work accomplished and meaningful test data. The problem of coordinating the regular work of the school with summer work in reading is rendered much simpler if the school has its own summer program.

In setting up a summer reading program one of the first considerations should be the financial details. Some communities offer free tax-supported programs, with residents of surrounding communities paying a fixed fee if additional places are available. Other reading programs charge sufficient amounts to pay teachers' salaries. Usually, but not always, the use of buildings and materials are supplied at no charge.

Closely connected with the financial side of the summer reading program is the matter of enrollment. Summer instruction is best devoted to true reading-disability cases in a situation closely approximating a reading laboratory or clinic. Frequently children who have not been successful in a regular reading class can forge ahead with this type of instruction. Some communities, especially those supporting a program through taxation, will demand that larger numbers be enrolled. In such cases, teachers are forced into a reading-class organization. While there is nothing wrong with this, the amount that can be accomplished is, of course, lessened. Frequently a combination of the two can be arranged.

From the above, it will be obvious that certain decisions must be made before setting up a summer reading program. Among these considerations are the answers to the following questions:

1. How is the program to be financed?

2. Are trained teachers (including the school's reading specialist) available?

3. Can the program be coordinated with existing work in reading?

4. Are materials fresh and new to children without stealing from those to be used later?

5. Will the necessary cumulative records be available?

6. Can the numbers involved be kept small enough to permit effective instruction?

The Junior-High Reading Program. The triple instructional program suggested here for the junior high school consists of developmental, corrective, and remedial phases. The developmental side is, in theory at least, the oldest of the three. The remedial phase was added when it became evident that a substantial number of boys and girls could profit from individual and small-group instruction. The corrective program is a more recent addition, made necessary in part by inequalities existing in the developmental approach to reading. The corrective phase of instruction seeks to prevent the incidence of reading problems by providing all seventh graders, except those enrolled in the remedial program, with work in reading. Provision is made for continuing combined corrective-remedial instruction for those who can profit from it in eighth and ninth grades.

Such a triple program, organized according to local conditions, may present a somewhat idealistic attack upon the reading problems of the junior high school. Not all schools will be able to establish a comparable program at once, but it should serve as a target.

Senior High

Reading instruction for members of the senior high is largely contingent upon the reading program of the junior high school.

While local conditions—including the philosophy of the administration and the availability of funds—may occasionally make the postponement of reading instruction necessary, the earlier instruction is started, the better it is for the individuals concerned. There are three main reasons for this statement: (1) The individual tends to be less frustrated the earlier he receives help. (2) Materials tend to be more available at lower grade ranges. (3) The earlier an individual receives instruction, the sooner he is able to profit from reading assignments given in his regular classes.

For these three reasons, some teachers and administrators may be tempted to neglect reading instruction in the senior high school on the theory that it is the province of the earlier grades. However, transfers from school systems having inadequate reading programs, the phenomenon of late development especially among boys, the necessity of continuing instruction already begun in the junior high, and the advisability of instituting some instruction designed to prepare students for college reading situations—all of these point up the desirability of providing further work in reading in the senior high school.

Variety of Provisions for Reading. Senior high schools, in their search for a solution to the problem of organizing reading instruction, have developed a variety of procedures. Strang [19] lists seven different approaches to the problem. These include (1) developmental reading in all classes, (2) reading taught as a special subject, (3) special English section for reading instruction, (4) voluntary enrollment in a reading laboratory program, (5) required enrollment in laboratory-type program, (6) one teacher working most of the school day with a group of poor readers, and (7) assignment to clinic. To these might be added the organization of reading clubs, which usually attract the better readers, and a vertical modification of point 6, in which the same teacher works with the same group of poor readers for two or more years. Blair [2], Simpson [16], and Strang [20] list numerous descriptions of successful reading programs. In general they consist of various combinations of the above provisions. The most common combination is that grouping developmental reading in all subjects, reading instruction in special sections of regular English classes, and some provision for remedial work.

Developmental Reading. As in the junior high school, the best provision for continuation of reading instruction at the senior high level is for every teacher to provide reading materials within the known abilities of each member of his class and to instruct students in reading techniques pertinent to his subject [19]. As in the earlier grades, such provision is made easier by homogeneous grouping on the basis of teacher judgment, school achievement, and general or specific reading ability. Once more, the teaching of a homogeneous group should not be used as an excuse for providing the same reading experiences for the whole class.

Special English Section. The existence of the special English section to provide continued instruction in reading is a partial admission that complete faith is not placed in the developmental side of the reading program. The objections advanced to this provision for reading instruction at the junior high level tend to apply equally when such a plan is used in the senior high school. However, if the English teachers are adequately trained in reading, and if instruction is given in those phases of reading encountered in all subjects, there remain only two objections. The first is that such procedures detract from the English program; the second is that such provision for reading does not reach all students.

A definite attempt to enlist the interest of all teachers in reading would free the English department from an unnecessary burden and would provide instruction for all according to their abilities. Poor readers are as much a problem in social studies, science, and mathematics classes as they are in English classes. Until all teachers become actively interested in reading, the special English section for poor readers is probably the easy solution, as it appears to be the procedure a majority of schools are adopting [2].

Remedial Reading. The third provision for reading instruction in senior high school is usually some form of remedial teaching. This may well be a reading laboratory program with students volunteering or being assigned to it out of study hall or library periods. Two groups of students will profit from such reading experience.

The first group for whom remedial reading is indicated are the students who, despite previous reading instruction, have not yet reached their indicated capacity. There may be several reasons for this. Possibly the family has been reluctant to seek psychiatric help, or the student has been slow to mature, especially in seeing the necessity for reading. Another possibility is that, because of sheer force of numbers, some students were neglected in earlier reading programs.

The second group for whom the reading laboratory may prove advantageous is composed of transfers from school systems lacking adequate reading instruction or from a junior high school within the system which, because of overcrowding, split sessions, or poor economic background, has not provided the required work in reading.

As schools begin earlier to provide the necessary help for boys and girls having reading difficulty, and as more teachers become proficient in developmental reading, the necessity for establishing the reading-laboratory approach may be less essential. However, for years to come, some form of individual reading instruction will be imperative.

Terminal Reading. A fourth type of reading program might be included for those for whom high school is terminal. The advisability of such a program depends largely on the success of developmental reading instruction, especially the guided free reading done in English classes. These young people should read fast enough and with enough comprehension for reading to be enjoyable. Only if reading is pleasurable are they at all likely to continue to read in adult life. At the same time, these terminal students may need extra help in developing the reading skills which will be demanded by their future employment.

Preparation for Demands Made by College Reading. Finally, a fifth type of reading instruction should be included in senior high programs for students planning to enter college. In the past, many schools have provided for such students special courses which include much of the content of college freshman subjects. This tendency to skim the cream from college material on the theory that college work will then be easier is an unfortunate though well-meant practice. It is likely to cause the student to feel that college is a rehash of high school with the result that the interest factor, so important in reading and learning, is diminished. Bad study habits are fostered. The young college student is tempted to neglect reading material with which he is already partially familiar. He half prepares assignments only to find, when entirely new material is encountered, that he has lost many of the required study skills. He then questions the preparation he received in the secondary school [23].

This objection to the anticipation of college material does not extend to the courses offered by secondary schools in the Advanced Placement Program. Presumably students selected for such work have adequate reading skills; if they do not, such instruction should be provided prior to the advanced work.

Rather than preparing students for college work by giving them a smattering of the material to be found in freshman courses, high schools should develop the reading and study skills which will help students not only get into college but to remain there. Self-discipline is one of these study skills. Closely allied to this is a respect for hard work acquired by having done some—preferably more than just a little. Objective tests and examinations have increased the tendency "to mistake information for education, to turn out 'quiz experts' who are crammed full of useful detail but who have not been trained how to think" [1]. Many high school courses are superficial. Fewer courses, deepened rather than enriched for better-than-average students, would improve preparation for college.

A good developmental reading program will do much to force a student to work up to his capacity, but some schools are not depending on this alone. Just as corrective reading classes are being introduced into junior high schools, so refresher courses are being scheduled in the second semester of the eleventh grade or the first semester of twelfth grade. The content of such a class, designed to provide practice in the language arts, will vary with the student, the type of college he plans to attend, his subject specialities, and his present mastery of reading, speaking, thinking, and writing.

An elective course could be provided in senior English classes, although teachers from other departments might teach it from time to time. It would not be an English course in the usual sense, but would include note taking from different subject lectures, preparation of term papers, and a series of reading tasks designed to improve the individual's reading for various purposes in widely different types of material. Part of the emphasis may be on speed of comprehension, as many of the course descriptions in Simpson [16] indicate; but the primary emphasis should probably be on organizing ideas obtained from several sources into reports and term papers. This is the skill often termed *creative reading.*

COLLEGE READING INSTRUCTION

The purpose of this section on college reading programs is to afford the Reading Improvement Committee a brief but comprehensive view of the variety of provisions for reading instruction offered to the secondary school graduate. The question is raised whether a reading-conscious school should count on such instruction. The existence of college reading programs does not lessen the desirability of offering reading instruction in high school for college-bound students.

Provisions for College Reading Instruction. The most common provision for affording help in reading is a short course, eight weeks to a semester in duration, aimed at improving the student's speed of comprehension. Some colleges make such a course compulsory for all except a few who stand high in standardized reading tests. Other colleges require it for students whose reading is not in line with their other abilities. Sometimes students are referred by faculty or advised to take the course by members of the student personnel office.

Another provision, found in some college programs, is having reading instruction built in to a required freshman course or orientation program. These provisions vary from those emphasizing mechanical equipment for speeding up reading to elaborate courses offering counseling on emotional and adjustment problems in addition to reading instruction [20].

Remedial reading as it is known in the secondary school assumes a minor role in college reading programs. Since college is selective to a greater or less degree, college staff members often feel that if a student cannot do the work expected of him he should not be in college. Some colleges, however, do recognize the necessity of offering individual instruction.

Many college instructors require large amounts of collateral reading in conjunction with the preparation of reports and term papers, or to supplement the textbook and lectures. Most colleges tend to leave the amount up to the individual instructor, but at least one college [5] is advocating the required reading of six general background books in each of the freshman and sophomore years and an equal amount in the last two years to be read in connection with the student's major field.

All types and methods of organizing college reading programs are to be found. Many of the discussions of the merits of various forms of instruction will furnish the Reading Improvement Committee with additional suggestions for high school courses. The yearbooks of The South West Reading Conference for Colleges and Universities, now the National Reading Conference for Colleges and Adults, probably afford the best picture of college reading programs [3]. Despite the title of this organization, representative public school systems are invited, and reading problems common to high school and college are considered.

Secondary School Attitude toward College Reading Programs. Certainly school guidance departments should be informed of the provisions colleges make for the continuation of reading instruction. To this end, colleges should include specific descriptions in their catalogues.

A student going to college has a number of important personal adjustments to make. For almost the first time in his life, he is faced with the necessity of making a completely new set of friends. He is usually away from home for his first protracted stay. He is on his own financially, emotionally, physically, and morally. The home and community no longer exert a measure of control, or at least the control is less direct.

At the very time he has gained his freedom, he is forced to meet what, for him, may be unpleasant realities. A carefully worked out daily study schedule becomes a must, since a majority of college classes meet two or three times per week rather than every day. The demands placed upon reading are much greater in college than in high school. Study halls and parental supervision are conspicuous by their absence. For these reasons, however adequate a college reading program may be, the instruction comes at a time when the college boy or girl is going through a critical adjustment period.

As the competition for admission to college grows stronger, the high school is called upon increasingly to help make students' reading and study skills as effective as possible. This is not because college reading programs are inadequate, but because to do otherwise is to run the danger that students will be overwhelmed by the demands made on their reading before they have the opportunity to improve their reading skills. The numbers involved make the scheduling of reading instruction early in the freshman year impractical in many instances.

No criticism of college reading programs is intended, but the forward-looking high school will seek to provide reading and study skills which function effectively so that, at a time of personal adjustment, the young college student will not "face the increased required reading assignments with limited resources and mixed feelings" [13].

ADMINISTERING THE REORGANIZATIONAL PROGRAM

All teachers, the Reading Improvement Committee, and the administrator will want to keep perspective while seeking to effect the reorganization of the reading program. Blair [2] contains many suggestions which, while applying specifically to remedial programs, have general application also. A series of "do's" and "don't's" for administrators [20] should serve as a guide to action while pointing out some of the pitfalls.

The following are some of the more important considerations to be kept in mind:

1. The recognition of need for reading improvement should come from teachers, parents, and students, as well as from the administration. The situation in which change is dictated from above should be avoided.

2. Once a faculty, or a substantial part of it, has indicated a realization of the need for improvement, the administrator should give enthusiastic support in terms of time, money, and personal effort.

3. Avoid the feeling that individuals and divisions of the school are being criticized. Concentrate on the parts of the program that are effective and build on these.

4. Change just for the sake of change is not desirable. An effective program is the result of careful and deliberate organization, based on a realized need.

5. Make use of the combined resources of the teaching staff and the community. Educate by involvement.

6. When the time comes to hire a reading specialist, make sure he is fitted for the job by personality as well as training. Give him a free hand in organizing remedial and special-class reading. Do not expect miracles overnight.

7. Make sure reading materials are adequate. To provide staff, schedule classes, and then to fail in supporting the program with materials is false economy.

8. Give tangible support to the Reading Improvement Committee. A professional library, consultant services, and in-service training courses are evidences of real support.

9. Provide time. At first regularly scheduled meetings may be devoted to consideration of reading problems. Special meetings help, but when a faculty really grapples with the reading question, released time every school day for a year is not too much.

10. Schedule work in reading within the school day. It is neither fair nor realistic to expect boys and girls or teachers to become enthusiastic about a program that the administration obviously regards as an extra.

11. Avoid embarrassing girls and boys. Sell them on the self-improvement aspect rather than the compulsory you're-so-bad-you-have-to approach. Select names for classes that are simple statements of fact without implications.

12. Remember the individual. Any reorganization should improve his reading as a learning tool, make him independent, free him to explore new fields and respond to new ideas, and enable him to understand the world around him as well as to understand himself.

13. Avoid slavishly copying a reading program reported as successful in another school system. Be eclectic; select parts of several programs and incorporate special features to meet individual situations.

14. Share know-how in professional meetings, reporting successful practices, arranging visitation, or inviting demonstration.

SUMMARY

The reorganization of a school reading program should be shared by the administrator and the Reading Improvement Committee. Such a committee should be representative of all subject-matter departments and all levels of the school so that the work may be a cooperative undertaking. Boys and girls and parents also should be involved. Problems in areas allied to reading, including testing, promotion, reporting, and curriculum, will be considered.

Some of the changes discussed by the committee will concern the basic organizational pattern of the school. The principal changes concern the primary grades, although some will affect all twelve grades. Grade designations may be abolished and the time limits for completing the work of the primary grades may be made elastic. Because the proposed changes may be somewhat radical, care must be taken to inform and include the community.

Many of the changes are possible within the present organizational framework. At the *primary grade* level these are (1) re-examination of the reading readiness program, (2) the establishment of a reading-levels approach to reading instruction, either with or without grade designations, and (3) the school systems not prepared to move quite so fast can use the levels approach to reading as a step toward the abolition of the conventional grade names at a later date.

The *intermediate grade* reading program needs to be improved so that continuous and continuing reading instruction is afforded every boy and girl. A variety of ways exist which attempt to provide for individual differences. Continuation of the primary grade reading-levels approach amounts to a form of homogeneous grouping and is one of the better provisions. Instruction in work-study reading skills and remedial instruction usually commence at the third or fourth grade.

At the *junior high* level the reading program should be reorganized to provide reading instruction in three ways: developmental, corrective, and remedial. At the seventh grade, corrective classes can be provided by means of the reading home room, special section of English, double English period, or the special reading class.

Corrective or preventive reading may also be continued in the eighth and ninth grades for those who are in need.

Of the many possible provisions for reading existing at the *senior high* level, the most common are the developmental, the special section of regular English class, and the remedial. To these, schools might consider adding a course for certain terminal students to enable them to leave school reading well enough so that reading is enjoyable and the level of reading is adequate for occupational demands. Another course in reading is suggested to equip students who are going to college with the reading skills which will be increasingly demanded. This suggestion is advanced not because of inadequacies in college reading programs but because proficiency in reading is desirable from the commencement of college work.

Each and every staff member, in assisting a school toward an improved reading offering, must keep a sense of perspective. To aid them in doing this, the fourteen points mentioned in this chapter will serve as a guide to action.

REFERENCES

1. Baruch, Bernard: *My Own Story*, Henry Holt and Company, Inc., New York, 1957.

* 2. Blair, Glenn Myers: *Diagnostic and Remedial Teaching*, rev. ed., The Macmillan Company, New York, 1956.

3. Causey, Oscar S. (ed.): *Significant Elements in College and Adult Reading Improvement*, Seventh Yearbook of the National Reading Conference for Colleges and Adults, Texas Christian University Press, Fort Worth, Tex., March, 1958.

4. Conant, James Bryant: *The American High School Today*, McGraw-Hill Book Company, Inc., New York, 1959.

5. "Dartmouth Cites New Study Plan," *New York Times*, Apr. 12, 1959.

* 6. Durrell, Donald D.: *Improving Reading Instruction*, World Book Company, Yonkers, N.Y., 1956.

7. Early, Margaret J.: "About Successful Reading Programs," *English Journal*, vol. 46, pp. 393–405, October, 1957.

8. Freudenreich, Carl J.: "How Can a Junior High School Staff Get a Schoolwide Developmental Program Under Way?" in Arno Jewett (ed.), *Improving Reading in the Junior High School*, Proceedings of Conference, December 13–14, 1956, U.S. Depart-

ment of Health, Education, and Welfare, Washington, 1957, pp. 37–46.

° 9. Hand, Harold C.: "Relationship of Guidance to Instruction," in *Guidance in the Curriculum,* 1955 Yearbook of the Association for Supervision and Curriculum Development, National Education Association, Washington, 1955, pp. 3–11.

10. Harris, Albert J.: "Grouping and Promotion in Relation to Progress in Reading," in William S. Gray and Nancy Larrick (eds.), *Better Readers for Our Times,* International Reading Association Conference Proceedings, vol. 1, Scholastic Magazines, New York, 1956, pp. 69–73.

° 11. Harris, Albert J.: *How to Increase Reading Ability,* 3d ed., Longmans, Green & Co., Inc., New York, 1956.

12. Jones, James J.: "The Principal and Public Relations," *Education Administration and Supervision,* vol. 41, pp. 313–317, May, 1955.

13. Kingston, Albert J., Jr.: "The Relationship of High School and College Reading Programs," in Oscar S. Causey (ed.), *Significant Elements in College and Adult Reading Improvement,* Seventh Yearbook of The National Reading Conference for Colleges and Adults, Texas Christian University Press, Fort Worth, Texas, March, 1958, pp. 24–29.

14. National Council of Teachers of English, The Commission on the English Curriculum: *The English Language Arts in the Secondary School,* Appleton-Century-Crofts, Inc., New York, 1956.

15. Pygman, C. H.: "Discussion: Grouping and Promotion in Relation to Progress in Reading," in William S. Gray and Nancy Larrick (eds.), *Better Readers for Our Times,* International Reading Association Conference Proceedings, vol. 1, Scholastic Magazines, New York, 1956, pp. 74–75.

16. Simpson, Elizabeth A.: *Helping High-school Students Read Better,* Science Research Associates, Inc., Chicago, 1954.

17. Stewart, L. Jane, Frieda M. Heller, and Elsie J. Alberty: *Improving Reading in the Junior High School,* Current Problems in Education Series, Appleton-Century-Crofts, Inc., New York, 1957.

18. Strang, Ruth: "Interrelations of Guidance and Reading Problems," *Education,* vol. 75, pp. 456–461, March, 1955.

° 19. Strang, Ruth, and Dorothy Kendall Bracken: *Making Better Readers,* D. C. Heath and Company, Boston, 1957.

° 20. Strang, Ruth, Constance M. McCullough, and Arthur E. Traxler: *Problems in the Improvement of Reading,* 2d ed., McGraw-Hill Book Company, Inc., New York, 1955.

21. Thompson, Ethel: "The Ungraded Plan Helps Provide for Continuity of Learning," *NEA Journal,* vol. 47, no. 1, pp. 16–18, January, 1958.

22. Toops, Myrtle Dewey: "Core Program Does Improve Reading Proficiency," *Education Administration and Supervision,* vol. 40, pp. 494–503, December, 1954.

* 23. Townsend, Agatha (ed.): *College Freshmen Speak Out,* Committee on School and College Relations of the Educational Records Bureau, Harper & Brothers, New York, 1956.

24. White, Margaret L.: "A Reading Program Organized by Reading Levels," *Newer Practices in Reading in the Elementary School,* Seventeenth Yearbook of the National Elementary School Principal, National Education Association, Department of Elementary School Principals, Washington, 1938, vol. 17, pp. 520–527.

25. Woodring, Paul: *A Fourth of a Nation,* McGraw-Hill Book Company, Inc., New York, 1957.

* See Appendix A for annotated list of books for the professional library in schools.

Appendix A

ANNOTATED BOOK LIST
FOR PROFESSIONAL LIBRARY

This list has been composed with the smaller school in mind. Many worth-while books have been left out of the list. The annotations are intended merely as a guide to the main contributions of a particular book and not as an evaluation of that book.

1. Association for Supervision and Curriculum Development: *Guidance in the Curriculum.*
2. Blair, Glenn Myers: *Diagnostic and Remedial Teaching.*
3. Bond, Guy L., and Eva Bond: *Developmental Reading in High School.*
4. Bullock, Harrison: *Helping the Non-reading Pupil in the Secondary School.*
5. Dunn, Anita, Mabel Jackman, and Bernice Bush: *Fare for the Reluctant Reader.*
6. Durrell, Donald D.: *Improving Reading Instruction.*
7. Durrell, Donald D., and Helen Blair Sullivan: *High Interest– Low Vocabulary Booklist.*
8. Gray, William S.: *On Their Own in Reading.*
9. Harris, Albert J.: *How to Increase Reading Ability.*
10. Hildreth, Gertrude: *Readiness for School Beginners.*
11. Hunnicutt, Clarence William, and William J. Iverson: *Research in the Three R's.*
12. Jordan, A. M.: *Measurement in Education.*
13. McKee, Paul: *The Teaching of Reading in the Elementary School.*
14. New Jersey Secondary School Teachers' Association: *All Teachers Can Teach Reading.*
15. Robinson, Helen M.: *Why Pupils Fail in Reading.*
16. Spache, George D.: *Are We Teaching Reading?*
17. Strang, Ruth, and Dorothy Kendall Bracken: *Making Better Readers.*

18. Strang, Ruth, Constance M. McCullough, and Arthur E. Traxler: *Problems in the Improvement of Reading.*

19. Townsend, Agatha: *College Freshmen Speak Out.*

20. Woolf, Maurice D., and Jeanne A. Woolf: *Remedial Reading
Teaching and Treatment.*

21. Yoakam, Gerald A.: *Basal Reading Instruction.*

1. Association for Supervision and Curriculum Development:
Guidance in the Curriculum, National Education Association, Washington, 1955.

This report is written from the point of view of the guidance
department. Its importance in a list of professional books on reading is that much of what it says parallels information given in books
for the reading specialist, but it often uses different terminology.
It can be used to help a faculty see that reading involves the
curriculum and is an important aspect of guidance.

2. Blair, Glenn Myers: *Diagnostic and Remedial Teaching,* rev.
ed., The Macmillan Company, New York, 1956.

Along with a fairly complete listing of remedial materials, Blair
supplies numerous accounts of junior and senior high school reading
programs. He also includes data on the frequency of use of different types of organization of reading classes. Thus the Reading
Improvement Committee can make a rapid survey of what other
school systems are doing. Chapters on remedial teaching of arithmetic, spelling, handwriting, and English fundamentals should prove
useful to individual teachers.

3. Bond, Guy L., and Eva Bond: *Developmental Reading in
High School,* The Macmillan Company, New York, 1941.

This is one of the earlier books on developmental reading at the
secondary level. Its suggestions for subject-matter teaching through
reading remain current. Chapters on the interest factor in reading
situations, differentiated attack, and independence in reading are
not equaled in more recent books.

4. Bullock, Harrison: *Helping the Non-reading Pupil in the
Secondary School,* Bureau of Publications, Teachers College, Columbia University, New York, 1956.

This book of 175 pages seeks to explain the nonreading pupil
who is defined not as a nonreader but as a boy or girl who reads so
far below the material required by the teacher that he or she is, to
all intents and purposes, a nonreading pupil.

In addition to worth-while descriptions of typical pupils, teachers will find much that is enlightening in the author's description of various types of teachers and their approach to reading.

5. Dunn, Anita, Mabel Jackman, and Bernice Bush: *Fare for the Reluctant Reader,* CASDA, State College for Teachers, Albany, N.Y., 1953.

A reading list of sure-fire favorites with boys and girls who are not in love with reading. Books are arranged by interest center and grade level. Difficulty is determined by popularity of titles with reluctant readers. For this reason, the listing is not as scientific as the Durrell-Sullivan book list and is designed for use in supplementary reading programs. Details of a guided free reading program are given.

6. Durrell, Donald D.: *Improving Reading Instruction,* World Book Company, Yonkers, N.Y., 1956.

This book seeks to explain many of the causes of poor reading in the elementary school in simple and straightforward fashion. Of particular significance are the sections dealing with common weaknesses at various levels in the program. Much attention is given to reading readiness, including visual and auditory perception, and to word recognition and word analysis. The contributions of the reading consultant and the supervising principal are considered briefly.

7. Durrell, Donald D., and Helen Blair Sullivan: *High Interest–Low Vocabulary Booklist,* Boston University, Boston, Mass., 1952.

The vocabulary difficulty and the interest level are both given for each book listed. A good source of materials for specific use with retarded readers who need accurate grade placement with high interest appeal. School librarians and teachers of slower sections will find this list invaluable in making book recommendations, but its principal value is in the suggestions it offers for individual reading for clinic cases.

A more recently revised list by Sullivan and Tolman is to be found in the *Journal of Education,* vol. 139, no. 2, December, 1956, under the title "High Interest–Low Vocabulary Materials." Both lists should be obtained if possible.

8. Gray, William S.: *On Their Own in Reading,* Scott, Foresman and Company, Chicago, 1948.

The subtitle, "How to Give Children Independence in Attacking New Words," reveals the purpose of the book. The first section stresses word perception through context clues, word-form clues, structural and phonetic analysis, and the dictionary. The second section details a five-level application of word-analysis skills. The book contains useful suggestions for primary teachers, and it is of special importance to teachers of the intermediate and secondary grades.

9. Harris, Albert J.: *How to Increase Reading Ability*, 3d ed., Longmans, Green & Co., Inc., New York, 1956.

This book covers a wide range of reading instruction from reading readiness to remedial work in secondary schools. It contains detailed plans for group instruction for elementary teachers and diagnosis and remediation for reading-disability cases, as well as good treatment of the teaching of word recognition. Elementary teachers, special-reading-class teachers, and reading specialists will find it a useful reference book. It contains a very complete listing of reading, intelligence, and screening tests, plus a handy list of publishers' addresses.

10. Hildreth, Gertrude: *Readiness for School Beginners*, World Book Company, Yonkers, N.Y., 1950.

This is one of the definitive books in the area of reading readiness. It discusses the philosophy as well as the practical application of readiness theories. The expanded readiness program is developed. It should be of value to kindergarten and primary teachers and elementary supervisors and principals who wish to strengthen the reading program in the reading readiness area.

11. Hunnicutt, Clarence William, and William J. Iverson (eds.): *Research in the Three R's*, Harper & Brothers, New York, 1958.

Research in the Three R's seeks to acquaint teachers with basic findings of research in the general area of reading. A knowledge of experimental evidence enables a classroom teacher to move forward from an insecure see-if-it-works attitude to a more assured position supported by the experimentation of others.

A secondary contribution of this book is information which will enable the teacher to answer many of the criticisms of public school practices in reading.

Approximately half the book deals with reading while the second half is divided about evenly between writing and arithmetic.

12. Jordan, A. M.: *Measurement in Education*, McGraw-Hill Book Company, Inc., New York, 1953.

Measurement in Education combines the history and principles of testing with detailed examination of representative tests. Achievement, intelligence, and special-purpose tests are included for all grades of elementary and secondary school. This book has been selected with the testing problems of the smaller centralized school in mind.

Larger school systems, where divisions of elementary and secondary are apt to be more pronounced, will find *Measurement and Evaluation in the Elementary School* and its companion volume, *Measurement and Evaluation in the Secondary School*, both by Greene, Jorgenson and Gerberich, better suited to their particular needs.

13. McKee, Paul: *The Teaching of Reading in the Elementary School*, Houghton Mifflin Company, Boston, 1948.

The introductory chapters present the nature of the process of reading. The major part of the book details a suggested program of instruction from kindergarten through sixth grade. It is not concerned with remedial instruction, but it should serve as a good source of in-service training material for elementary teachers.

14. New Jersey Secondary School Teachers' Association: *All Teachers Can Teach Reading*, 1035 Kenyon Avenue, Plainfield, N.J., 1951.

A sixty-two page booklet for use in arousing a secondary school staff to the possibilities of reading instruction in school subjects. Different reading skills are briefly explained, generalizations are made, and concrete suggestions are offered.

15. Robinson, Helen M.: *Why Pupils Fail in Reading*, University of Chicago Press, Chicago, 1946.

This book suggests several possible causes of failure in reading. Among these are visual, neurological, auditory, and speech difficulties. In addition, factors of intelligence, the emotions, personality, and environmental and social characteristics are considered.

Robinson's book is based on the intensive study of thirty seriously retarded readers. While it is of primary interest to reading specialists, the book contains material for the classroom teacher interested in learning disabilities. The thesis advanced is that failure usually has a multiple causation.

16. Spache, George D.: *Are We Teaching Reading?* University of Florida, Gainesville, Fla., 1956.

Spache assembles the evidence for use in correcting some of the false impressions that have arisen concerning contemporary reading instruction. Although the booklet consists of but thirty-one pages, the reader will find here a handy way of getting at research studies which need to be brought to the attention of the general public.

17. Strang, Ruth, and Dorothy Kendall Bracken: *Making Better Readers*, D. C. Heath and Company, Boston, 1957.

This serves as a very readable introduction to problems of developmental reading for secondary teachers. The reading program of the elementary school and the range of ability and interest are discussed in preparation for considering the contributions of subject-matter teachers to reading. Reading is treated as the responsibility of the whole school staff. Many suggestions for grouping and specific classroom techniques aid the teacher in seeing what provisions can be made in his own classes. Appendixes include valuable information on tests, materials of instruction, and mechanical equipment.

18. Strang, Ruth, Constance M. McCullough, and Arthur E. Traxler: *Problems in the Improvement of Reading*, 2d ed., McGraw-Hill Book Company, Inc., New York, 1955.

This is one of the definitive books in the field of secondary reading instruction. Part 1 concerns the whole school program and gives accounts of successful reading plans. Part 2 treats the reading problem from the angle of subject-matter teachers, and Part 3 considers the aspects of appraisal and remediation.

Problems in the Improvement of Reading is not easy reading, but it does contain a wealth of reference material which teachers who are taking in-service training courses may wish to consult. This book is frequently used as a basic text in developmental reading classes in college.

19. Townsend, Agatha (ed.): *College Freshmen Speak Out*, Committee on School and College Relations of the Educational Records Bureau, Harper & Brothers, New York, 1956.

College freshmen criticize their secondary school preparation for college reading situations. This book should be required reading for complacent secondary school teachers who may feel that their responsibility ends when they succeed in getting boys and girls into college.

20. Woolf, Maurice D., and Jeanne A. Woolf: *Remedial Reading Teaching and Treatment*, McGraw-Hill Book Company, Inc., New York, 1957.

This book deals mainly with remedial programs at the secondary level. The approach is unique in that copious use is made of case histories, counseling interviews, reports of in-service workshops and seminars. Classroom and clinical techniques are focused on boys and girls with reading disabilities. Suggestions are included for remedial programs in many different types of schools, so that this book may be of valuable assistance to school systems engaged in setting up or reorganizing their remedial instruction. Administrators will gain a thorough concept of the case study and the interview and through this information should be better able to appreciate the time-consuming nature of one phase of the reading specialist's position.

21. Yoakam, Gerald A.: *Basal Reading Instruction*, McGraw-Hill Book Company, Inc., New York, 1955.

The book is divided into three parts. In Part 1, fundamental principles of reading instruction are discussed. Part 2 is concerned with eight major abilities in the reading process, many being developed concurrently. Teachers and administrators will derive much assistance from this straightforward approach to reading instruction. Part 3 deals with developing an integrated program and with appraising progress made in reading instruction.

The appendix contains information on the Yoakam readability formula which appears to be fully as reliable as most of the other formulas, and much less time-consuming.

In addition to the publications listed above, there are a number of magazines and conference reports which are worthy of consideration. Among the magazines which, from time to time, contain articles on reading are the *Elementary School Journal, Elementary English,* and the *English Journal* (secondary).

The Supplementary Educational Monographs, published by the University of Chicago Press, cover specific reading topics from kindergarten to college. *Corrective Reading in Classroom and Clinic,* vol. 79, is a good example; but there are many others in the series. Some of these, unfortunately, are out of print.

Certain issues of the *National Elementary Principal* are devoted entirely to articles on reading. *Reading for Today's Children,* vol.

35, no. 1, September, 1955, is one such issue. Other education magazines also follow this practice of devoting a major part of a particular issue to the subject of reading.

The *Journal of Developmental Reading,* published quarterly by the Department of English, Purdue University, Lafayette, Indiana, is concerned with teaching practices for secondary school and college.

Teachers of senior high reading classes will find the yearbooks formerly published by the Southwest Reading Conference for Colleges and Universities supply information on college reading programs, much of which could be used to advantage in high school classes. The yearbooks are being continued by the National Reading Conference for Colleges and Adults and are published by Texas Christian University Press, Fort Worth, Texas.

The Reading Teacher, issued quarterly by International Reading Association, 5835 Kimbark Avenue, Chicago 37, Illinois, contains articles of interest to everyone connected with reading.

Finally, Scholastic Magazines publishes the International Reading Association Conference Proceedings each year under various titles.

Appendix B

SURVEY OF READING CLIMATE

PURPOSE OF CHECK LIST

This check list may be used by the Reading Improvement Committee to aid in evaluating the reading climate of the entire school. The procedure is more effective if several independent judgments are obtained. The school principals might collaborate on one for their respective schools. A lay member, or members, of the Reading Improvement Committee could make a second evaluation, while a third copy of the check list might be used by department heads, guidance personnel, supervisors, individual teachers, and others concerned. Alternatively the survey may be made by the special-interest subcommittees indicated in Chapter 1. Whichever method is decided upon, the survey should be made early in the consideration of the reading program so that it may serve as the basis for discussion.

Some duplication of items in the various parts of the check list is intentional so that certain phases of the reading program will be evaluated from more than one angle. Flexibility is provided for by the opportunity to write in other items and by the provision of the column under the heading Not applicable.

Many factors will have to be considered before the Reading Improvement Committee will be able to decide how many checks in the Acceptable, Inadequate, or Not applicable columns constitute a cause for action. No attempt is made here to weigh the importance of the various items, since this will tend to vary from school to school.

If the subtotal evaluation is made at the end of each section, these subtotals may be carried back to the first page of the check list as a summarization.

	Check (✔) for degree of consideration			
	Satis-factory	Accept-able	Inade-quate	Not appli-cable

Satisfactory—working well at present.
Acceptable—but could be improved.
Inadequate—needs attention.
Not applicable—does not concern a particular
  department or level of the school.

	Satis-factory	Accept-able	Inade-quate	Not appli-cable
I. Administration	—	—	—	—
II. Clinic facilities	—	—	—	—
III. Cumulative record	—	—	—	—
IV. General items	—	—	—	—
V. Health	—	—	—	—
VI. Public relations	—	—	—	—
VII. Reading instruction	—	—	—	—
A. Reading readiness	—	—	—	—
B. Primary reading	—	—	—	—
C. Intermediate reading	—	—	—	—
D. Junior high reading	—	—	—	—
E. Senior high reading	—	—	—	—
VIII. School library	—	—	—	—
IX. Staff	—	—	—	—
I. Administration				
A. Leadership	—	—	—	—
1. Community public relations	—	—	—	—
2. Teaching staff	—	—	—	—
B. Provision for professional growth of staff	—	—	—	—
1. Reading Improvement Committee	—	—	—	—
2. In-service training courses	—	—	—	—
3. Consultant services	—	—	—	—
4. Cooperation in making case studies	—	—	—	—
5. Other	—	—	—	—
C. Humanagement or personnel practices	—	—	—	—
1. Selection of staff	—	—	—	—
2. Assignment of staff	—	—	—	—
3. Supervision of first-year teachers	—	—	—	—
4. Other	—	—	—	—

	Check (✔) for degree of consideration			
	Satis-factory	Accept-able	Inade-quate	Not appli-cable
D. Budget provisions for reading	—	—	—	—
1. Reading survey	—	—	—	—
2. Testing materials	—	—	—	—
3. Basic reading materials	—	—	—	—
4. Special reading materials	—	—	—	—
5. Other	—	—	—	—
E. Curriculum	—	—	—	—
1. In line with local needs	—	—	—	—
2. In line with national needs	—	—	—	—
3. Grass-roots revision when necessary	—	—	—	—
4. Presents a challenge to many levels of ability	—	—	—	—
F. Coordination of reading program	—	—	—	—
G. Rate of progress	—	—	—	—
H. Other	—	—	—	—
SUMMARY OF ADMINISTRATION	—	—	—	—
II. Clinic facilities				
A. Survey of community resources	—	—	—	—
1. Child-guidance clinic	—	—	—	—
2. Speech clinic	—	—	—	—
3. Reading clinic	—	—	—	—
4. Psychiatric clinic	—	—	—	—
5. Other	—	—	—	—
B. Survey of possible sponsors for future clinics	—	—	—	—
C. Basis of referral	—	—	—	—
1. Probable waiting time for diagnosis	—	—	—	—
2. Probable waiting time for therapy	—	—	—	—
D. Provision for remedial therapy by school once diagnosis has been made	—	—	—	—
E. Provision for cooperation and follow-up	—	—	—	—
F. Other	—	—	—	—
SUMMARY OF CLINIC FACILITIES	—	—	—	—

	Check (✔) for degree of consideration			
	Satis- factory	Accept- able	Inade- quate	Not appli- cable
III. Cumulative record				
A. Contents of particular importance in reading	—	—	—	—
1. Complete test data	—	—	—	—
2. Anecdotal record	—	—	—	—
3. Health information	—	—	—	—
4. Screening-test results	—	—	—	—
5. Specific information on individual pupil's reading levels	—	—	—	—
a. Exact place in basal readers or reading level (elementary)	—	—	—	—
b. Skills mastered	—	—	—	—
c. Skills needing attention	—	—	—	—
6. Other	—	—	—	—
B. Plans for continuation of cumulative folder	—	—	—	—
1. Summarized for secondary school use *or*	—	—	—	—
2. Folder worked out with elementary principals	—	—	—	—
C. Uses made of cumulative record to improve reading instruction	—	—	—	—
1. Elementary				
a. To provide continuing reading instruction	—	—	—	—
b. To reduce range of ability in formation of grade sections	—	—	—	—
c. Other	—	—	—	—
2. Secondary				
a. Aid in formation of homogeneous groups	—	—	—	—
b. Selection of corrective work	—	—	—	—
c. Selection of remedial work	—	—	—	—
d. Other	—	—	—	—
SUMMARY OF CUMULATIVE RECORD	—	—	—	—

	Check (✔) for degree of consideration			
	Satis-factory	Accept-able	Inade-quate	Not appli-cable
IV. General items				
A. Testing program	—	—	—	—
1. Reading tests	—	—	—	—
a. Survey type	—	—	—	—
b. Analytic type	—	—	—	—
2. Intelligence tests	—	—	—	—
a. Group	—	—	—	—
b. Individual	—	—	—	—
3. Special purpose tests	—	—	—	—
4. Other	—	—	—	—
5. Balanced testing program	—	—	—	—
6. Test results used to improve instruction	—	—	—	—
B. Grouping	—	—	—	—
1. Heterogeneous	—	—	—	—
2. Homogeneous by	—	—	—	—
a. School achievement	—	—	—	—
b. Reading ability	—	—	—	—
c. Teacher judgment	—	—	—	—
d. Other basis	—	—	—	—
3. Core	—	—	—	—
4. Other	—	—	—	—
C. Scheduling	—	—	—	—
1. Class size	—	—	—	—
2. Avoidance of block schedul-ing	—	—	—	—
D. Guidance department coordinates reading program	—	—	—	—
E. Classrooms	—	—	—	—
1. Provision for lighting	—	—	—	—
2. Provision for shading windows	—	—	—	—
F. Reading classroom or laboratory	—	—	—	—
1. Equipment	—	—	—	—
2. Reading materials	—	—	—	—
3. Use made by teachers of read-ing center	—	—	—	—
G. Other	—	—	—	—
SUMMARY OF GENERAL ITEMS	—	—	—	—

	Check (✔) for degree of consideration			
	Satis-factory	Accept-able	Inade-quate	Not appli-cable
V. Health				
A. Yearly physical examination	—	—	—	—
B. Screening for visual abnormalities	—	—	—	—
1. By whom performed	—	—	—	—
2. Equipment used	—	—	—	—
C. Screening for hearing abnormalities	—	—	—	—
1. By whom performed	—	—	—	—
2. Equipment used	—	—	—	—
D. Screening for speech abnormalities	—	—	—	—
1. By whom performed	—	—	—	—
2. Facilities available for correction	—	—	—	—
E. Reports to parents	—	—	—	—
1. Method of reporting	—	—	—	—
2. Follow-up of referral	—	—	—	—
F. Cooperation with members of medical profession	—	—	—	—
G. Other	—	—	—	—
SUMMARY OF HEALTH	—	—	—	—
VI. Public relations				
A. General public	—	—	—	—
1. Philosophy of education	—	—	—	—
2. Understanding of nature of school program	—	—	—	—
3. Other	—	—	—	—
B. Topical information for parents and/or PTA	—	—	—	—
1. Reading readiness	—	—	—	—
2. Reporting	—	—	—	—
3. Promotion policy	—	—	—	—
4. Reading instruction	—	—	—	—
5. Remedial reading instruction	—	—	—	—
6. Bases of grouping	—	—	—	—
7. Other	—	—	—	—
C. Methods of establishing good public relations	—	—	—	—
1. Individual conferences	—	—	—	—
2. Group meetings	—	—	—	—

	Check (✔) for degree of consideration			
	Satis-factory	Accept-able	Inade-quate	Not appli-cable
3. PTA program	—	—	—	—
4. Involvement of parents in work of the school	—	—	—	—
5. Other	—	—	—	—
SUMMARY OF PUBLIC RELATIONS	—	—	—	—
VII. Reading instruction				
A. Reading readiness	—	—	—	—
1. Coordinated approach whole school day	—	—	—	—
a. Background experiences broadened and shared to aid reading	—	—	—	—
b. Group games and dramatizations	—	—	—	—
c. Nursery rhymes and songs	—	—	—	—
d. Story period and story-telling	—	—	—	—
e. Visual-perception skills	—	—	—	—
f. Auditory-perception skills	—	—	—	—
2. Materials of reading	—	—	—	—
a. Workbooks and similar materials	—	—	—	—
b. Seat work	—	—	—	—
c. Library books	—	—	—	—
d. Teacher's manual and local guides	—	—	—	—
e. Other	—	—	—	—
3. Health examination	—	—	—	—
a. General physical	—	—	—	—
b. Vision screening	—	—	—	—
c. Hearing screening	—	—	—	—
d. Speech screening	—	—	—	—
e. Other	—	—	—	—
4. Testing program	—	—	—	—
a. Intelligence tests	—	—	—	—
b. Reading readiness tests	—	—	—	—
5. Formation of reading groups	—	—	—	—

	Check (✔) for degree of consideration			
	Satis-factory	Accept-able	Inade-quate	Not appli-cable
a. Continuation of readiness activities	—	—	—	—
b. Retesting upon teacher judgment	—	—	—	—
6. Cumulative folder started	—	—	—	—
7. Parental conferences	—	—	—	—
SUMMARY OF READING READINESS	—	—	—	—
B. Primary reading	—	—	—	—
1. Materials of reading	—	—	—	—
a. Basal readers	—	—	—	—
b. Cobasal readers	—	—	—	—
c. Supplementary books for individual reading	—	—	—	—
d. Workbooks	—	—	—	—
e. Teacher's manual	—	—	—	—
2. Reading skills	—	—	—	—
a. Phrasing, enunciation, and pronunciation in oral reading	—	—	—	—
b. Comprehension in all reading situations	—	—	—	—
c. Word-attack skills	—	—	—	—
3. Reading levels observed—grouping flexible	—	—	—	—
4. Remedial work by classroom teacher	—	—	—	—
5. Testing program	—	—	—	—
6. Cumulative folder continued	—	—	—	—
7. Parental conferences	—	—	—	—
SUMMARY OF PRIMARY READING	—	—	—	—
C. Intermediate reading	—	—	—	—
1. Materials of reading	—	—	—	—
a. Basal reading instruction continued	—	—	—	—
b. Work-study-type reading instruction	—	—	—	—

| | Check (✔) for degree of consideration | | | |
	Satis- factory	Accept- able	Inade- quate	Not appli- cable
c. Special supplies and instructional games	—	—	—	—
2. Skills and understandings	—	—	—	—
a. Structural and phonetic analysis	—	—	—	—
b. Word meaning	—	—	—	—
c. Location skills	—	—	—	—
d. Individualized supplementary reading	—	—	—	—
e. Other	—	—	—	—
3. Reading levels observed	—	—	—	—
a. Oral reading with comprehension	—	—	—	—
b. Silent reading with comprehension	—	—	—	—
4. Remedial reading	—	—	—	—
a. By classroom teacher	—	—	—	—
b. By reading specialist	—	—	—	—
5. Testing program	—	—	—	—
6. Cumulative folder continued	—	—	—	—
a. Used by classroom teacher in formation of reading groups	—	—	—	—
b. Used in assigning to sections for next year	—	—	—	—
7. Parental conferences	—	—	—	—
SUMMARY OF INTERMEDIATE READING	—	—	—	—
D. Junior high school reading	—	—	—	—
1. Three-track program	—	—	—	—
a. Developmental, all subject-matter teachers	—	—	—	—
b. Corrective, special reading classes	—	—	—	—
c. Remedial, disability cases and selected slow learners	—	—	—	—
2. Developmental reading program	—	—	—	—

	Check (✔) for degree of consideration			
	Satis-factory	Accept-able	Inade-quate	Not appli-cable
a. Recognition of reading levels	—	—	—	—
b. Recognition of reading difficulties inherent in subject	—	—	—	—
c. Determination of textbook difficulty	—	—	—	—
d. Classroom libraries	—	—	—	—
e. Adjusted materials	—	—	—	—
f. Other	—	—	—	—
3. Corrective reading classes	—	—	—	—
a. Scheduling of reading classes	—	—	—	—
(1). Home-room period	—	—	—	—
(2). Special English section(s)	—	—	—	—
(3). Double-period English class	—	—	—	—
(4). Special reading class	—	—	—	—
(5). Other	—	—	—	—
b. Supervision and assistance from reading specialist	—	—	—	—
c. Materials for reading instruction	—	—	—	—
(1). Published materials	—	—	—	—
(2). Teacher-prepared materials	—	—	—	—
d. Credit for work in reading	—	—	—	—
e. Other	—	—	—	—
4. Remedial program	—	—	—	—
a. Materials for reading instruction	—	—	—	—
(1). Special purpose	—	—	—	—
(2). Instructional games	—	—	—	—
(3). Mechanical equipment	—	—	—	—
b. Instruction within school day	—	—	—	—
c. Individual and small-group work	—	—	—	—

	Check (✔) for degree of consideration			
	Satis- factory	Accept- able	Inade- quate	Not appli- cable
d. Provision for referral through guidance department	—	—	—	—
5. Testing program	—	—	—	—
6. Cumulative folder continued	—	—	—	—
7. Conferences	—	—	—	—
a. Student	—	—	—	—
b. Parent in special cases	—	—	—	—
c. Special-service personnel	—	—	—	—
d. Subject-matter teachers	—	—	—	—
SUMMARY OF JUNIOR HIGH READING	—	—	—	—
E. Senior high school reading	—	—	—	—
1. Three-track program	—	—	—	—
a. Developmental, all subject-matter teachers	—	—	—	—
b. Corrective, special reading classes	—	—	—	—
c. Remedial, disability cases and slow learners	—	—	—	—
2. Developmental reading program	—	—	—	.
a. Recognition of reading levels	—	—	—	—
b. Recognition of reading difficulties inherent in subject	—	—	—	—
c. Determination of textbook difficulty	—	—	—	—
d. Classroom libraries	—	—	—	—
e. Adjusted materials	—	—	—	—
f. Other	—	—	—	—
3. Corrective reading classes for				
a. Terminal students—functional	—	—	—	—
b. College preparatory students	—	—	—	—
(1). Within English class	—	—	—	—
(2). One-semester elective	—	—	—	—
(3). Language arts approach	—	—	—	—

	Satis-factory	Accept-able	Inade-quate	Not appli-cable

Check (✔) for degree of consideration

	Satis-factory	Accept-able	Inade-quate	Not appli-cable
(a). Reading	—	—	—	—
(b). Note taking	—	—	—	—
(c). Term-paper writing	—	—	—	—
(d). Oral reports	—	—	—	—
4. Remedial program	—	—	—	—
a. Instruction within school day	—	—	—	—
b. Continuation of junior high program	—	—	—	—
5. Testing program	—	—	—	—
6. Cumulative folder continued	—	—	—	—
7. Conferences	—	—	—	—
a. Student	—	—	—	—
b. Parent in special cases	—	—	—	—
c. Special-service personnel	—	—	—	—
d. Subject-matter teachers	—	—	—	—
SUMMARY OF SENIOR HIGH READING	—	—	—	—
VIII. School library				
A. Budget for book purchase	—	—	—	—
B. Physical facilities	—	—	—	—
1. Reference room	—	—	—	—
2. Browsing corner	—	—	—	—
3. Committee rooms	—	—	—	—
4. Other	—	—	—	—
C. Available for individuals and scheduled groups at all times	—	—	—	—
D. Study hall held at a place other than the library	—	—	—	—
E. Classroom libraries	—	—	—	—
F. Teachers share in compilation of book orders	—	—	—	—
G. Teachers make use of librarian's services in preparation of units	—	—	—	—
H. Other	—	—	—	—
SUMMARY OF SCHOOL LIBRARY	—	—	—	—
IX. Staff				
A. Professional training in reading	—	—	—	—

	Check (✔) for degree of consideration			
	Satis-factory	Accept-able	Inade-quate	Not appli-cable
1. College courses in developmental reading	—	—	—	—
2. In-service training courses	—	—	—	—
B. Professional enthusiasm	—	—	—	—
1. Attendance at conferences	—	—	—	—
2. Attendance at workshops	—	—	—	—
3. Cooperation with reading specialist	—	—	—	—
4. Cooperation with guidance department	—	—	—	—
C. Developmental learning philosophy	—	—	—	—
1. Recognition of reading levels	—	—	—	—
2. Provision for differences in ability	—	—	—	—
3. Achievement in line with capacity	—	—	—	—
D. Success with different types of grouping	—	—	—	—
1. Achievement	—	—	—	—
2. Special needs	—	—	—	—
3. Interest	—	—	—	—
4. Tutorial	—	—	—	—
E. Provision for first-year teachers	—	—	—	—
1. Adequate supervision	—	—	—	—
2. Work with experienced teacher in buddy system	—	—	—	—
F. Research	—	—	—	—
1. Action-type classroom research	—	—	—	—
2. Reporting of research	—	—	—	—
G. Use made of school library and librarian	—	—	—	—
H. Use made of classroom libraries	—	—	—	—
I. Use made of professional library	—	—	—	—
J. Other	—	—	—	—
SUMMARY OF STAFF	—	—	—	—

Appendix C

ADDITION TO CUMULATIVE FOLDER

The addition to the cumulative folder should not be copied as it appears here, since the present school folder will usually contain some of the information. Rather, it should be used as a check sheet to determine what additional information should be provided. Once this has been done, a suitable page may be mimeographed. In most cases, space for recording data will be more generous than that provided in the accompanying form.

ADDITION TO CUMULATIVE FOLDER (CHECK SHEET)

School year	Read- ing tests*	Intelli- gence tests*	Vision	Hear- ing	General health	Reading achievement (Books read)†	Reading strength	Correc- tive work
K								
1								
2								
3								
4								
5								
6								
						Reading progress	Corrective work	
7								
8								
9								
10								
11								
12								

* Give test name, form, date, and subtest scores.
† Give titles of books read and pages completed.

Appendix D

REPORT FORMS FOR READING CONTROL

To: Study hall teacher or librarian   Date_____
From: Reading teacher
_____ will be working in the reading laboratory
(Room _____) on M T W TH F at _____ o'clock.
This will be today only, the rest of the week, until further notice.

                            Signed_____

To: Principal's office   Date_____
From: Reading teacher
_____ will not be at regularly assigned study hall
or library. He (she) will be working in the reading laboratory
(Room _____) on M T W TH F at _____ o'clock.
This will be today only, the rest of the week, until further notice.

                            Signed_____

To: Reading teacher   Date_____
From: Guidance office
_____ has requested help in reading. He (she)
is in grade _____, attendance is regular, irregular. He (she)
is free M T W TH F at _____ o'clock and is to be found
in Room _____ at that time.

                            Signed_____

To: Guidance department   Date_____
From: Classroom teacher

_____, grade _____, appears to be having
difficulty in _____ because of his reading. His
reading level is _____ and the material he is reading
is _____.

                        Signed_____

To: Principal's office and Guidance office   Date_____
The following have been working to improve their reading skills
during the past month:

Names	School grade	Reading levels	Times per week	Dis- position

                 Signed_____
                        Reading teacher

LISHA KILL JUNIOR HIGH SCHOOL
Waterman Avenue
Albany 5, New York

Dear

Your son has been placed in remedial reading class _____ day(s) a week. These classes are held for those students, who, our records show, are capable of reading better than they do. It is not enough that they be able to say the words; they must be able to understand, interpret, select pertinent information and organize it for use.

Your son is constantly checked and rechecked during the class periods to determine in what areas he has progressed or in what skill he still needs help. The reading program has several goals: 1) to make reading more accurate, 2) to make reading faster, 3) to increase vocabulary and understanding, 4) to promote skills that will help in attacking other subjects independently, and 5) to make reading a source of enjoyment and a means of satisfying curiosity.

_____ seems to   _____be making little progress

_____be making progress slowly

_____be making progress rapidly

_____have a good attitude & is
trying to improve

Below are some of the basic areas included in the reading program. Those in which he has shown improvement are marked with a *plus*. Those in which he needs help are marked with a *minus*. Those not checked at all indicate that no marked deficiency was noted in that area.

	1	2	3	4
recognizing basic words				
vocabulary				
attacking new words				
concentrating and sticking to a job				
selecting main ideas				
paying attention to key words				
following directions				
drawing inferences and conclusions				
organizing ideas				
applying what he reads				
speed				

_____ was discharged _____ because _____

Please feel free at any time to call me or come in to talk about _____ program. Please comment (on back) and return.

Sincerely yours,

(Signed)_____

Reading teacher

NOTE: Sample forms used by permission. Similar forms are available for the opposite sex.

NAME INDEX

SUBJECT INDEX